ALTERNATIVE MONETARY REGIMES

ALTERNATIVE MONETARY REGIMES

EDITED BY

Colin D. Campbell

AND

William R. Dougan

The Johns Hopkins University Press

Baltimore and London

© 1986 The Johns Hopkins University Press
All rights reserved
Printed in the United States of America

The Johns Hopkins University Press, 701 West 40th Street,
Baltimore, Maryland 21211
The Johns Hopkins Press Ltd., London

Table on p. 113: From Michael B. Connolly and John McDermott, eds.,
The Economics of the Caribbean Basin. Copyright 1985 Praeger Publishers.
Reprinted by permission of the publisher.

Poem on p. 204: Robert Creeley, "I Know A Man," from *For Love:
Poems, 1950–1960* and *Poems, 1950–1965*. Copyright 1962 Robert Creeley.
Reprinted by permission of Charles Scribner's Sons
and Marion Boyars Publishers Ltd, respectively.

∞™ The paper used in this publication meets the minimum requirements
of American National Standard for Information Sciences—Permanence
of Paper for Printed Library Materials, ANSI Z39.48-1984.

Library of Congress Cataloging-in-Publication Data
Main entry under title:
Alternative monetary regimes.

Bibliography: p.
Includes index.
1. Monetary policy—Addresses, essays, lectures. 2. Foreign
exchange administration—Addresses, essays, lectures. 3. Gold
standard—Addresses, essays, lectures. I. Campbell,
Colin Dearborn, 1917– . II. Dougan, William R.
HG230.3.A44   1986   332.4′6   85-30034
ISBN 0-8018-2887-2 (alk. paper)
ISBN 0-8018-2889-9 (pbk. : alk. paper)

Contents

Contents

Contributors

Robert Z. Aliber Professor, Graduate School of Business, University of Chicago; Professor, Amos Tuck School of Business Administration, Dartmouth College

Robert J. Barro Professor, University of Rochester

Phillip Cagan Professor, Columbia University

Colin D. Campbell Professor, Dartmouth College

Carl F. Christ Professor, Johns Hopkins University

Kenneth W. Clements Professor, University of Western Australia

Richard N. Cooper Professor, Harvard University

Michael R. Darby Professor, University of California, Los Angeles

William R. Dougan Visiting Professor, Center for the Study of the Economy and the State, Graduate School of Business, University of Chicago

David I. Fand Professor, Wayne State University

Stanley Fischer Professor, Massachusetts Institute of Technology

Robert E. Hall Professor, Stanford University and Hoover Institution

Kent P. Kimbrough Professor, Duke University

Axel Leijonhufvud Professor, University of California, Los Angeles

David E. Lindsey Associate Director, Division of Research and Statistics, Board of Governors of the Federal Reserve System

J. Huston McCulloch Professor, Ohio State University

Allan H. Meltzer Professor, Graduate School of Industrial Administration, Carnegie-Mellon University

Anna J. Schwartz National Bureau of Economic Research, Inc.

Leland B. Yeager Professor, Auburn University

J. Richard Zecher Vice President and Chief Economist, The Chase Manhattan Bank

Preface

THE PAPERS and comments contained in this book were presented at a conference at Dartmouth College on August 22–24, 1984. Approximately fifty economists from the academic community, government, and journalism attended the conference. We are indebted to them for contributing to an informative discussion.

The idea for an exchange of opinions on alternative monetary regimes originated with Ellis L. Phillips, Jr., chairman of the Ellis L. Phillips Foundation of Lyme, New Hampshire. Among the many activities supported by the foundation are programs on monetary policy and inflation. The conference was sponsored jointly by the Phillips Foundation and Dartmouth College.

This volume is intended for general readers and for college and university students beyond the usual introductory course in money and banking. Its timeliness is underscored by the revival of interest in the gold standard. Two of the chapters are devoted to an examination of the record of the gold standard and a comparison with developments since its demise. Also, a major topic discussed in this volume is an alternative to the gold standard that is being widely debated—requiring the Federal Reserve authorities to adhere more closely to an announced rule prescribing a money growth rate, a GNP growth rate, or a stable price level. The attention given by economists to such matters has been increasing because of two major theoretical developments: the growing acceptance of the importance of monetary policy and the rational expectations approach to macroeconomics. According to the rational expectations approach, the predictability of government policies has important effects on the functioning of the economy.

The volume consists of an introduction and six chapters. The introduction provides readers with some theoretical background for understanding how the predictability of monetary policy may affect the attainment of two principal economic goals: full employment and price-level stability. The introduction also outlines the major concepts and issues covered in the subsequent chapters. In order to present a diversity of viewpoints, the major essay in each chapter is followed by two comments.

Chapter 1 presents two monetary theories of inflation: Robert Barro's theory that inflation is the inevitable result of the Federal Reserve System's discretion over monetary policy and Phillip Cagan's related but distinct view that inflation is due to the conflict between the Federal Reserve's short-run goal of reduced unemployment and its long-run goal of price stability. Barro, Cagan, and Axel Leijon-hufvud favor greater reliance on simple rules to stabilize prices and less emphasis on discretionary money-supply management to pursue short-term stabilization. They differ, however, in the degree of short-term latitude that they would grant to the monetary authorities.

In Chapter 2, two different types of gold standard are described. Anna Schwartz covers the historical gold standard, in which the government bought and sold gold at a fixed price, and examines its performance and the necessary conditions for its restoration. In their comments, Huston McCulloch and Richard Zecher analyze a type of gold standard in which gold coins are the basic type of money and the supply of money is created by the marketplace rather than by the government.

Chapter 3 focuses on the international aspects of monetary regimes. Richard Cooper, Kenneth Clements, and Robert Aliber discuss the implications of exchange-rate policy for domestic monetary policy, stressing the distinction between those countries that fix their exchange rates to the currency of a reserve-center country and those that serve as reserve centers.

Allan Meltzer, Carl Christ, and Stanley Fischer in Chapter 4 evaluate the predictability of money and prices under different monetary regimes and compare the gold standard to both the Bretton Woods regime following World War II and the current regime of fluctuating exchange rates. The discussion is based on Meltzer's empirical results for six separate periods in the United States from 1890 to 1980.

Chapter 5 focuses on the policies of the Federal Reserve System since the early 1970s. David Lindsey, Kent Kimbrough, and David Fand examine Federal Reserve actions during this period and discuss whether monetary policy would have been better if the Federal Reserve had been guided by a relatively restrictive rule.

In Chapter 6 Leland Yeager and Michael Darby discuss Robert Hall's radical proposal for a new monetary regime aimed at making future prices more predictable while at the same time providing sufficient flexibility to combat unemployment. Hall would pay interest on bank reserve deposits at the Federal Reserve banks, use the predicted ratio of the price level to the rate of unemployment over the next twelve months as the Federal Reserve's target, and use—as the Federal Reserve's instrument of control—the differential between the Treasury bill rate and the rate of interest paid on reserve deposits.

The essential question underlying this volume is how the workings of the monetary and financial systems in the United States and other countries can be improved. Given the decline in inflation since 1980 and the expansion of real output since 1983, one might well ask why such a question is of current interest. There are two important reasons. First, inflation continues to be a threat even though prices in the United States are not rising as rapidly as they did before 1982. The current rate of inflation is higher than it was in the 1950s and early 1960s, and the relatively low rate of inflation from 1982 to 1985 could be temporary—the result of special conditions such as the decline in oil prices and its effects on real output in the United States and on the appreciation of the dollar. Second, the building of a consensus on so complex an issue as monetary reform is a slow process. Because successful monetary reform requires a broad base of political support for the changes made and continued support and understanding in the future, it is necessary that nonspecialists understand the issues. Debate over monetary policy seems likely to occupy an increasingly prominent position in the public arena. Our hope is that this volume will contribute to that debate by illuminating some of the issues that must be addressed.

ALTERNATIVE MONETARY REGIMES

Introduction

COLIN D. CAMPBELL AND
WILLIAM R. DOUGAN

THE PAST few years have witnessed a resurgence of interest in monetary reform as an important policy issue. The current interest in alternative monetary arrangements arises from two sources. The first of these is dissatisfaction with experience since the early 1970s—high and variable rates of inflation, similarly high and even more variable interest rates, sharp fluctuations in foreign exchange rates, and large swings in the level of real economic activity. The other source of interest in the fundamental structure of monetary policy, especially among economists, is the widespread acceptance of the hypothesis of rational expectations, which questions the effectiveness of many types of government policies, including monetary control actions.[1] As Lucas (1976) has pointed out, policy changes affect the economy in two ways: by changing the values of the policy instruments themselves and by modifying people's expectations, thereby altering their reactions to future changes in the policy instruments.

It has long been recognized that unanticipated inflation contributes to the variability of an individual's real wealth. The degree to which inflation is correctly anticipated depends in large measure on the predictability of monetary policy. For example, if people expect the money supply to grow 10 percent during the coming year, they will expect a similar rate of inflation. This expected rate of inflation affects both the prices at which they are willing to buy or sell assets (e.g., bonds) and the prices they agree on in drawing up contracts governing future transactions (e.g., wages to be paid over the next three years). If individuals' forecasts of inflation turn out to be correct, then the outcomes of their various transactions will be as intended. Inflation-adjusted interest rates will yield savers the rate of return they expected, and the wages paid by firms will be consistent with full employment of labor.

1. The term *rational expectations* was introduced to economics by Muth (1961). He maintained that "expectations, since they are informed predictions of future events, are essentially the same as the predictions of the relevant economic theory" (p. 316). That is, if x_t^e is the aggregate expectation of the variable x in period t, and Ex_t is the value of x_t predicted by the relevant theory, then the hypothesis of rational expectations is that $x_t^e = Ex_t$.

1

Figure 1

Supply Curve of the Representative Producer

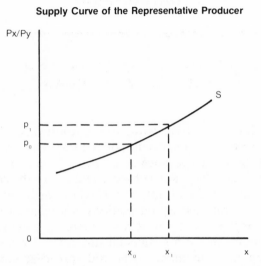

Contrast this outcome with a situation in which actual money growth and inflation turn out to be greater than anticipated. Borrowers will receive windfall gains, and lenders will suffer equivalent losses. Employers will earn above-normal profits, while employees find that their real income is lower than they had expected. Such variations in real wealth due to the unpredicted component of inflation are undesirable in and of themselves in a society of risk-averse individuals.

Besides effects on the distribution of wealth, the predictability of the behavior of the various monetary aggregates may affect the timing and severity of fluctuations in real GNP. The possible effect of money-supply variability on real output can be illustrated by an example based on the work of Friedman (1968; 1976, Chapter 12), Phelps (1970), and Lucas (1972), as depicted by Figure 1.

The horizontal axis in Figure 1 represents units of commodity x produced by an individual who specializes entirely in the production of x and offers it for sale at prices quoted in dollars.[2] The vertical

---

2. When prices are quoted in this way, they are determined on the basis of the basket of other goods or services they can command. This "real" price of a commodity is unaffected by a pure inflation or deflation, since in such circumstances all "nominal" prices (that is, prices quoted in currency units) rise or fall in the same proportion, leaving their ratios unchanged. Thus, if a person's wage increases from $4 to $5 an hour and the prices of the goods and services purchased all rise 25 percent, the prices of those items in terms of an hour's worth of labor remain the same.

axis represents the price of x relative to an index of the prices of all the goods and services consumed by the individual, the bundle y, and is labeled Px/Py. The curve labeled S shows the quantity of x that the individual will produce for every possible value of Px/Py. The individual's decision on how much time, effort, and expense to devote to the production of x will depend in part on the quantity of goods that others are willing to offer in exchange for x. As shown by the supply curve in Figure 1, the amount of x produced and offered for sale increases as Px/Py increases.

When monetary policy is uncertain, a major difficulty in deciding how much of x to produce is that it is costly for an individual to monitor continuously the prices of all the goods and services that person consumes. Let us suppose that the producer depicted in Figure 1 has been producing at the rate of x_0 in response to the relative price p_0 when there occurs a sudden increase in customers' willingness to offer dollars for x. If this demand shock represents a change in consumers' actual valuation of x relative to other goods, then the increased spending represents an increased willingness to offer other goods in exchange for x. The result is a higher relative price, such as p_1. Under such conditions the optimal response of a producer of x is to increase the rate of output to x_1.

On the other hand, if the increased willingness of customers to offer dollars for x is due to a monetary expansion, then a similar demand shock is occurring in the markets for the goods in y. In this case, since there has been no change in consumers' relative valuations of commodities, the result is an increase in all nominal prices but no change in relative prices. The optimal response for the representative producer of x is to continue to produce at the rate x_0. Lucas (1973) has shown that when a producer cannot tell what proportion of a current demand shock is due to a real disturbance, the best rule for that producer to follow is to presume that a fraction θ of that disturbance is real, where θ is the proportion of the total variation in the nominal price of x that on average has been due to the variation in the relative price of x.

If the pattern of monetary disturbance is predictable, θ will prove to be an accurate estimate of the proportion of any particular demand shock that is due to real forces, and the supply decisions of individuals will turn out to be correct.[3] Several important results follow from

---

3. As Robert Barro points out in Chapter 1, those decisions may not be correct for the society as a whole if supply decisions are distorted for some other reason. Suppose, for example, that x represents the amount of labor supplied by an individual. Since leisure cannot be taxed directly, an income tax results in a level of employment that is inefficiently low in the sense that the marginal product of another hour worked

3

this proposition. First, a change in total spending (whether due to changes in money supply or money demand) that is exactly what people expect will have no effect on the overall rate of output or employment.[4] Second, total output and employment will rise above trend when total spending is greater than expected and will fall below trend when total spending is less than expected. Since nominal prices will change in the same direction as total spending (neglecting the effects of secular changes in total output), periods of unusually high aggregate output and low unemployment will also be periods of unexpectedly high inflation.

These propositions constitute what is referred to as the *natural rate hypothesis*, which Friedman (1968) proposed as an explanation of the widely noted negative correlation between inflation and unemployment known as the *Phillips curve* and illustrated in Figure 2.[5] According to this hypothesis, there is a different short-run Phillips curve for every expected rate of inflation.

In the hypothetical economy depicted in Figure 2, the natural rate of unemployment (the rate that prevails whenever expected inflation equals actual inflation) is 7 percent.[6] If we consider the long run to be the period over which expectations catch up to reality, the long-run Phillips curve is a verical line passing through the full-employment point.[7]

To understand why short-run Phillips curves are negatively sloping, consider an economy that has not experienced any inflation, so that all demand shocks have been real disturbances and $\theta = 1$. Suppose the central bank initiates a new policy of monetary expansion sufficient to generate a steady 10 percent inflation if fully anticipated.

---

by an individual is worth more (by the amount of tax paid on the wage received) than the value the person places on an hour of leisure.

4. Such invariance of real economic variables to fully anticipated nominal disturbances is commonly referred to as *neutrality*. Neutrality derives from the assumption not merely that expectations are rational but also that all markets are in equilibrium. Also, neutrality applies only to disturbances that do not change relative prices. Certain types of fiscal policies, such as changes in marginal tax rates, may affect real variables, even if their effects on total spending are fully anticipated.

5. The Phillips curve is named for A.W. Phillips, who documented the strong negative correlation between unemployment and the rate of change of nominal wages in the United Kingdom from 1861 to 1957 (Phillips 1958).

6. The numerical value of the natural rate may vary over time within a given country as well as across countries at a given time. It can be affected by, among other things, the composition of the labor force, provisions for unemployment insurance, and minimum-wage laws.

7. This assumes that the natural rate is invariant to the rate of inflation. Friedman (1977), however, argues that the long-run Phillips curve may be positively sloped as a result of heightened uncertainty over relative prices.

Figure 2

Phillips Curves for a Hypothetical Economy

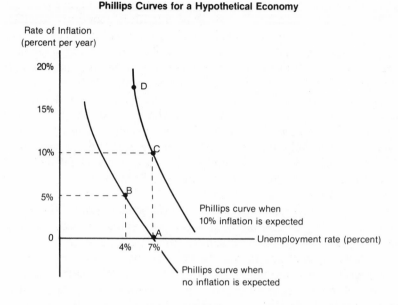

Producers will attribute all of the demand shock to real factors and will respond with an appropriate increase in output. If the supply curve of the typical producer resembles the curve S in Figure 1, this demand shock will result partly in higher nominal prices and partly in increased production. The increase in production will require an increase in employment because higher product prices make firms willing to pay higher wages, thereby inducing some workers to accept jobs they would not have accepted at a lower wage. If the initial rise in nominal prices averages 5 percent and the associated decline in unemployment is 3 percent, the economy will move from point A to point B in Figure 2. The resulting inflation rate is less than 10 percent because the higher incomes from the increased production of goods and services increase the amount of money people are willing to hold.

The increases in output and employment due to surprise inflation result from people's erroneous interpretation of nominal price and wage increases as if they were real. As the rise in the general price level becomes apparent, however, perceived real prices and wages decline. Producers cut back production in accordance with their supply curves, and unemployment increases, causing the Phillips curve to shift to the right. When the full inflationary impact of the new monetary policy is understood, the expected rate of inflation equals

5

its actual value (10 percent), and unemployment returns to its natural rate. The new long-run equilibrium is at point C in Figure 2.

By contrast, consider an otherwise identical economy in which inflation has been the source of half the movement in prices, so that $\theta = 0.5$. Suppose that the central bank has been expanding the money supply at a rate that has generated a steady 10 percent inflation. If the central bank accelerates money growth sufficiently to generate 20 percent inflation if fully anticipated, the temporary reduction in unemployment will be smaller than in the previous example, even though the increment to the rate of money growth is still 10 percent. Since $\theta = 0.5$, only half of the new demand shock will be viewed as a real disturbance. The unemployment rate will still fall below 7 percent, but not as low as 4 percent. The inflation rate will rise to more than 15 percent, although it will still fall short of its new long-run value.[8] This short-run equilibrium is depicted as point D in Figure 2. In short, the more inflation an economy has experienced, the less of a surprise any given increment to inflation is likely to be.

As Lucas (1976) points out, the very essence of a policy is that it is a predictable response of the government or the central bank to a particular set of circumstances. Since it is not possible for a central bank to pursue a policy that consistently surprises people, then the basic question for the design of monetary policy is, What is the best set of predictable actions, contingent or otherwise, for the monetary authorities to follow? The set of predictable actions that policymakers choose to follow constitutes the *monetary regime* of the country. The debate over monetary policy, then, is fundamentally a debate over alternative regimes. Each of the chapters in this volume illuminates some aspect of the problem of choosing an appropriate monetary regime.

Rules versus Discretion

A fundamental issue in the design of a monetary regime is how much discretion ought to be granted to the monetary authorities. In Chapter 1, Robert Barro analyzes the inherent logic of a purely discretionary regime, a system in which the monetary authorities are free to determine the rate of change in the money supply. This discretionary regime appears to be very similar to the current Federal Reserve regime, although Barro does not say so explicitly.

8. This neglects the added complication that the demand for money may be sufficiently interest-elastic to induce temporary overshooting of the new steady-state inflation rate as nominal interest rates rise due to the increase in expected inflation.

Barro's principal conclusion is that a central bank with discretionary authority will increase the growth of the money supply beyond the level consistent with price stability. If the economy's natural rate of unemployment is inefficiently high because labor markets are distorted by taxes, minimum wages, or other such policies, unanticipated inflation can bring a temporary gain in economic well-being, and policymakers attempting to further the public interest may choose to follow an inflationary monetary policy. In addition, a surprise inflation has the beneficial effect of retiring part of the outstanding stock of government debt through a nondistorting lump-sum tax rather than taxes, such as income or excise taxes, that reduce the allocative efficiency of the economy.

Under a discretionary regime, however, once these incentives for the monetary authorities to inflate become understood and individuals expect the authorities to generate inflation, the Phillips curve shown in Figure 2 will move to the right. As a result, if the central bank expands the money supply by the expected amount, none of the sought-after benefits will be realized. The rate of inflation will be higher without any gain in employment. If instead the central bank does not accelerate the growth of the money supply, the result will be higher unemployment. In either case, policymakers face a dilemma—they must choose between permanent inflation or a recession of uncertain duration.

The problem raised by Barro is not that people misperceive the current rate of inflation, as in the previous discussion of the Phillips curve, but rather that people understand the central bank's incentives to generate inflation and therefore do not believe that the monetary authorities will refrain permanently from a policy of "surprise" inflation. Under discretion, the central bank has no unambiguous way in which it can commit itself credibly to a noninflationary policy. Even if the monetary authorities were to announce their future money-growth targets, they must somehow convince the public that they will not subsequently revise those targets when they become inconvenient. It is not impossible for a central bank with discretionary authority to follow a credible noninflationary policy, but the type of behavior necessary to convince the public of its determination would most likely resemble a nondiscretionary path. That is, the authorities to some extent would have to limit the scope of their discretion by adhering to a fairly restrictive rule or set of rules governing the determination of the money supply. A major difficulty in designing an optimal monetary regime is that we do not know enough about the rate at which central-bank credibility is eroded by the exercise of discretionary power.

To illustrate the elusive nature of the tradeoff between rules and discretion, consider a rule requiring the central bank to expand the money supply at a constant annual rate of k percent. Suppose that a period of rapid financial innovation results in a permanent increase in the demand for money. Strict adherence to the k percent rule would result in a period of unusually low inflation and unusually high unemployment if the reduction in inflation were not fully anticipated. If the monetary authorities were to deviate temporarily from the k percent growth path of the money supply, they could mitigate or eliminate the increase in unemployment. Offsetting this potential gain from discretionary money-supply management are two potential costs. First, the authorities might misjudge the magnitude or the permanence of the money-demand shock and therefore destabilize rather than stabilize output and inflation. Second, any such foray into policy activism will to some extent undermine the credibility of the central bank's commitment to the k percent rule. If these costs of activism are smaller than the associated gains in a particular set of circumstances, then the optimal monetary regime will allow for a deviation from the k percent growth path contingent on the presence of those circumstances. Examples of such contingent deviations from a rule mentioned by Barro occurred when countries on the gold standard suspended convertibility of their currencies into gold during major wars and resumed convertibility at the prewar price after an appropriate postwar deflation. The art of designing an optimal monetary regime consists primarily of gauging what kinds of contingencies can be accommodated without undermining the credibility of the central bank's commitment to a constant price of gold or rate of money-supply growth or similar rule.

The Gold Standard

To develop a sense of the optimal allowance for contingent departures from an underlying rule, it is necessary to study the actual workings of past monetary regimes. In Chapter 2, Anna Schwartz summarizes the history of the gold standard and examines the proposal that the United States return to such a standard.

Under a gold standard, the U.S. government is committed to keeping the price of gold fixed and is willing to convert the dollar into gold at a fixed price. In such a regime, the Treasury must maintain gold reserves sufficient for the volume of sales that may be necessary from time to time to peg the price of gold successfully, and the U.S. Treasury would be required to sell gold whenever the price of gold tended to rise. If the Treasury were to pursue a discretionary policy that resulted in inflation, the prices of all goods and services (including gold) would rise. This rise in the price of gold would necessitate gold sales by the Treasury and could eventually deplete the Treasury's gold reserves. Thus, with a gold standard the government cannot conduct a truly discretionary monetary policy.

A primary advantage of the gold standard is its presumed tendency toward a predictable long-run value of the monetary unit. This predictability depends on the predictability of the increase in the supply of gold. The commitment of the U.S. Treasury to exchange gold for currency or currency for gold at a fixed price means that the purchasing power of a currency unit is always equal to the purchasing power of a corresponding amount of gold. Money is "as good as gold" because the monetary authorities assure that they are perfect substitutes. Since the aggregate price level is inversely related to the purchasing power of the monetary unit, it is also inversely related to the value of gold relative to other commodities. If gold rises in value because the price level has fallen, the incentives to mine more of it increase.

As long as there is a positive elasticity of supply of gold with respect to its value in terms of other goods, a gold standard will lead to an increase in the rate of growth of the money supply as the general level of prices of goods and services falls. That is, unusually low nominal prices will increase the money growth rate and unusually high nominal prices will decrease the money growth rate. For the price level to maintain a constant long-run value, the long-run supply of gold would have to be perfectly elastic. Under less elastic gold-supply conditions, the price level would fluctuate around a long-run deflationary trend. While such reversion of the price level toward its trend value is presumed to be a characteristic of commodity standards in general and not merely a gold standard, the era of the gold standard represents our most important experience with such a regime, and gold is the commodity most commonly advocated by supporters of a commodity standard.

The long-run predictability of the supply of gold and thus the price level under a gold standard may be substantially reduced if the cost of producing gold is subject to shocks such as discoveries of new ore deposits or technological improvements in the extraction process, both of which occurred during the historical gold standard. To the extent that such developments are induced by deflation, they are merely manifestations of the money-supply response to be expected under a gold standard. If they are exogenous shocks, however, they demonstrate that unpredictable swings in the value of money are possible under a gold standard.

To evaluate the relative effectiveness of a rule fixing the price of gold as a means of stabilizing the general price level and avoiding excessive fluctuation in aggregate production, Schwartz compares the performance of the economy under the historical gold standard with the experience of the United States and the United Kingdom following World War II. Although the era of the gold standard was characterized by substantially lower average rates of inflation than in the period following World War II, there was also greater variability of real per capita income. As Allan Meltzer points out in Chapter 4, it is impossible to know how much of the difference in output volatility between these two periods is due to the difference in monetary arrangements and how much to other factors such as the transition from an agricultural to an industrial society. However, the greater short-run variability of the rate of inflation under the gold standard as compared to the period following World War II could have caused greater variability in real output if more variable inflation is harder to forecast than less variable inflation.

As Schwartz points out, a shift from discretionary monetary management to a true gold standard would represent a drastic change in monetary regimes. So substantial a change in policy would require a degree of political consensus that she thinks is not attainable in the foreseeable future. Even if the United States returned to a gold standard, it is not at all certain that prices would actually be more predictable than under alternative arrangements.

Foreign Exchange Rates

An important aspect of a country's monetary regime is the way in which it provides for the determination of the value of the domestic currency in terms of foreign currencies. In Chapter 3, Richard Cooper discusses both the internal and external implications of fixed exchange rates. Under such a system, the monetary authorities are committed to maintaining a fixed rate of exchange between the domestic currency and the currency of another country. Although the major currencies now float against each other relatively freely, many smaller countries peg their currencies to one of the major currencies.

Cooper makes two central points about exchange-rate policy and monetary policy. First, under a commitment to a fixed exchange rate, central-bank management of the domestic money supply is constrained by balance-of-payments considerations. An excessive expansion of the stock of domestic credit will ultimately cause a reduction in the central bank's holdings of the currency to which its monetary unit is pegged. To avoid exhausting their foreign reserves, the monetary authorities must curtail their domestic money creation to the rate that will maintain equilibrium in the balance of payments. Cooper considers in detail the likely consequences of a fixed exchange rate for a small or medium-sized country and finds that the answer depends on far too many factors to yield a single optimal policy for all countries.

Cooper's second major point is that while fixing the value of its currency against another currency eliminates discretionary money-supply management in the pegging country, it does not do so in the reserve-currency country. Therefore, merely fixing exchange rates does not by itself establish a world monetary regime. To establish a predictable monetary regime, an international system of fixed exchange rates must specify the way in which the stock of the monetary unit to which the currencies are pegged is determined. Under an international gold standard, the rate of gold production would largely determine the rate of world inflation or deflation in the long run. During the Bretton Woods era, the United States, in its role as the reserve-currency country, largely determined the rate of growth of the world money supply.

Cooper's analysis suggests a question that is potentially important for the United States: Should the rate of inflation under a discretionary regime with floating exchange rates be expected to differ systematically from the rate of inflation that would be generated in the same country if it were the reserve-currency country in a system of fixed exchange rates? To answer this question requires the extension of a positive theory of discretionary monetary policy to the case of an international system such as Bretton Woods. Analyses by Gordon (1975) and Toma (1982) have emphasized the potential importance of political and institutional factors in determining the rate of inflation under discretionary monetary policy. If the influence of foreign central bankers on the monetary policy of the reserve-currency country were to alter that policy in a predictable way, an international system of fixed exchange rates would provide a monetary regime for the reserve-currency country that would differ from a discretionary system with floating exchange rates.

Comparative Uncertainty under Different Monetary Regimes

Of the various criteria by which alternative monetary regimes should be evaluated, the degree of uncertainty of the future course of the general price level associated with each regime is among the most important. In Chapter 4, Allan Meltzer examines data for the United States from 1890 to 1980, dividing the period into six different monetary regimes. He uses a multistate Kalman filter to distinguish three types of changes in variables over time: transitory changes in the levels of variables, permanent changes in levels (which are transitory changes in growth rates), and permanent changes in growth rates. Meltzer estimates people's forecasts of money, income, and prices in a given period as the predictions of such filters applied to past values of those variables. The parameters of the forecasting equations are revised as the passage of time reveals unexpected changes in the variables to be permanent rather than transitory.

To compare the predictability of money, income, and prices under the different monetary regimes, Meltzer estimates the average errors that would be made in forecasting the levels and rates of change of those variables in each of the six periods. He finds that nearly 20 percent of the variation in the price level under the gold standard was purely transitory compared to about 1 percent in the post–World War II era. If the one-period-ahead forecast errors were equal in the different regimes, the regime with the greatest proportion of transitory forecast errors would offer the greatest degree of long-term predictability.

What Meltzer finds, however, is that the one-term-ahead forecast errors were so much larger under the gold standard than under either the Bretton Woods or the floating-exchange-rate regimes that the long-term price level under the last two regimes was more predictable despite the fact that nearly all price-level shocks were permanent under those regimes. This result highlights the important distinction between ex post price-level stability, which was far greater under the gold standard, and ex ante price-level predictability, which appears to have been greater under policies since 1951. Thus, the Federal Reserve appears to have used its discretionary authority in the post–World War II period to pursue policies resulting in higher but more predictable rates of inflation.

Meltzer's conclusion should be qualified in several ways. First, as he points out, the data for the gold-standard years contain substantially more measurement errors than do the data for later periods. Second, the finding of reduced long-term price-level uncertainty since 1951 is inconsistent with the observed decline in the average length of bond maturities relative to earlier periods. Finally, it is not clear whether the filtering technique employed accurately incorporates the extent to which individuals expected the price level to revert toward its trend value in the long run, especially if the length of time required for this reversion to manifest itself is subject to random fluctuation. Despite these qualifications, Meltzer's findings are important because they call into question one of the major benefits usually attributed to a monetary system based on gold.

The Federal Reserve System

In Chapter 5, David Lindsey evaluates Federal Reserve discretion over monetary policy since 1970. During the 1970s, as the inadequacies of targeting monetary policy on interest rates became apparent, the Federal Reserve and the U.S. Congress paid increasing attention to the use of the growth rates of monetary aggregates as policy targets. This culminated in the October 1979 change in target variables from the federal funds rate to nonborrowed bank reserves. Since such a change was viewed as necessary to restrain money growth to its announced target rate, the period from October 1979 to the fall of 1982 is sometimes viewed as an example of what can be expected under a constant-money-growth rule. Whether this period is actually a good sample is questionable, since, as Lindsey points out, M1 (currency plus checkable deposits) growth was actually highly erratic.

Lindsey believes that much of the variability in M1 and in short-term interest rates between 1979 and 1982 resulted from instability in the demand for money due largely to important institutional changes such as the nationwide authorization of NOW accounts (interest-earning deposits on which checks may be written). An unanticipated increase in the quantity of money demanded tends to contract the level of employment and output unless it is fully accommodated by an increase in the money supply. Under such conditions, the Federal Reserve could attempt to avoid the contraction in real output by departing from its announced monetary growth target.

The drawbacks of such intervention are the possible overreaction by the monetary authorities and the possible damage to the credibility of the authorities' commitment to the stated long-term money-growth path. Since the fall of 1982, when the Federal Reserve, in Paul Volcker's words, "put a greater premium on judgment and less [on] 'automaticity,'" both interest-rate volatility and unemployment have declined without a resurgence of inflation (Volcker 1983, p. 174). These developments lead Lindsey to endorse a regime in which the central bank targets its policies on monetary aggregates but retains sufficient discretion to depart from those targets under particular economic circumstances.

A Proposal for Reform

In the final chapter of this book, Robert Hall proposes a basic change in the way that monetary policy is carried out. It is an interesting example of the scope that exists for monetary reform. His purpose is to describe the optimal monetary regime for an economy in which prices move sluggishly, causing monetary changes to affect real output. Hall's system is designed to attain three objectives: microeconomic efficiency, stability, and macroeconomic efficiency. The first goal, which requires that money earn a market rate of interest, would be reached by having the Federal Reserve pay a rate of interest on bank reserves equal to slightly less than the three-month Treasury bill rate and by allowing all financial institutions to issue interest-bearing notes in small denominations. The second goal, stability of financial institutions, would be largely attained by the saturation of the economy in reserves that would result from paying interest on them.

Finally, to reduce fluctuations in real output, Hall would have the monetary authorities adjust the price level up or down in a constant proportion to increases or decreases in the rate of unemployment from its normal level. The central bank would alter the price level by changing the differential between the interest rate it pays on reserves and the three-month Treasury bill rate. Lowering the interest rate paid on reserves, for example, would cause a reduction in the ratio of reserves to deposits desired by financial intermediaries, thereby inducing banks to create more loans and deposits. Additionally, the reduction in interest on reserves would lower the interest rate paid by financial institutions on deposits and the new type of interest-bearing notes, thereby reducing the quantity of money demanded. Both effects would cause the price level to rise.

Summary

The basic issue underlying this book is the degree of discretion that should be granted to the monetary authorities. The major source of disagreement is the desire for both predictability and flexibility. The purpose of this volume is to provide a theoretical framework for understanding these issues and to summarize the available empirical evidence that is necessary to judge the merits of alternative monetary systems. As this volume illustrates, there is no broad consensus on the changes that should be made in our present monetary regime. However, any change from the current system should take heed of the problems and possibilities discussed in the chapters that follow.

REFERENCES

Friedman, Milton. "The Role of Monetary Policy." *American Economic Review* 58 (March 1968), 1–17.

———. *Price Theory*. Chicago: Aldine Publishing Co., 1976.

———. "Nobel Lecture: Inflation and Unemployment." *Journal of Political Economy* 85 (June 1977), 451–72.

Gordon, Robert J. "The Demand for and Supply of Inflation." *Journal of Law and Economics* 18 (December 1975), 807–36.

Lucas, Robert E., Jr. "Expectations and the Neutrality of Money." *Journal of Economic Theory* 4 (April 1972), 103–24.

———. "Some International Evidence on Output-Inflation Tradeoffs." *American Economic Review* 63 (June 1973), 326–34.

———. "Econometric Policy Evaluation: A Critique." In *The Phillips Curve and Labor Markets*, Karl Brunner and Allan H. Meltzer, eds. Carnegie-Rochester Conference Series on Public Policy, vol. 1. Amsterdam: North-Holland, 1976. Pp. 19–46.

Muth, John F. "Rational Expectations and the Theory of Price Movements." *Econometrica* 29 (July 1961), 315–35.

Phelps, Edmund S., et al. *Microeconomic Foundations of Employment and Inflation Theory*. New York: W. W. Norton & Co., 1970.

Phillips, A. W. "The Relation between Unemployment and the Rate of Change of Money Wage Rates in the United Kingdom, 1861–1957." *Economica* 25 (November 1958), 283–99.

"Statement by Paul A. Volcker, Chairman, Board of Governors of the Federal Reserve System, before the Committee on Banking, Housing and Urban Affairs of the U.S. Senate, February 16, 1983." *Federal Reserve Bulletin* 69 (March 1983), 167–74.

Toma, Mark. "Inflationary Bias of the Federal Reserve System: A Bureaucratic Perspective." *Journal of Monetary Economics* 10 (September 1982), 163–90.

ONE

Rules versus Discretion

THE TRADITIONAL debate over rules versus discretion focused on the capability and objectives of the monetary authorities. Advocates of rules referred to imperfect knowledge about the economy and to policymakers' propensities to further inappropriate ends, possibly motivated by special interests.[1] But if the policymakers were intelligent and well-meaning, there was no obvious defense for a rule that tied their hands in advance. Discretion seemed to be synonymous with flexibility, which one had no reason to deny to smart, benevolent policymakers.

This perspective on rules versus discretion was changed by Kydland and Prescott (1977), who looked at rules as a form of commitment. A commitment amounts to a binding contract, which specifies in advance the actions that someone will take, possibly contingent on a variety of exogenous circumstances. In contrast, under discretion, a person promises only to take those actions that will best further one's objectives later. (Such promises are easy to enforce.) Discretion is the special case of a rule or contract in which none of today's provisions restrict a person's future actions. In the area of private business dealings, we tend to think about optimal forms of contracts and regard pure discretion as unusual. Similarly, in the context of public policy, the perspective becomes the optimal form of rules or prior restrictions—even smart, benevolent policymakers are likely to desire and use an ability to make binding promises.

Kydland and Prescott discuss various areas of public policy in which commitments are important. An example is patents, which encourage inventions but also restrict the supply of goods ex post. Under pure discretion, a policymaker who has no past commitments and cares about social welfare would (once and for all) invalidate all old patents but continue to issue new ones. However, the perception of a policy of this type by potential inventors has adverse effects on new inven-

I AM GRATEFUL to the National Science Foundation for support of underlying research.
    1. See, for example, Friedman (1960, Chapter 4).

tions, which soon become old inventions. Hence, the optimal policy contains a mechanism to preclude or at least inhibit the abolition of old patents. Then the details of this policy involve the standard tradeoff between the incentive to invent and the ex post restriction of supply.

The manner of committing future actions varies with the area of public policy. In some cases, such as the duration and scope of patents, the rules are set out in formal law. Then the costs of changing laws (possibly coming under the constitutional restrictions against ex post facto laws) enforces the government's commitments. However, in the case of the Gold Standard Act in 1933 the existence of a law proved to be inadequate protection for those who held gold or made contracts denominated in gold.[2]

More often a government's commitments rely on the force of reputation, whereby people's expectations of future policy are tied in some fashion to past behavior. For instance, if a government defaults on its debts, potential bondholders are deterred by the perception that future defaults are more likely. Presumably this consideration is the main deterrent to default by many sovereign debtor countries today. (*Sovereign* must mean lacking in formal collateral.) As a general matter, the precise connection between past actions and expectations of future behavior is difficult to formalize in a model.

Monetary Policy under Discretion

A major contribution of Kydland and Prescott was the recognition that monetary policy involves the same issues about commitments as do such areas as patents, default on government debt, and imposition of levies on previously accumulated capital (via changes in property taxes or in other taxes that fall on capital). In the case of patents, it is obvious that a policymaker must worry about the link between current actions—such as eliminating past patents or changing the form of patent law—and people's perceptions about the value of presently issued patents (which motivate inventions). Similarly, monetary authorities must consider the interplay between today's choices—whether to engineer a monetary expansion or to change the "law" governing monetary policy—and people's beliefs about future money and prices.

Consider the example of the Phillips curve discussed in Kydland

---

2. For a discussion of the abrogation of gold clauses in public and private contracts, see Yeager (1966, p. 305). Additional discussions are in Nussbaum (1950, pp. 283–91) and McCulloch (1980).

and Prescott (1977) and in Barro and Gordon (July 1983, August 1983). These models involve the following main ingredients. First, monetary policy works by affecting the general price level. Second, unexpected increases in the price level (but not expected changes in prices) expand real economic activity. In other words, there is an "expectational Phillips curve." Third, the "representative person" and hence the benevolent policymaker value these expansions of activity at least over some range (which means that existing distortions make the "natural" level of output too small). Fourth, inflation itself is harmful—people value it only as a device to create unexpected inflation and thereby higher levels of economic activity.[3]

This model is structurally similar to the example about patents. At any point in time, the policymaker is motivated to generate unexpected inflation in order to stimulate the economy. (The analogue is the expansion of supply via the abolition of past patents.) But people understand these incentives in advance and therefore form high expectations of inflation. Hence, the policymaker must choose a high rate of inflation just to stay even, that is, in order for the actual rate of inflation to be equal to the expected rate of inflation. Finally, this high inflation imposes costs on the economy. (The parallel is the decrease in inventions because of the expectation that current patents will not be honored later.)

Barro and Gordon (July 1983, August 1983) analyze the equilibria for monetary policy and inflation for the Phillips curve model. In the case of pure discretion, the monetary authorities have no mechanisms for committing the future behavior of money and prices. Rather, they have a free hand to maximize social welfare at each point in time, while treating past events as givens. In this situation, there is an incentive in each period to create surprise inflation in order to generate an economic boom. But individuals understand this motivation and formulate their expectations accordingly. In this model, actual inflation cannot end up being systematically higher or lower than expected inflation.

Overall, two conditions must be satisfied in equilibrium. First, people's expectations of inflation are correct on average (that is, expectations are rational). Second, although the monetary authorities retain the power in each period to fool people via inflation surprises, they are not motivated to exercise this power. In order for this second condition to hold, the monetary authorities' drive to create unexpected inflation must, in equilibrium, be balanced by the

3. The analysis can be extended to incorporate the standard inflation tax or other real effects from anticipated inflation. Then the best rate of inflation need not be zero.

cost of inflation itself. In other words, inflation must be high enough so that the marginal cost of inflation equals the marginal benefit from inflation surprises. Only then will the chosen rates of inflation and monetary growth be consistent with the policymaker's desire to maximize social welfare at each point in time. The important point is that this equilibrium involves inflation that is high, but not surprisingly high. The economy bears the costs of high inflation but does not receive the rewards that would arise from unexpected inflation.

The high-inflation equilibrium as described depends on the presence of benefits from surprise inflation but does not rest solely on the existence of the (expectational) Phillips curve. Surprise inflation also amounts to a capital levy on assets, such as money and government bonds, that are denominated in nominal terms. Hence, at a point in time, unexpected inflation is like a lump-sum tax and works as a device to generate government revenue. Given that other taxes are distorting, the policymaker (and the representative person in the economy) would value the use of this lump-sum tax. Accordingly, this model parallels the previous one based on the Phillips curve, even though the source of benefit from unexpected inflation is different. There is an analogous discretionary equilibrium with high inflation.[4] But as before, this high inflation corresponds to high expected inflation. That is, there is no tendency for inflation to be surprisingly high.

In the model based on the Phillips curve, the incentive to create surprise inflation hinges on the desire to expand economic activity. This incentive depends on some distortions that make the natural rate of output too low. The disincentive effects from income taxes and transfer programs are possible sources of such distortions.[5] Similarly, in the model in which the government values surprise inflation as a lump-sum tax, there must be an underlying environment in which alternative taxes are distorting. In both cases, the existence of initial distortions underlies the prediction of high inflation. Calvo (1978) discusses the general role of existing distortions in these types of models. The bad outcomes under discretion depend on the presence of these distortions.

Barro and Gordon (August 1983) view the high-inflation equilibrium in a discretionary monetary regime as a positive theory of monetary policy and inflation under present-day monetary arrangements. Aside from predicting "high" average inflation and monetary growth,

4. See Barro (1983) for an elaboration of this model.
5. These taxes and transfers themselves may be warranted as necessary counterparts of (valuable) government expenditures. Hence, there is no implication that the government is failing to optimize on the fiscal side.

the model indicates the reactions to changes in the benefits from unexpected inflation or in the costs of actual inflation. For example, a rise in the natural rate of unemployment can raise the benefits from lowering unemployment through surprise inflation. It follows that a secular rise in the natural unemployment rate would lead to a secular rise in the mean rates of monetary growth and inflation. Similarly, the monetary authorities would value reductions of unemployment during recessions. The implication is that monetary growth would vary countercyclically, although such a policy can end up with no effect on the amplitude of business cycles.

A higher stock of nominally denominated public debt raises the benefits from capital levies via surprise inflation. The model implies that more public debt will lead to higher monetary growth, inflation, and nominal interest rates (although not to a rate of inflation in excess of the expected rate). In other words, the prediction is that deficits will be partly monetized. A similar analysis suggests that indexation of the public debt for inflation—which removes some of the benefits from surprise inflation—will lead to lower rates of inflation and monetary growth. Finally, a higher level of government spending tends to raise the benefits from lump-sum taxation (because the deadweight losses from other taxes would be higher). This change leads again to higher rates of inflation and monetary growth. That is, the endogenous response of monetary growth implies that government expenditures are inflationary.

The model assumes that actual inflation is costly but does not explain the source of these costs. Two frequently mentioned possibilities are the administrative expenses for changing prices and the transaction costs associated with economizing on cash holdings. The positive analysis of monetary policy does imply that a downward shift in the costs of inflation will lead to more inflation. If people think that inflation is not a serious problem, then the economy will end up with a lot of inflation.

This analysis of a discretionary monetary regime implies also that each flicker in the benefits from inflation surprises or in the costs of inflation will be reflected in variations in inflation. In contrast to an environment in which the government stabilizes prices, there will be substantial random fluctuations of inflation and monetary growth. Further, the greater the random fluctuations in the variables that influence the benefits from inflation shocks, the larger the variances of prices and money. For example, if there are frequent supply shocks (which alter the natural rate of output), then inflation and monetary growth will be volatile.

Monetary Rules

The results under discretion contrast with those under rules, that is, under regimes where the policymaker can and does make commitments about future monetary growth and inflation. Under discretion, the equilibrium involved high inflation but no tendency toward surprisingly high inflation. Hence, the economy suffered the costs from high inflation but secured none of the benefits from inflation surprises. Clearly, the monetary authorities can improve on this outcome by committing themselves ex ante to low inflation. If this commitment is credible—that is, if it is adequately enforced—then people also anticipate low inflation. The equilibrium would exhibit low and stable inflation,[6] with the same average amount of surprise inflation (zero) as before. These results support a form of constant-growth-rate rule, although applied to prices rather than to the quantity of money per se.

There is a tension in this type of rules equilibrium because the policymaker may retain the capacity to produce large social gains at any point in time by "cheating," that is, by generating surprisingly high inflation. There may then be a temporary economic boom or at least a substantial amount of government revenue obtained via a distortion-free tax. But if such cheating were feasible and desirable, people would understand the situation beforehand. In this case, the low-inflation equilibrium would not be tenable. Rather, there would be a high-inflation, discretionary equilibrium, as described previously. That is why the enforcement power behind a low-inflation rule is crucial. There must be a mechanism for binding the policymaker's hands in advance, so that (surprisingly) high inflation cannot be chosen later, even if such an outcome looks good ex post. The rationale for this binding of hands applies even though (or actually especially if) the policymaker is well-meaning. This type of commitment is necessary in order for low inflation to be credible and for the economy to achieve the equilibrium with low inflation.

Although the low-inflation, rules equilibrium is superior to the high-inflation, discretionary equilibrium, the rules equilibrium is still not first-best. The benefits from inflation surprises—for example, from lower unemployment or from the generation of distortion-free government revenue—reflect some external effects that have not been eliminated. In fact, it is the desire to approach the first-best

6. More generally, one can choose the average inflation rate that is optimal from the standpoint of the usual inflation tax.

solution via inflation surprises ex post that threatens the viability of the low-inflation equilibrium. The pursuit of the first-best tends to push the economy away from the second-best of a rule with low inflation, and toward the third-best of discretionary policy with high inflation. Again, this perspective highlights the importance of the enforcement power that makes a rule sustainable.

The optimal rule might set prices contingent on exogenous events, rather than being noncontingent. For example, wartime can be accompanied by high inflation, which constitutes surprisingly high inflation from the standpoint of earlier times at which the war was not anticipated. In an equilibrium, the counterpart must be surprisingly low inflation during peacetime. This type of contingent rule may be desirable because it generates lots of easy revenue via the capital levy from unexpected inflation during emergencies. In particular, it is possible to hold down distortions from the income tax at important times, such as wars.[7] Although the necessary accompaniment is a loss of revenue during nonemergencies, the net effect of this contingent policy is likely to be beneficial.[8] Under the gold standard, governments did in fact tend to go off gold during wars. This procedure enables a government to pursue the type of contingent policy for inflation that I sketched above. Although the movement off gold during wars was not necessarily a violation of the rules, the subsequent return to gold at the previous parity was probably an important part of the enforcement process.

A difficulty with contingent rules is that they may be difficult to verify. In particular, it is easy to confuse contingencies with the type of cheating that I have described.[9] Further, the policymaker would

7. The government's ability to run deficits lessens this incentive but does not eliminate it. Contingent on a bad draw, such as a war, it tends to be desirable to trigger the distortion-free capital levy.

8. There is such an outcome in the model of Lucas and Stokey (1983). They consider a form of contingent public debt, which ends up paying off well during peacetime and badly in wartime. If government bonds are nominally denominated and noncontingent (for reasons that escape me), the contingent behavior of inflation achieves the same end.

9. Fischer (1980) argues that governments may find it advantageous to preserve some possibilities for cheating, rather than committing themselves fully not to cheat (even if such commitments were feasible). An interpretation of Fischer is that contingent rules are preferred to noncontingent ones, as in the previous example where governments inflate during wars or other national emergencies. A second possible interpretation is that randomization of policy may sometimes be useful. Although randomized policies were nonoptimal in the models of monetary policy in Barro and Gordon (July 1983), Weiss (1976) offers an example in which a randomized income tax would be desirable. On the other hand, Skinner (1984) argues empirically that randomization of the income tax is, in fact, harmful on net.

be inclined to explain away high inflation as the consequence of some emergency rather than as a failure to conform with the rules. These considerations favor a rule that is relatively simple, such as a constant-growth-rate rule for either prices or money. The contingencies should be limited to well-defined events, such as major wars. Although this limitation may miss some gains from contingent action, the greater ease of enforcement makes it less likely that the situation will degenerate into a high-inflation, discretionary equilibrium.

The Policymaker's Reputation

Barro and Gordon (July 1983) have examined a regime in which the monetary authorities' reputation is substituted for formal rules. Under these conditions, people's expectations of future inflation depend on past performance. Unlike the case of pure discretion, the monetary authorities' choice of today's inflation rate assigns a weight to the effect on future inflationary expectations. Such considerations motivate the monetary authorities to hold down the rates of inflation and monetary growth.

This model involves a reputational equilibrium in which the outcome for inflation is a weighted average of that under discretion and that under a constant-growth-rate rule. The higher the monetary authorities' discount rate, the greater the weight attached to the discretionary result. From a positive standpoint, the findings are qualitatively in line with those under discretion. The main difference is that the reactions of inflation to various shocks—such as shifts in the natural rate of unemployment or in the size of government— are now smaller in magnitude. Hence, the variances (as well as the means) of inflation and monetary growth are smaller than those under discretion.

A difficulty with a regime based on the monetary authorities' reputation is the potential for multiple equilibria. There is a bootstrap character to the reputational equilibria, whereby if people base future beliefs on the policymaker's actions, the policymaker may be motivated (in a range of cases) to validate these beliefs. The various equilibria conform with rational expectations as well as with period-by-period optimization by the monetary authorities. Although one of the possible reputational equilibria tends to generate the best results overall, it is unclear how the economy (perhaps guided by the policymaker) would settle on this particular equilibrium.

There may be a unique reputational equilibrium in cases where past performance conveys information about the policymaker's own preferences—as in the model of Backus and Driffill (1984), who built on the work of Kreps and Wilson (1982). This analysis relies on differences in the personal characteristics of the potential policy-makers, which probably leaves little scope for systematic theoretical analysis.

On the one hand, it seems that the equilibria supported by reputation are uncertain approximations to the outcomes delivered by formal rules when supported by appropriate enforcement mechanisms. But, on the other hand, it appears that reputation, rather than a formal rule, prevails in many areas of public policy. This suggests that the costs of establishing and enforcing formal rules should not be ignored.

Types of Monetary Rules

Consider now the choice among types of monetary rules, rather than between rules and discretion. The choices among rules may be divided between quantity rules and price rules. In the former category, the policymaker aims for a target path of a monetary aggregate, such as the monetary base, M1, or a still broader concept of money. Friedman's (1960, Chapter 4) proposal for a constant-growth-rate rule for M2 falls into this class. From October 1979 until late 1982, the Federal Reserve System claimed to be following a policy of this type, stated in terms of monetary targets. But it is hard to see from the data that the growth of the monetary aggregates from quarter to quarter became more stable. On the other hand, during this period, interest rates showed unprecedented volatility, which many people believe was related to the Federal Reserve System's new policy.

Under a price rule, the monetary authorities would use their direct instruments of control—which might be not only open-market operations and changes in the discount rate but also a pegged exchange rate or a set price of gold—to achieve a desired path for some target price. The target might be a general index of prices, the prices of specified commodities, an interest rate, or the exchange rate itself. Examples of price rules are the gold standard, other commodity standards, a regime with a fixed exchange rate, and Irving Fisher's (1920) "stable-money" proposal for varying the price of gold in order to stabilize the overall cost of living. A policy of pegging a nominal interest rate is also a price rule but an incomplete one, because a rule to peg interest rates requires additional specifications in order to pin down the levels of prices and other nominal variables (see Sargent and Wallace 1975 and McCallum 1984). An interest-rate rule is not really a substitute for a rule that specifies the quantity of some monetary aggregate or the level of some price.

People are typically concerned with current and future prices rather than with the quantities of the monetary aggregates per se. People care about changes in the rate of inflation and nominal interest rates but usually not about how much M1 is outstanding. Hence, the case for a quantity rule must rely on ease of implementation and verification.[10] Even this argument is compromised by the monetary authority's tendency to shift from one target aggregate to another (see Hetzel 1984). A regime based on shifting quantity targets involves feedback from unspecified ultimate targets to money, rather than actually being a quantity (of money) rule.

A principal reason for a price rule focusing on a narrow band of prices, such as gold or an exchange rate, is that such regimes are relatively easy to operate and monitor. Otherwise, it would be preferable to stabilize a broad index of prices, possibly using the price of gold (as in Fisher 1920) or some other specific price target in order to attain the desired behavior of prices in general.

At the risk of engaging in normative economics, I would advocate a modified Fisherian regime in which open-market operations (rather than the price of gold) are used to achieve a target path for a general price index such as the GNP deflator.[11] This type of regime involves a form of feedback in which a price level above target triggers lower growth of the monetary base, and vice versa, for a price level below target. The objective might involve a moving path of prices, which allows for nonzero inflation. However, the ease of monitoring the system (and preventing once-and-for-all discretionary adjustments to the level of prices) argues for specifying the target as a constant price level. This setup would also produce the most convenient monetary unit, namely, one that maintains a nearly constant purchasing

---

10. I do not mean to argue that a constant-growth-rate rule for money, if implemented in the 1950s, would have been inferior to actual monetary policy. A quantity rule is likely to be better than discretion. Also, the difference between a quantity rule, say for M1, and a rule for stabilizing the general level of prices derives from movements in the real demand for M1. Shifts in the real demand for M1—especially the changes in velocity that are induced by shifting nominal interest rates—would probably have been mild if the monetary authority had adhered to a constant-growth-rate rule. However, when starting with high and volatile nominal interest rates, there are serious problems in the implementation of a quantity rule. There is the possibility of severe deflation during the transition to lower inflation, since real cash balances must rise dramatically. The advantage of a price rule is that it allows for large infusions of nominal money during the transition. In addition, since this monetary expansion arises only in response to the actual behavior of prices, there is no threat to the credibility of the system.

11. Simons (1936), who was concerned mostly with the superiority of rules over authorities, also favored a price rule rather than a quantity rule.

power.[12] On the other hand, the government's seigniorage would be severely limited. Finally, it would be possible to permit deviations from the target price level during major wars. This kind of provision parallels the practice under previous monetary regimes for governments to depart from gold in wartime.

A credible price rule of this type works to stabilize prices even if there are lags in observations of price indexes or in the effects of (exogenous changes in) money on the price level. In particular, if prices rise above target, then people would know that future monetary actions would bring prices back down to target. This expectation of deflation would raise the current real demand for money and thus lower the current price level. In other words, there would be a form of stabilizing speculation that would improve the functioning of the system. (The Swiss may have been relatively successful in controlling inflation because of a system of this type rather than having a constant-growth-rate rule for money. See Grossman 1984.)

Overall, the proposed price rule would generate a near zero mean inflation rate and a small forecast variance of future price levels. In such a regime the prices of individual commodities would be accurate guides for the allocation of resources. As recommended by Hayek (1945), monetary policy would provide a stable economic background that would enhance the flow of information and thereby promote efficiency.

Hall (1980) and Taylor (1984) have suggested that monetary policy aim at stabilizing nominal GNP, rather than the general price level. Since nominal GNP is the product of real GNP and the GNP deflator, this rule prescribes inverse feedback of money to two things: excesses of real GNP over target and excesses of the deflator over target. In contrast, the price-stabilization rule dictates feedback only to the level of prices—given the price level, fluctuations in real GNP do not induce any reactions of monetary instruments.

In order to evaluate proposals for stabilizing nominal GNP, it is necessary to ask why feedback from real GNP to money is desirable. In particular, reacting to real output would cause the monetary authorities to do less well at stabilizing the price level. There would be occasions when the policymaker would have to accept departures of the price level from target in order to achieve the desired response of money to fluctuations in real output. There would have to be some gain from these monetary reactions to real output to justify the increase in fluctuations in the general price level.

12. See Hall (1982) for a related discussion.

In the theories associated with the new classical macroeconomics such as those of Sargent and Wallace (1975), the regular reaction of money to real activity does not smooth out the business cycle.[13] Since people know that recessions inspire monetary accelerations, there are no systematic surprises. If only the surprise movements in money matter for real variables, there would be no implications for the business cycle. It follows that it would be preferable to limit monetary policy to the objective of stabilizing the general price level. Any broadening of this objective threatens people's accurate perceptions of prices (which has adverse real effects) but provides no offsetting benefits.

On the other hand, Keynesian theories with sticky prices suggest that regular feedback from output to money can (usefully) smooth out fluctuations in real economic activity. Although such a policy would mean an increase in the volatility of prices, it is nevertheless worthwhile for money to react systematically to variations in real GNP.

In effect, the proposal to stabilize nominal GNP is an attempt to unite the principal warring factions of macroeconomists. The new classicists are supposed to be happy because monetary policy would be governed by a rule, and that rule does entail stabilization of some nominal magnitude. Then the feedback response of money to real GNP is to be regarded as a minor nuisance, most of which the private sector, it is hoped, can filter out.

Keynesians are supposed to be happy with the proposal to stabilize nominal GNP because it allows for an active response of money to recessions and booms. Presumably most Keynesians would also accept the feedback from prices to money, although they may not opt for the equal weighting given to fluctuations in real GNP and fluctuations in the general price level. The main thing that Keynesians would have to give up is their commitment to discretionary monetary policy, which seems little to ask.

The choice between the two objectives—stabilizing the general price level versus stabilizing nominal GNP—corresponds to the weights one attaches to the validity of the two competing viewpoints about macroeconomics. (Surely one of these views must be correct.) If one attaches little weight to Keynesian theories with sticky prices, the policymaker's preferred objective would be stabilization of the general price level.

13. This is also the conclusion of purely real theories of business cycles. In other models, monetary activism can affect the character of the business cycle but not in a desirable manner. In these cases, feedback from output to money should be avoided.

Robert J. Barro

Positive versus Normative Theories
of Government Policy

I have been vague about whether I am engaging in positive or normative economics (which doubtless reflects my uncertainties, rather than a desire to conceal truth). Gordon and I (July 1983) intended to carry out a positive analysis of monetary policy, given that the existing institutions dictated an environment of discretion. That is, the policymaker could not opt for a rule under which there would be meaningful commitments about the future growth of money or prices. Given these institutional constraints, we analyzed the day-to-day operating characteristics of the monetary authorities. At this level, it did not seem that the advice of economists would be especially relevant.

Gordon and I also contrasted the results under discretion with those under rules, that is, under alternative institutions in which the monetary authorities could make some commitments about the future growth of money and prices. For this comparison between discretion and rules to be interesting, both regimes must be feasible. That is, there must be a choice of erecting institutions that do or do not permit commitments about future money and prices. This choice should be as much subject to positive analysis as are those about day-to-day operations under a given institutional mode. Further, if an economist labels the actual institutional selection as inferior to other arrangements, what does that labeling mean? Conceivably, the economist may have unearthed new knowledge, but other possibilities are more likely. Although Buchanan and Tullock (1962) and Buchanan (1962) argue that the advice of economists is more pertinent at the level of institutional choice than at the level of day-to-day operations, it is unclear what positive theory of institutional choice they have in mind.

Perhaps the answer is that economists' advice does have some role but one that is measured in the same way as the contribution of other factors of production. Namely, economists' market wages—rather than claims to save the economy billions of dollars through policy advice—tell us something about the group's productivity. Although the wages of economists are fairly high, they still represent a negligible proportion of the GNP.[14]

---

14. Perhaps economists are like the water of the water-diamond paradox. If there were only a few economists, then their overall wage income might be enormous. But economists are in such abundant supply (being cheap to produce) that their wage rate is driven down to a meager level.

REFERENCES

Backus, David K., and J. Driffill. "Inflation and Reputation." Queens University, Kingston, Ontario, February 1984.

Barro, Robert J. "Inflationary Finance under Discretion and Rules." *Canadian Journal of Economics* 16 (February 1983), 1–16.

Barro, Robert J., and David B. Gordon. "Rules, Discretion and Reputation in a Model of Monetary Policy." *Journal of Monetary Economics* 12 (July 1983), 101–21.

———. "A Positive Theory of Monetary Policy in a Natural Rate Model." *Journal of Political Economy* 91 (August 1983), 589–610.

Buchanan, James M. "Predictability: The Criterion of Monetary Constitutions." In *In Search of a Monetary Constitution*, Leland B. Yeager, ed. Cambridge: Harvard University Press, 1962. Pp. 155–83.

Buchanan, James M., and Gordon Tullock. *The Calculus of Consent*. Ann Arbor: University of Michigan Press, 1962.

Calvo, Guillermo A. "On the Time Consistency of Optimal Policy in a Monetary Economy." *Econometrica* 46 (November 1978), 1411–28.

Fischer, Stanley. "Dynamic Inconsistency, Cooperation and the Benevolent Dissembling Government." *Journal of Economic Dynamics and Control* 2 (February 1980), 93–107.

Fisher, Irving. *Stabilizing the Dollar*. New York: Macmillan, 1920.

Friedman, Milton. *A Program for Monetary Stability*. New York: Fordham University Press, 1960.

Grossman, Herschel I. "Counterfactuals, Forecasts, and Choice—Theoretic Modelling of Policy." *NBER Working Papers*, No. 1381, June 1984.

Hall, Robert E. "Monetary Policy for Disinflation, Remarks Prepared for the Federal Reserve Board," Stanford University, Stanford, California, October 1980.

———. "Explorations in the Gold Standard and Related Policies for Stabilizing the Dollar." In *Inflation: Causes and Effects*, Robert E. Hall, ed. Chicago: University of Chicago Press for the National Bureau of Economic Research, 1982. Pp. 111–22.

Hayek, Friedrich A. "The Use of Knowledge in Society." *American Economic Review* 35 (September 1945), 519–30.

Hetzel, Robert L. "The Formulation of Monetary Policy." Federal Reserve Bank of Richmond, Virginia, 1984.

Kreps, David, and Robert Wilson. "Reputation and Imperfect Information." *Journal of Economic Theory* 27 (August 1982), 253–79.

Kydland, Finn E., and Edward C. Prescott. "Rules Rather than Discretion: The Inconsistency of Optimal Plans." *Journal of Political Economy* 85 (June 1977), 473–91.

Lucas, Robert E., and Nancy L. Stokey. "Optimal Fiscal and Monetary Policy in an Economy without Capital." *Journal of Monetary Economics* 12 (July 1983), 55–93.

McCallum, Bennett T. "Some Issues Concerning Interest Rate Pegging,

Price Level Determinacy, and the Real Bills Doctrine." *NBER Working Papers*, No. 1294, March 1984.

McCulloch, J. Huston. "The Ban on Indexed Bonds, 1933–77." *American Economic Review* 70 (December 1980), 1018–21.

Nussbaum, Arthur. *Money in the Law, National and International.* Brooklyn: The Foundation Press, 1950.

Sargent, Thomas J., and Neil Wallace. " 'Rational' Expectations, the Optimal Monetary Instrument, and the Optimal Money Supply Rule." *Journal of Political Economy* 83 (April 1975), 241–54.

Simons, Henry C. "Rules versus Authorities in Monetary Policy." *Journal of Political Economy* 44 (February 1936), 1–30.

Skinner, John W. "Uncertain Tax Policy and Economic Efficiency." University of Virginia, Charlottesville, Virginia, March 1984.

Taylor, John B. "What Would Nominal GNP Targeting Do to the Business Cycle?" In *Understanding Monetary Regimes*, Karl Brunner and Allan H. Meltzer, eds. Carnegie-Rochester Conference Series on Public Policy, vol. 22. Amsterdam: North-Holland, 1985. Pp. 61–84.

Weiss, Laurence. "The Desirability of Cheating Incentives and Randomness in the Optimal Income Tax." *Journal of Political Economy* 84 (December 1976), 1343–52.

Yeager, Leland B. *International Monetary Relations*. New York: Harper & Row, 1966.

The Conflict between Short-run and Long-run Objectives

PHILLIP CAGAN

I AGREE with Barro's theme that even though price stability is a desirable objective of monetary policy, it eludes us because we allow other objectives to interfere with its attainment. Barro refers to the study he did with Gordon (August 1983) to describe the model he uses. In this model, monetary expansions that are unanticipated produce a temporary reduction in unemployment at the expense of long-run inflation. The irresistible temptation by the authorities thus to reduce unemployment by cheating on their honest desire to achieve price stability is known, however, and taken into account by the public. Given the public's expected rate of inflation, a lower rate of inflation would result in unemployment, so a stable equilibrium, in which the benefit of any reductions in unemployment is outweighed by the social costs of raising the inflation rate even further, is reached. This equilibrium is inferior to one of price stability with the same unemployment rate, which can be reached, however, only by somehow convincing the public that the authorities will not cheat.

I question whether a stable equilibrium is reached in this process. Let me amend and extend Barro's model by using it to describe the traditional view of this process. Then I shall comment on the conflict between short-run and long-run objectives.

Barro's Model Reformulated

In Barro's model, the economy ends up in an unsatisfactory situation of inflation without any reduction in unemployment. The preferred position of lower inflation and the same unemployment is not reached because the authorities cannot be trusted to foreswear unannounced stimulus to reduce unemployment. It is a little hard to believe, however, that the preferred outcome would not be achieved. (For a similar skepticism, see Taylor 1983.) The authorities have to convince the public that they will not cheat on their commitment to price

31

stability, to be sure, but that credibility problem is not insuperable. Its emphasis in the current literature misdirects our attention to the wrong problem. It is not deception that keeps the desired goal of price stability out of reach. It is the public's insistence, shared and accepted by the authorities, not to subordinate low unemployment to other objectives. Proposals for a binding commitment to price stability are really a mechanism to give the authorities an excuse to impose a policy that the public, or at least its politically elected representatives, does not want.

But these objections to Barro's model can be easily taken care of. Let me substitute for the rational-expectations, market-clearing framework of his model the traditional notions of price inflexibility and long lags in the effect of monetary policy. These are not Keynesian concoctions, as Barro's discussion might suggest. They were an accepted view before Keynes. Not all older views are Keynesian. As a matter of fact, when I entered the profession years ago, it was difficult to get anyone outside Chicago to take seriously an assumption of fully rational economic behavior and price-clearing competitive equilibrium. Times do change. Now any contrary assumption is all but greeted with derisive catcalls. To avoid that, let me introduce price inflexibility as a hypothetical assumption to be judged by the predictability of its implications. It may or may not be a realistic assumption, depending on one's point of view. Similarly, a lag in the complete response of prices to monetary actions longer than the one period used in current theoretical models of rational expectations is also perhaps no longer accepted, but I have believed in the monetary lag for too long to change now. In any event, no one says how long each period is in those models. Could each period be two years?

If we put price inflexibility and long lags into Barro's model, it describes the following scenario. Although price stability is highly desired, the public also wants monetary policy to stimulate the economy when cyclical unemployment develops. This stimulation is known to reduce unemployment. It is also known that because of long lags, the stimulus has a delayed effect and is often continued by mistake longer than necessary to counteract the unemployment. The nation is willing to risk overstimulus to avoid unemployment, though the degree of risk willingly incurred can change from time to time. Overstimulus expands the economy too much and results in inflation. Periodic episodes of inflation are not reversed and produce a secular rise in the price level. Thus the model produces an upward trend in prices, not because of cheating but because the authorities are unable to achieve both full employment and complete price stability and are unwilling or politically unable to abandon the former. The attempt

to counteract cyclical unemployment without generating later inflationary pressures could in theory succeed, but it is difficult and usually fails, as we know from experience. Moreover, if unemployment
has any negative weight in the nation's welfare function, preserving
price stability in the face of price shocks like the OPEC oil price
increase is impossible.

In this reformulated version of Barro's model, a stable equilibrium
appears unlikely. When inflation develops, the authorities can be
counted on to slow it down, but they are hesitant to press down too
hard and are certainly unwilling to reverse an increase in prices by
deflating them. Inflationary pressures from a previous overstimulus
may not be eliminated before the next bout of unemployment. The
overstimulus syndrome is therefore implanted on higher and higher
initial rates of inflation. There is a tendency, therefore, toward esca-
lation of inflation. If the rate of inflation gets high enough, the resolve
to bring it down may stiffen, and the objective of low or lower
inflation may predominate for a while, as since 1980.

Are we seeing today a permanent shifting of the relative weight
attached to short-run and long-run objectives? Will the outcome shift
toward less price instability? Perhaps it will. But for any given negative value of cyclical unemployment except zero, there will always
be a perceived gain in countering prevailing unemployment and a
danger of overdoing the stimulus.

Can this process be stopped by nondiscretionary methods of the
kind Barro discusses? Yes, of course it can. Will it? I doubt it. I see
no evidence that the public is willing to accept nondiscretionary
policies and to give up the option to deal not only with severe unemployment but also financial crises. There is today a heightened awareness of the advantages of price stability, and perhaps a new desire
to avoid the worst excesses of fine tuning. But no government today
would surrender its freedom to deal as it sees fit with macroeconomic
problems and would never say that it would. Wars are not the only
contingencies that governments want the option to deal with, and as
Barro notes, any attempt to list all contingencies destroys the credibility of a nondiscretionary policy and, moreover, becomes hopelessly imprecise.

A serious problem with nondiscretionary policies, which specify
automatic responses to deviations of a price index from constancy,
is overshooting. If a lag exists, a policy response initiated when the
price index changes takes considerable time to reverse the change
in prices, which in the meantime continues to call forth automatic
responses. By the time these finally take effect, they are likely to
have overdone the correction and have to be reversed. Overshooting

makes such automatic policies less appealing. Although it is not certain that under the historical gold standard overshooting was a problem, corrections of price movements were exceedingly slow.

It is possible to design a response that takes the lag into account and avoids overshooting, but given the present state of knowledge, no automatic response can be expected to do the job of preserving price stability and yet never overshoot. In the literature the theoretical systems that avoid overshooting in automatic policies assume a degree of informational feedback that is unrealistic.

Short-run and Long-run Objectives

The fundamental problem that Barro addresses is the conflict between short-run and long-run objectives. The short-run objectives are to alleviate disturbances that hit financial markets and to counteract cyclical unemployment. The long-run objective is price level stability. As explained, devotion to the former can cause serious misses of the latter.

But contrary to some discussions, these objectives are not completely incompatible. It is possible to stabilize prices over the long run and still take discretionary measures for the short-run objectives so long as policy gives priority to the long-run effect on prices. This can be done because of the long lag in the effect on prices and the relative unimportance of minor variations in monetary growth in the short run, given expectations of long-run stability. Because of this theoretical compatibility, central banks will never abandon interest-rate smoothing completely. In monetary targeting, short-run variations in the rate of growth of the money supply can be used to absorb financial disturbances and fight cyclical unemployment so long as a target for the growth rate of the money supply consistent with price stability is achieved over a period of one to two years. Mistakes of overpursuing the short-run objectives are of course a problem, but short-run deviations from the long-run target need not, if controlled properly, be a source of mistakes. If the target is accurate and not widely missed, there will be no overshooting.

One of the attractions of monetary targeting is that it offers the possiblity of resolving to some extent the conflict between short-run and long-run objectives. Monetary growth can be targeted to achieve price stability in the long run and yet allow discretionary deviations within limits devoted to short-run objectives. It is important, of course, to avoid inflationary mistakes because a deflationary correction is costly and not likely to be undertaken. Yet, given the primitive state of forecasting and the long lag in monetary effects, monetary targeting comes closest to providing an accurate guide to long-run objectives.

The recent emphasis on targeting GNP rather than targeting monetary growth puzzles me. A GNP growth path has been an objective of policy since the end of bond pegging in the early 1950s. The desired growth path of prices and real output implies a desired growth path for nominal GNP. Given the time lag in influencing GNP by monetary policy, there must be a way of guiding policy instruments ahead of time. Monetary targeting is such a method. A method often proposed supposedly as an alternative is to set all the policy instruments as directed by a sophisticated econometric model that exists either in a computer or in the heads of the authorities. If such a model exists and we have confidence in it, by all means it should be used to set the instruments, including the monetary target. But we all know the limitations of these models. If econometric models are reliable enough to guide policy, why do we have more than one such model predicting the same variables? In any event, the use of model feedback does not offer a serious alternative to monetary targets for the long run. Once that target is set, feedback of institutional or structural changes that would call for a modification in the target can be documented only infrequently, and econometric models fitted to the past do not provide such information.

Feedback from econometric models does provide an alternative to monetary targets in the short run, since there is a choice between continual adjustments to the feedback and a policy of staying put with a fairly constant monetary growth rate. As stated, so long as the long-run target is adhered to, short-run deviations are not incompatible with the objective of price stability and the use of monetary targeting to achieve it. The only question is whether the feedback is successful in achieving the short-run objectives and whether it tends to interfere with the long-run target. There is a vast literature on this issue. A cautious activism appears to rule current monetary policy. It should be ever mindful of the Brainard (1967) principle that the less certain is the model and information on which policy must be based, the less active should be the policy. Or Murphy's law may be more appropriate: if it is possible for policy activism to foul up, it will.

Because monetary targeting offers a way to resolve the conflict between short-run and long-run objectives, it is unfortunate that recent shifts in money demand and the possibility of further shifts owing to financial innovations have weakened confidence in the reliability of monetary targeting. If the Federal Reserve authorities lack confidence in monetary targeting and therefore are unwilling to put primary reliance on it, what other indicator can they follow to ensure that the policy adopted will not turn out to be inflationary? Interest rates, which are the only other indicators on which the Federal Reserve is disposed to rely have been inadequate. Monetary policy really should have an indicator of whether current actions are consistent with the later attainment of its price goals. I have written elsewhere (1979), as have others, about the reasons for this weakening of confidence in monetary targeting and will not repeat them. My own view is that the weakening of confidence is justified but that monetary targeting, even with occasional discretionary adjustments for shifts in the trend of velocity, is still the best we can do and should be retained.

The current retreat from monetary targeting, combined with the previous recognition of the failure of interest-rate targeting to achieve long-run objectives, leaves no accepted principle on which the conduct of monetary policy is to be based. Monetary policy today appears to give recognition to a variety of principles on which its conduct might be based but in fact is based on allegiance to none. Of course, some monetary policy will be pursued, with or without an accepted principle. It has operated in the past without one, whether successfully or not. But experience has shown that without an accepted principle there is little chance of settling on a reasonable resolution of the conflict between short-run and long-run objectives or of giving a clear indication to the public of how exactly that conflict will be resolved.

One outcome seems sure: without a better method of pursuing price stability than trial and error, there will be overshooting and frequent serious misses, which will not be reversed. Consequently, there is little prospect of achieving even approximate price stability. Without an operating principle designed to achieve price stability, we might still hope for, and exhort the monetary authorities to impose, vigorous policies to dampen inflationary pressures whenever they arise. If the authorities are reasonably careful, they might be able to achieve a noninflationary economy that is only periodically interrupted by episodes of rising prices. That is hardly secular price stability, but that is probably the best we shall be able to achieve under our present monetary procedures. At worst we shall experience continuing episodes of high and fluctuating inflation rates. Those are the logical implications of our unresolved conflict between short-run and long-run objectives.

REFERENCES

Barro, Robert J., and David B. Gordon. "A Positive Theory of Monetary Policy in a Natural Rate Model." *Journal of Political Economy* 91 (August 1983), 589–610.

Brainard, William. "Uncertainty and the Effectiveness of Policy." *American Economic Review* 57 (May 1967), 411–25.

Cagan, Phillip. "Financial Developments and the Erosion of Monetary Controls." In *Contemporary Economic Problems*, William Fellner, ed. Washington, D.C.: American Enterprise Institute for Public Policy Research, 1979. Pp. 117–51.

Taylor, John B. "Comments." *Journal of Monetary Economics* 12 (July 1983), 123–25.

Rules with Some Discretion

AXEL LEIJONHUFVUD

THE MAIN PART of Barro's paper discusses earlier work by himself and David Gordon. That work models the behavior of the monetary authorities and is concerned with such questions as the incentive compatibility of monetary rules, that is, whether it is possible to find rules that are credible because the authorities will have no incentive to break them.

In "Rules, Discretion and Reputation in a Model of Monetary Policy" (July 1983), Barro and Gordon considered a model of monetary policy under full discretion. The rational expectations equilibrium of this model gave a high inflation rate on the average combined with (futile) attempts at countercyclical policy. A policy rule, if binding, would improve matters.

In "A Positive Theory of Monetary Policy in a Natural Rate Model" (August 1983), Barro and Gordon showed that a reputational equilibrium for the model yields a solution halfway between this full discretion case and the rule-bound case.

These attempts to model the behavior of the policymaking authorities and their interaction with the public are an interesting branch of the recent literature. We will see more work along these lines; indeed, I am afraid that we will see more of it than is instructive, for it is possible to ring almost endless changes on models of this kind.

Yet, interesting as these incentive compatibility problems are, it is difficult to know whether they are the first thing we should worry about in discussing the choice (or design) of a monetary regime. In Barro's model, the policymakers are assumed to have an incentive to break the announced rule in order to create surprise inflation and, therefore, an increase in employment. Unanticipated inflation makes the representative consumer work more than he would like to if he knew what was going on. But why should the representative consumer, in his role as the representative voter, reward the policymaker for swindling him into working too much? (The policymaker expects to be rewarded, and in Barro's model, this is a rational expectation.) Barro asks us, in fact, to consider a world in which inflation is to be

38

deplored but unanticipated inflation encouraged. But why should rational agents dislike anticipated and like unanticipated inflation in a world where the first is basically neutral while the second fools them into behaving inoptimally? The Kydland-Prescott-Calvo-Barro line on this question is that the representative voter has already made the mistake of imposing an income tax on himself, which has induced him to goof off, so that he is actually grateful to be fooled into working more. It is a clever answer—too clever by half, maybe. It tells us that we should stop looking for policies that might result in stable money and predictable nominal values, for if we found one and used it, it would thwart the representative person's rational desire to be fooled into not working less than he truly wants.

This conclusion would spell a somewhat pitiful and inglorious end to monetary theory as we have known it. Before abandoning the time-honored enterprise, we might ask how we got ourselves painted into this particular corner. Two sets of interrelated issues are important:

1. The choice of monetary regime, I agree, has to be discussed as a choice between rational expectations equilibria that yield different time-paths for inflation and unemployment. That said, however, the question becomes how much understanding of the system the rational expectations approach obliges us to impute to agents.

2. The analytical setting not only of Barro's paper but of most of the recent discussion is a model world in which, in the absence of nominal shocks, unemployment stays at its natural rate and in which monetary policy can be effective only insofar as it generates nominal surprises. The second issue is whether this is the appropriate model for the choice of regime questions.

On the first issue, it has come to be regarded as naive to suppose that economists might understand the economy better in some respects than economic agents—so naive, in fact, that if you want to earn top dollar as an economist, you must profess to know nothing of value, for if you claim otherwise, both your colleagues and the representative agent will infer that you must think you know some things that certainly ain't so. A marginal social product of zero is the upper bound. Everyone has tired of the old anecdote about the two economists and the bill on the sidewalk: "Look, there lies a $100 bill!"— "No, there doesn't." The modern version would go: "I think I've learned something useful."—"No, you didn't!" Barro's paper ends up on this note: "If an economist labels the actual institutional selection as inferior to other arrangements, what does that labeling mean? Conceivably the economist may have unearthed new knowledge, but other possibilities are more likely."

My own old-fashioned view on all this is by and large the naively optimistic one that people are not terribly smart and tend to bungle things. I also believe, therefore, that economic performance, like most things, might be improved upon. I admit a slight complication to this rosy view of the matter—namely, that economists belong to the set of people who tend to bungle things. In particular, I see the inflation and monetary instability of the last twenty years as one Big Muddle created by people who did not understand what they were messing with, aided and abetted by an economics profession that did not—and still does not—understand the economic and social consequences of monetary instability.

On the second issue, monetarist natural rate of unemployment models have received far more attention than they merit. The evidence is, of course, overwhelming that the Phillips curve shifts with inflationary expectations. At the time of the controversy, the monetarist natural rate model was the perceived alternative to the stable Phillips tradeoff models; it was lent too much credibility by their demise. The actual evidence *for* it does not, I think, compel us to take it seriously.

In particular, we do not have strong reasons to believe either that aggregative fluctuations occur only in response to nominal shocks or that all changes in money (however measured) should be interpreted as exogenous nominal shocks that should have no real aggregative consequences as long as only nominal prices adjust appropriately. Consider, for instance, convertible monetary standards. External convertibility will suffice—open economies with fixed exchange rates. Here the monetary authorities are powerless to change the nominal scale of the economy by pumping money into it. The money supply is essentially endogenous, so purely nominal shocks will at least not come from this direction. Rational nominal expectations are inelastic with respect to both the current price level and the current money stock. Business fluctuations occur primarily in response to real shocks (such as the old Keynesian standby, the "shift in the marginal efficiency of capital") and are characterized by the endogenous co-movement of money and trade credit with real activity. Employment varies with the perceived real rate of return. The central bank, although unable to make nominal income any number it might want since it does not control the nominal scale of the system, does have some limited, short-run ability to affect real income through its influence on the real price and availability of credit. This potentially useful power to influence real magnitudes is at its maximum when fully anticipated and at its minimum when unanticipated. Economists who look, instead, for a useful role for the central bank based on its capacity, under an inconvertible fiat standard, to create nominal surprises have, I am afraid, gotten the whole subject of monetary stabilization policy backwards.

Consider, then, our use of rules in some other areas of endeavor. Most team sports, for instance, are played subject to a set of rules large enough to make a small book. Why do we let a group of middle-aged, out-of-shape men impose constraints on the actions of these superb athletes? The rule books go far beyond merely forbidding deliberate mayhem. Why not leave the rest to the discretion of the people who will be in the best position to judge what is the best thing to do?

Imagine experimenting with the game by successively tearing the pages out of the rule book (starting at the back) and observing the caliber of play as the structure of the game is loosened up. Pretty soon the play will deteriorate and get sloppy as the allowable options open to each player in any given situation multiply. The interaction between players on the floor becomes increasingly unreliable, and the game will be less fun to play and less fun to watch. Gradually, unintentional injuries will become more frequent. Eventually, when the last page is gone, if not sooner, the players will no longer know what game they are supposed to be playing. (You might also consider tightening the rules until the game becomes a ceremony prescribed by strict protocol: each team takes turns marching in slow procession up the court to deposit the ball in the basket, etc.)

Presumably all basketball players optimize all the time, and presumably they have better information in any given situation than the rule-makers. Yet we have no philosophical difficulties in discussing the pros and cons of changing the rules at the margin. And we have a good idea of why we do not leave professional basketball to be determined as a reputational equilibrium among players without imposed rules and without umpires.

The monetary regime that we have allowed to develop in this country is (in some relevant respects) like a ballgame with rules much too loose to permit fast, reliably coordinated, relatively injury-free play. Private sector agents do not know what to expect in the way of nominal shocks from the monetary authorities in the future; consequently, they are unable to make reliable inferences about the real outcome of present longer-term commitments. The policymakers cannot infer the expectations of a public that does not know what to expect; consequently, they are unable to make reliable inferences about the effects of their own actions. And economists, finally, find that they do badly trying to predict the sequential outcomes of this unreliable interaction between policymakers and the public. *Every-*

one does badly. And everyone stands to gain by changing the game. Even middle-aged, out-of-shape economists might be able to draft rule changes that improve the game and are incentive-compatible all around.

Now if business cycles occur also for nonmonetary reasons and if central banks have some power, even if limited and temporary, to change the real cost of credit, then we might want them to have the discretion to use this power for stabilization purposes. On the other hand, the monetary authorities must also simplify their behavior if they are to be able to use their "real" powers at all reliably. In particular, we want them to cease creating nominal surprises. How can these desiderata be combined?

Congress should legislate a maximum for the monetary base that the Federal Reserve could have in existence at any given time (Leijonhufvud 1984). This ceiling on the base should be made to rise (like the Friedman rule) x percent per year, x being computed as the difference between some long-run average for the growth rate of real output and the trend in the velocity of base money. On the date that the legislation goes into effect, the initial legal maximum base should be set 10, 15, or perhaps even 20 percent above the actual base as of that date.

This rule leaves some room for discretion. It also leaves open the choice of short-term policies and operating procedures. As long as the Federal Reserve finds itself well below the ceiling, it can expand or contract, and it can execute either policy by using either quantity targets or interest targets. But while the authorities would retain short-term discretion as long as they are below the ceiling, the possibility that U.S. monetary policy might come to follow a long sequence of predominantly inflationary moves is eliminated.

A central bank operating under a law establishing a ceiling for the monetary base would have to treat the difference between the maximum legal base and the actual base as if it were its foreign exchange reserves and the bank were operating in a fixed exchange rate system. It could pursue an expansionary policy (or step in as lender of last resort) only as long as it had excess reserves. If, in trying to help the economy out of one recession, it were to go so far as to hit the ceiling, it would have to plan on a prolonged period of expanding at less than the permissible Friedmanian rate in order to accumulate the ammunition needed to be of help in another.

The longer-term nominal expectations of the public in the resulting monetary regime should come to approximate the expectations that are rational under a gold standard—with the added benefit that the public does not have to worry about the vagaries of world gold production and the like. Although the main purpose of my proposal is to reduce the long-term nominal uncertainty that is surely the major problem with our present "random-walk monetary standard," it may have the added benefit of reducing the amount of short-term speculation on the course of monetary policy. The market's intense fascination with month-by-month, or even week-by-week, variations in the money supply is a recent phenomenon. Once it is clear that Friday money supply announcements do not signal changes in the stance of the authorities over the longer term, short-term inflation expectations should also become less volatile and more coherent. To the extent that this is achieved, our ability to predict the consequences of macroeconomic policy measures will improve. And everyone will be better off for it.

REFERENCES

Barro, Robert J., and David B. Gordon. "Rules, Discretion and Reputation in a Model of Monetary Policy." *Journal of Monetary Economics* 12 (July 1983), 101–21.

————. "A Positive Theory of Monetary Policy in a Natural Rate Model." *Journal of Political Economy* 91 (August 1983), 589–610.

Leijonhufvud, Axel. "Constitutional Constraints on the Monetary Powers of Government." In *Constitutional Economics: Containing the Economic Powers of Government*, Richard B. McKenzie, ed. Lexington, Mass.: D.C. Heath Co., 1984. Pp. 95–113.

TWO

Alternative Monetary Regimes:
The Gold Standard

ANNA J. SCHWARTZ

THE GOLD standard has recently been the subject of much discussion. The discussion is largely attributable to dissatisfaction with the high and variable rates of inflation and interest rates, the low productivity growth, and the turbulence in foreign exchange markets since 1970. These undesired developments are associated with the existing discretionary fiat money regime, and they have encouraged examination of a monetary regime linked to gold, the vestiges of which the world abandoned early in the 1970s.

The desirability of a return to the gold standard is a controversial issue. Informed judgment of this issue requires an understanding of past experience. In addition, examination of the operation of the historical gold standard has intellectual interest. Scholars differ in their explanations of the functioning of the gold standard and in their assessments of its performance.

The historical gold standard evolved over centuries. It was a regime in which a particular weight of gold served as the supreme type of money with which all lesser types of money—government fiduciary issues, bank notes, and deposits—were interconvertible. During the gold standard era, the institutions and practices related to payments for the settlement of debts underwent evolutionary change.

In this chapter, we analyze the historical gold standard and its relevance to the solution of current economic problems. The first section surveys the evolution of the historical gold standard from the final decades of the nineteenth century to the collapse of the Bretton Woods system in the early 1970s. The second section presents the evidence on the performance of the gold standard as viewed by its advocates and opponents. The third section examines the necessary conditions for the restoration of the gold standard. Conclusions are summarized in the fourth section.

Evolution of the Gold Standard

Gold standards have varied historically depending on the presence or absence of the following elements:

1. a national money unit
2. nongold national money issued by either the government or by a fractional-reserve commercial banking system
3. a central bank
   a. with gold reserves only
   b. with mainly foreign exchange reserves
4. convertibility of nongold money into gold coin or gold bars
5. classes of holders for whom nongold money is convertible

National Money Units. Although a gold standard without national money units is conceivable—coins would circulate by weight with no price in a national money unit attached and prices would be expressed in weights of gold—the countries that adopted the gold standard before 1914 defined their national money units as a specific weight of gold. This set the price of an ounce of gold in terms of that unit. In 1879, for example, when the United States restored the link between the dollar and gold, after a 17-year interruption, the dollar was defined as 23.22 grains of fine gold. There are 480 grains of gold in a fine troy ounce. Thus the price of a fine troy ounce of gold was $20.67 (480 ÷ 23.22 = 20.67). In all countries with a gold standard, prices of gold were set in terms of the country's national money unit—dollars, pounds, marks, francs, and other monetary units. Each government was committed to buying gold from the public at its fixed price and to converting the gold into coin. Each government was also committed to selling gold to the public at a slightly higher price. The difference between the purchase and sale prices is called *brassage*, the government's fee for manufacturing coins.

The external value of a national currency under the gold standard was determined by comparing it with another widely used currency. For instance, the pound sterling was worth $4.8665 before World War I and from 1925 to 1931. Since the dollar was defined as 23.22 grains of fine gold and a pound sterling as 113.0016 grains of fine gold, a pound sterling had 4.8665 as much gold by weight as a U.S. dollar. The exchange rate between these two currencies was a fixed rate because the gold weight of each currency did not vary (or, equivalently, the price of gold per ounce in terms of each currency did not change). Varying the weights of gold represented by a currency would have meant changes in the price of gold in that country.

The link between currencies was gold at a fixed price. Imbalances in international payments might be settled by claims in the form of bills of exchange in national currencies of other countries that had fixed gold equivalents. (A bill of exchange on a British firm, for example, is an order on the firm to pay a certain amount of British pounds to the exporter on a certain date. American exporters typically drew up such bills of exchange when they sold goods to foreign firms.) If the demand for and supply of a national currency did not balance, gold flows would be activated.

Thus, whenever the dollar price of a British pound at the official exchange rate of $4.86 deviated by more than 1 or 2 percent above or below the official rate (these limits were referred to as the gold points and represented the cost of packing, insuring, and shipping gold between the two countries), it paid either to convert U.S. dollars into gold and transfer it abroad, or else to convert British pounds into gold and transfer it here. If U.S. demand for cheaper British goods increased, for example, this raised the dollar price of bills of exchange denominated in pounds. Once the dollar price of the pound reached $4.92, the U.S. gold export point, it paid importers to convert U.S. dollars into gold, ship the gold to England, and purchase pounds at $4.86. Conversely, at the U.S. gold import point, which might have been as low as $4.83, it paid exporters to convert pounds sterling into gold, ship the gold to the United States, and purchase dollars. Gold shipments in either direction would thus restore the price of foreign exchange to parity.

Therefore, not only new gold output but inflows or outflows related to movements in the balance of payments affected the size of the domestic money supply. A reduction in a country's money supply and ultimately in its price level enhanced the country's appeal as a source of goods and services to foreigners and reduced the domestic demand for foreign goods and services. An increase in a country's money supply and ultimately in its price level diminished that country's appeal as a source of goods and services to foreigners and increased the domestic demand for foreign goods and services. Because of this automatic adjustment process, the duration and size of imbalances of international payments tended to be self-limiting. Gold flows served to equalize price movements across countries.

Economists debate the details of this process. Some argue that the gold flows before 1914 were minimal and that prices worldwide adjusted rapidly. There was one world price level, and the external adjustment process posed no greater problem than interregional adjustment of prices within a country. These refinements need not detain us.

Nongold National Money. As the gold standard evolved, substitutes for gold were developed. The motive for substitution was a reduction in the real resources employed in mining gold. Paper money substitutes may be produced with much smaller real resources. The substitutes included fiat currency issued by governments and commercial bank notes and deposits, with gold reserves of the government and the banks equal to a fraction of their monetary liabilities. The incentive to limit the size of the fraction of gold reserves was strengthened during trend periods when the supply of gold did not keep pace with the demand for it for both monetary and nonmonetary uses.

Fractional gold reserves were held as evidence of the issuers' readiness to convert nongold money into gold at the pleasure of the holder, at a fixed price of gold, not a changing market price of gold. In this system, domestic disturbances, such as banking panics, could affect the size of a country's gold reserves. Public alarm about the adequacy of the gold reserve ratio could trigger an internal drain of gold when holders of bank notes and bank deposits chose to shift to gold. The aftermath of such episodes was that the government and the banks subsequently took action to contract their monetary liabilities, and this resulted in an increase in their gold reserve ratios.

A fractional-reserve gold standard accentuated the effects of gold flows on the quantity of money. A $1 gold inflow, depending on the size of the reserve ratio, might increase the quantity of money as much as $8 or $10; a $1 gold outflow might reduce the quantity of money by as much as $8 or $10, with parallel effects on domestic spending and prices.

International capital flows, however, alleviated to some extent either the size of gold flows or their consequences. Short-term capital flows served to reduce and smooth the immediate flows of gold that would otherwise have been required to settle payments imbalances. Long-term capital flows enabled developing countries to borrow real resources from developed countries by running a persistent excess of imports of goods and services over exports of goods and services without entailing gold flows. In the event of a rise in the domestic quantity of money, in the short run, interest rates would tend to decline, inducing investors to shift funds to foreign money markets. The size of the change in export prices relative to import prices that would otherwise have occurred would be reduced by the resulting capital outflow.

In a fractional-reserve banking system combined with a gold standard, domestic and international convertibility of claims on the monetary authorities was the mechanism to ensure that the growth of the money supply was held in check.

Central Banks with Gold Reserves. Central banks in Europe predated the gold standard. After the gold standard was adopted, their behavior did not always exemplify the discipline a true gold standard imposes. They did not necessarily respond to a loss of gold due to balance of payments deficits by actions to reduce the quantity of money, or to a gain of gold due to balance of payments surpluses by actions to increase the quantity of money.

Scholars continue to debate the extent to which such behavior by the Bank of England and other central banks characterized the period before 1914. After World War I, the issue is not in doubt: central banks, including the Federal Reserve System, frequently chose not to permit gold flows either to expand or contract the quantity of money, or to do so to a lesser degree than full adjustment would have required. The gold standard was not automatic but became managed.

Central Banks with Foreign Exchange Reserves. Central banks also learned to economize on gold holdings by using other currencies as reserve assets, principally sterling before 1914, increasingly dollars thereafter. A central bank that held all or a large part of its international reserves in foreign exchange of a country that was on a gold standard was said to be on a gold exchange standard. The gold exchange standard was preferred because foreign exchange, in the form of deposits at foreign banks or foreign treasury bills, was earning assets, but gold holdings were not. A disadvantage of holding reserves in assets denominated in a foreign currency was that a central bank would incur losses when that currency was devalued.

The gold standard before World War I was often described as a sterling-gold exchange system and, under the Bretton Woods system after World War II, as a dollar-gold exchange system. Although both were fixed exchange rate systems in conception, the Bretton Woods system became a fixed but adjustable exchange rate system.

Under the Bretton Woods system, the par value of each national currency was established in agreement with the International Monetary Fund and was expressed either in terms of gold or in terms of U.S. dollars valued at 13.71 grains of fine gold. (The dollar of 23.22 grains of fine gold had been devalued by the United States under authority of the Gold Reserve Act of January 31, 1934, to 13.71 grains of fine gold—equivalent to $35 an ounce.) Members of the International Monetary Fund were responsible for maintaining the par value of their currencies, with the United States alone undertaking the free purchase and sale of gold at the fixed price of $35 per ounce. Other countries bought and sold their currencies for dollars to maintain their par values within the agreed limits. Settlement of international payments imbalances took place mainly by transfers of reserve assets in the major money markets.

Convertibility of many European currencies was first achieved under the Bretton Woods system in 1958. The system performed fairly effectively for only a few years. From the mid-1960s on, the Bretton Woods system was characterized by repeated foreign exchange crises. Periodically market participants anticipated that the existing par values were unsustainable and would shift funds from a weak currency to a strong currency, exacerbating the external position for both currencies. Countries with undervalued currencies resisted revaluation and countries with overvalued currencies resisted devaluation.

The system of fixed but adjustable exchange rates collapsed under the pressure of persistent balance of payments problems: deficits in the United States, the reserve center, and surpluses (and undervalued currencies) in some countries such as West Germany. The money supply in the United States grew at rates independent of the country's balance of payments position. This was contrary to the way the money supply would have behaved under an international gold standard. Unless dollar inflows were sterilized by their monetary authorities, surplus countries accumulated dollar reserves that expanded their monetary base. According to the surplus countries, the United States exported inflation through its balance of payments deficits.

Convertibility of Nongold Money into Gold. A gold coin standard with nongold substitutes existed in a number of countries before 1914. Gold coin circulated but was only a small part of the total money supply, and nongold money was redeemable in gold coin. As a way of economizing on the use of gold, many countries ceased to coin gold after 1914 (the United States, not until 1933). This terminated free coinage, the circulation of gold coins, and the legal tender status of gold coins. The objective was to concentrate all of a country's gold holdings into international reserves available for international payments. Nongold money became convertible into heavy gold bars. Such a gold standard is known as a *gold bullion standard.*

Classes of Holders. Under a gold coin standard with nongold substitutes, all holders—domestic and foreign—of nongold money could convert it into gold coin. Under a gold bullion standard, convertibility existed for both types of holders. Under the Bretton Woods dollar-gold exchange standard, the right of convertibility in the United

States was limited to foreign official institutions. Foreign official institutions held dollars for the purpose of intervention in foreign exchange markets so long as they were confident that they could obtain gold from the United States for dollars at their initiative. For a time, a gentleman's agreement among central banks in certain industrial countries not to present dollar balances for convertibility into gold staved off the denouement. The chronic deficits in the U.S. balance of payments and the unwanted accumulation of dollars by foreigners that threatened a drain of all U.S. gold finally led in 1971 to formal inconvertibility for all holders.

Initially, the United States and its trading partners made several attempts to restore a system of fixed exchange rates. After much negotiation, a readjustment of currency parities was arranged at a meeting at the Smithsonian Institution in Washington on December 17–18, 1971. Wider margins of fluctuations above and below the new so-called central exchange rates were permitted. The official dollar price of gold would henceforth be $38, a devaluation of the dollar of 7.9 percent. While the dollar remained inconvertible, the new official dollar price of gold implied a depreciation of the gold value of the dollar rather than an appreciation of the gold value of other currencies. The central exchange rates established at the Smithsonian meeting lasted only a short time as market participants expressed disbelief in them.

In February 1973, new central rates were set in a hurried round of negotiations. The official dollar price of gold was raised further to $42.22, leaving unchanged the gold value of other currencies. The new central rates did not staunch the flow of dollars abroad, and another crisis erupted in March 1973. As a result of this crisis, exchange rates pegged to the dollar were abandoned by the major industrialized countries. Amendments to the Articles of Agreement of the International Monetary Fund formally removed gold from its previous central role in international monetary arrangements. The International Monetary Fund's official gold price was abolished, as were par values, gold convertibility, and maintenance of gold value obligations.

Arguments for a Gold Standard. Supporters of the gold standard have several basic arguments in favor of a gold standard of whatever variant. The first argument is that gold has intrinsic value and therefore serves as a standard of value for all other goods. In addition, supporters view gold as a desirable store of value because new production adds only a small fraction to the accumulated stock. Because of this, prices denominated in gold do not vary greatly from year to year. Even if other forms of money such as government-issued or bank-issued paper currency and bank deposits exist, convertibility into gold at a fixed price would compel the monetary authorities to avoid inflationary policies.

An inflationary increase in government paper currency, for example, would tend to raise prices of goods and services in terms of paper currency, and induce money holders to convert their paper dollars to gold, putting pressure on the government's gold holdings. At the same time, with gold as a country's international reserve asset, adjustment to balance of payments deficits and surpluses would be automatic. An increase in the money supply by ultimately raising the price level would raise the price of exports relative to the price of imports, leading to a balance of payments deficit and a gold outflow. In addition, the increase in the money supply would lower domestic interest rates relative to those abroad, inducing a capital outflow and a further gold outflow. In such a monetary system, political manipulation of the money supply would be avoided.

Another argument in favor of the gold standard is that the rate of increase in the gold money supply would vary automatically with the profitability of producing gold and would assure a stable money supply and stable prices in the long run. A rapid increase in the output of gold due to gold discoveries or technological improvements in gold mining, for example, would raise the prices of all other goods in terms of gold, making them more profitable to produce than gold and ultimately leading to a reduction in gold output. The reduction in the purchasing power of gold, moreover, would lead to a shift in the demand for gold from monetary to nonmonetary uses, thus reinforcing the output effects. Conversely, a decline in prices of goods and services, due to technological improvements in the nongold sector, would increase the profitability of gold production, encouraging increased gold output, which would ultimately tend to raise the price level. The initial increase in the purchasing power of gold would also lead to a shift in the demand for gold from nonmonetary to monetary uses, thus reinforcing the output effects. Long-run price stability would be the result.

In the following section, we evaluate the evidence for these arguments.

Evidence on the Performance of the Gold Standard

Assessment of the performance of the historical gold standard is based on the following issues:

1. What was the behavior of prices under the gold standard? Price behavior can be analyzed from three perspectives:
   a. long-run price predictability—the ultimate return of the price level to its initial value
   b. long-run price stability—the price level neither rising nor falling over substantial periods
   c. short-run price stability
2. What was the behavior of short-run real output under the gold standard?
3. In the world's markets, did the gold standard transmit foreign shocks both of a monetary and nonmonetary character?
4. How great was the magnitude of resource costs associated with maintaining the gold standard?
5. Was the gold standard free from political manipulation?

Economists differ in their assessment of these issues. The gold standard is often described as a rule that governs monetary policy. The rule is that the domestic money supply must rise and fall in line with the rise and fall of gold reserves. Adhering to the gold standard rule is described as a form of precommitment by monetary authorities. As explained in Chapter 1, one respect in which economists differ in assessing the gold standard is in their judgment of the advantage of precommitment to a rule versus the advantage of discretionary actions by monetary authorities. As explained in Chapter 4, even those who favor precommitment are not unanimous in supporting the gold standard. Some prefer an alternative rule such as stable monetary growth. We now review the evidence concerning the five issues listed above.

Behavior of Prices under the Gold Standard. Table 2–1, row 1, shows that in both the United States and the United Kingdom the average annual rates of change in wholesale prices during the pre–World War I period were much lower than in the post–World War II period. Table 2–3 compares the negative average rates of change in the implicit price deflator in the United States and the United Kingdom from the 1870s to the 1890s with the average rates of inflation from the 1890s to World War I. Although the contrast in Table 2–1 between the close to zero rates of change of prices in the gold standard period from the 1870s to World War I compared with the inflation in the period from 1946 to 1979 has been interpreted by some (Bordo 1981, Cagan 1984) as demonstrating near-stability of prices under the gold standard, Cooper (1982) and Dornbusch (Report 1982, pp. 414–15) have pointed out that this conclusion is not supported by the standard deviation of price changes shown in Table 2–1, row 2.

Table 2–1. A Comparison of Selected Economic Variables from the 1870s
to World War I under the Gold Standard and from 1946 to 1979,
United States and United Kingdom

Measure	United Kingdom		United States	
	Gold standard, 1870–1913	Postwar, 1946–1979	Gold standard, 1879–1913	Postwar, 1946–1979
1. Average annual change in wholesale prices (percentage)[a]	−0.7	5.6	0.1	2.8
2. Standard deviation of price change (percentage)[b]	4.6	6.2[c]	5.4	4.8[c]
3. Average annual growth in real per capita income (percentage)	1.4	2.4	1.9	2.1
4. Coefficient of variation of annual percentage changes in real per capita income (ratio)[d]	2.5	1.4	3.5	1.6
5. Average unemployment rate (percentage)	4.3[e]	2.5	6.8[f]	5.0
6. Average annual growth in the money supply (percentage)[a]	1.5	5.9	6.1	5.7
7. Coefficient of variation of the growth in the money supply (ratio)[d]	1.6	1.0	0.8	0.5

SOURCES: Richard N. Cooper, "The Gold Standard: Historical Facts and Future Prospects," *Brookings Papers on Economic Activity* 13 (1982), 5. The table is drawn from Michael D. Bordo, "The Classical Gold Standard: Some Lessons for Today," Federal Reserve Bank of St. Louis *Review* 63 (May 1981), 14, and calculations from George F. Warren and Frank A. Pearson, *Gold and Prices* (New York: John Wiley & Sons, Inc., 1935), pp. 13–14, 87; Brian R. Mitchell, *Abstract of British Historical Statistics* (London: Cambridge University Press, 1962), pp. 367–68; Council of Economic Advisers, *Economic Report of the President, January 1982* (Washington, D.C.: Government Printing Office, 1982); and International Monetary Fund, *International Financial Statistics* (Washington, D.C.: IMF), various issues.

[a] Calculated as the time coefficient from a regression of the log of the variable on a time trend.

[b] Calculated as the standard error of estimate of the fitted equation $\ln P_t = a \ln P_{t-1}$, where P_t is the wholesale price index in year t.

[c] 1949–79.

[d] Calculated as the ratio of the standard deviation of annual percentage changes to their mean.

[e] 1888–1913.

[f] 1890–1913.

Table 2-2. Level and Percentage Change of Wholesale Price Indexes
for the United States, United Kingdom, Germany, and France,
Selected Years, 1816–1913

	United States	United Kingdom	Germany	France
Year		(1913 = 100)		
1816	150	147	94	143
1849	82	86	67	94
1873	137	130	114	122
1896	64	72	69	69
1913	100	100	100	100
Period		Percentage change		
1816–49	−45	−41	−29	−33
1849–73	67	51	70	30
1873–96	−53	−45	−40	−45
1896–1913	56	39	45	45

SOURCES: Richard N. Cooper, "The Gold Standard: Historical Facts and Future Prospects," *Brookings Papers on Economic Activity* 13 (1982), 9. Data for the United States and the United Kingdom are from George F. Warren and Frank A. Pearson, *Gold and Prices* (New York: John Wiley & Sons, Inc., 1955), pp. 87–88; data for Germany and France are from Brian R. Mitchell, *European Historical Statistics, 1750–1970* (New York: Columbia University Press, 1975), pp. 736–39.

Moreover, the latter argue that the very wide fluctuations in the wholesale price index from 1816 to 1913 shown in Table 2–2 in the United States, United Kingdom, Germany, and France are hardly a pattern of long-term stability. (A problem with Table 2–2 is that it includes dates for the four countries when they were not on the gold standard—1816 for the United Kingdom, 1873 for the United States, and the initial dates for both Germany and France.) Cagan (1984) has replied that although there was indeed a substantial decline in wholesale prices before 1896 followed by an even greater increase before 1914, during the post–World War II period, in which there was a loose or nonexistent tie to gold, wholesale prices quadrupled the rise under the gold standard.

Although the decline and rise in prices between the 1870s and World War I nearly canceled each other, that reversal is dismissed by gold opponents as accidental. Contemporaries, it is contended, could hardly have known that the price level following a period of decline would be restored by a period of price increase. Even if it were in part accidental, the tendency for declines or increases in prices to be reversed after a long lag is a basic characteristic of a commodity standard, as Cagan (1984) notes. Although the gold standard did not provide short-term or long-term price stability, it

Table 2–3. Rate of Change in Prices and Real Income between Cycle Phases,*
1873–1914, United States and United Kingdom

	Percentage change per year		
	Implicit price deflator (1)	Real income (2)	Real income per capita (3)
UNITED STATES			
Deflation			
From the 1873–78 contraction to the 1895–96 contraction	−1.5	3.6	1.4
From the 1878–82 expansion to the 1895–96 contraction	−1.3	2.5	0.3
Inflation			
From the 1895–96 contraction to the 1913–14 contraction	1.9	3.8	1.9
UNITED KINGDOM			
Deflation			
From the 1874–79 contraction to the 1893–1900 expansion	−0.6	2.3	1.4
Inflation			
From the 1893–1900 expansion to the 1913–14 contraction	0.8	1.6	0.8

SOURCES: Phillip Cagan, "The Report of the Gold Commission (1982)," in *Monetary and Fiscal Policies and Their Application*, Karl Brunner and Allan H. Meltzer, eds., Carnegie-Rochester Conference Series on Public Policy, vol. 20 (Amsterdam: North-Holland, 1984), pp. 247–67; Milton Friedman and Anna J. Schwartz, *Monetary Trends in the United States and the United Kingdom* (Chicago: University of Chicago, Press, 1982), based on Tables 5.7 and 5.8.

* The cycle phases are from the National Bureau of Economic Research reference cycles. See U.S. Department of Commerce, *Business Conditions Digest* (February 1984), p. 104.

did provide long-term price predictability—the price level returned to its initial level.

The use of the wholesale price index to measure price trends has been criticized by Reynolds (1983), a proponent of the gold standard. He claims that because the wholesale price index was dominated by farm commodity prices, it did not reflect changes in the purchasing power of gold; the decline in 1894–96 was only an "apparent" deflation. This criticism is not supported by other information about prices. The implicit price deflator paralleled the wholesale price index, and accounts of the period leave no doubt that the price movements as measured by the wholesale price index were not merely statistical artifacts.

The concept of the gold standard as a guarantor of price stability

Table 2–4. A Comparison of U.S. Business Cycles in 1879–1897
(Period of Deflation) and 1897–1914 (Period of Inflation)

Years	Duration in months		Average change in economic activity (percentage)	
	Expansions	Contractions	Expansions	Contractions
1879–1897	123 (56%)*	96 (44%)	21.7	−22.2
1897–1914	109 (52%)	101 (48%)	20.0	−18.7

SOURCES: Phillip Cagan, "The Report of the Gold Commission (1982)," in *Monetary and Fiscal Policies and Their Application*, Karl Brunner and Allan H. Meltzer, eds., Carnegie-Rochester Conference Series on Public Policy, vol. 20 (Amsterdam: North-Holland, 1984), pp. 247–67. Based on Geoffrey H. Moore, ed., *Business Cycle Indicators*, vol. I (Princeton: Princeton University Press for National Bureau of Economic Research, 1961), pp. 104, 671.

* Percentage of total period is in parentheses.

was criticized by prominent contemporaries. What occasioned the criticism was precisely the long-term secular price movements—the rise in prices associated with the mid–nineteenth-century gold discoveries and the decline in prices that began in the 1870s under an expanding international gold standard. In his (1863) pamphlet, "A Serious Fall in the Value of Gold Ascertained, and Its Social Effects Set Forth" (1884), William Stanley Jevons estimated that between 1848 and 1860 the value of gold fell 9 percent. In 1875 he questioned the use of metallic standards of value in view of the extreme changes in their values and urged as a reform a tabular standard of value, to be based on an index number.

In 1887 Alfred Marshall (1925, pp. 189, 192) discussed "the evils of a fluctuating standard of value" and concluded that "the precious metals cannot afford a good standard of value." He dismissed bimetallism as flawed and proposed as remedies for the fluctuating standard of value either symmetallism or a tabular standard. With the reversal of the secular price movement after 1896, concern shifted to the inflationary fluctuation of the standard. In 1913 the remedy that Irving Fisher (1913) proposed was the "compensated dollar," raising the gold content of the dollar (lowering the price of gold) to offset inflation, lowering the gold content of the dollar (raising the price of gold) to offset deflation.

It has been suggested by Cagan (1984) that the problem created by the tendency of gold (or any commodity) to drift in terms of its purchasing power, due to changes in the relative demands for and supplies of gold (or any commodity), is not serious since it can be solved by periodically adjusting the gold content of the dollar in line with Fisher's proposal. If the price index rose 2 percent, for example, the gold content of the dollar would be increased 2 percent. The reduced price of gold would reduce the value of the gold reserve and discourage inflows both from domestic and foreign gold holdings. This would reduce the growth rate of the money supply. Downward pressure on prices would eventually stabilize the price index and a long-run drift of prices would be avoided.

Implementing this proposal might have several undesirable effects: speculative buying and selling of gold, international complications if prices moved idiosyncratically in one country, and overshooting because of lags in the response of prices to changes in the money stock. Despite these problems, the main contention of the proponents of this proposal is that since there is a solution to the problem of long-run drift, drift cannot be a serious objection to the gold standard.

However imperfect the record of price behavior under the gold standard, the main argument in its favor is that inflation rates were never as high and variable as in the post–World War II period. Moreover, because the gold standard promoted long-term domestic and international price predictability, it provided incentives to private market agents to make long-term contracts, which are vital for the efficient operation of a market economy. In the inflationary environment since the mid-1960s, markets have increasingly shunned long-term contracts with a consequent loss of economic efficiency.

Behavior of Short-run Real Output. Table 2–1, rows 3 and 4, shows that the average annual growth in real per capita income was higher from 1946 to 1979 in both the United States and the United Kingdom than from the 1870s to World War I. Also, this table shows that the variability (coefficient of variation of annual percentage changes in real per capita income) was smaller from 1946 to 1979 than in the earlier period. Table 2–3, columns 2 and 3, shows that real output in the United Kingdom rose more rapidly during deflation than during inflation in the period from the 1870s to World War I; in the United States real output grew more rapidly during periods of inflation than in periods of deflation. Again, as in the case of price behavior, conflicting assessments have been made of these data on output behavior. Opponents of the gold standard interpret this evidence as showing both lower annual average growth in real per capita income and greater instability of the growth rate under the gold standard than during the post–World War II period. They also cite higher unemployment rates under the gold standard than during the later period (Table 2–1, row 5).

Proponents of the gold standard question the reliability of the estimates of national income and of unemployment in years past. Also, they cite the slowdown in real per capita income growth in 1979–82 as reversing the favorable comparison of the post–World War II period relative to gold standard years. In addition, they believe that the high unemployment in the 1890s may have resulted from the surge in immigration despite growing employment.

Banking panics were frequent under the gold standard, and sharp monetary contractions that produced output instability occurred in 1884, 1890, 1893, 1907, and 1914 (see Table 2–4). The issue is whether greater stability of monetary growth in the post–World War II period (Table 2–1, lines 6–7) is explainable by the shift from the gold standard. The improvement may instead reflect the establishment of the Federal Deposit Insurance Corporation, which stabilized money growth relative to growth of the monetary base (Barro 1984). If similar structural changes had been introduced under the gold standard, the low year-to-year variability in the world's monetary gold stock might have resulted in greater relative stability of money growth and of real variables.

The behavior of real output under the gold standard was not exemplary, but if allowance is made for factors unrelated to the gold standard that may account for the deficiencies, the record is respectable.

Monetary and Nonmonetary Foreign Shocks. Gold proponents extol the fixed exchange rates under the gold standard for the efficiencies resulting from a stable international money that integrated the world's commodity and capital markets.

To opponents of the gold standard, a disadvantage of these fixed exchange rates is that they transmitted monetary and nonmonetary disturbances to other countries. Before World War I, such disturbances typically were related to shifts in capital exports by Great Britain from one part of the world to another, for example, the shift from investment in U.S. railways to South American projects in the late 1880s or the significant decline in aggregate British capital exports to all countries in the 1890s. Also, business cycles tended to be synchronized under the gold standard. A boom in one country would lead to an increase in demand by its residents for goods and services in the rest of the world. The opposite happened when there was a recession. To preserve fixed exchange rates, gold flows required actions by monetary authorities or the banking system.

Changes in U.S. tariffs were a type of nonmonetary disturbance that was transmitted to the rest of the world. The Dingley Tariff of

1897 imposed the highest import duties in history to that date, and the Smoot-Hawley Tariff of 1930 raised tariff rates on imported commodities, notably agricultural imports, well above postwar levels. Since the United States was a relatively closed economy, keeping imports out of the United States injured its trading partners more than it did the United States. Smoot-Hawley not only reduced the exports of our trading partners and aggravated the decline in their terms of trade but also led to the eventual default of their foreign debts. The gold standard required short-term domestic adjustments to correct balance of payments disequilibria that arose from policies transmitted by fixed exchange rates from other countries.

An additional problem under the gold standard was that capital movements were sometimes uncontrollable and aggravated the underlying situation that generated the capital flows. Raising the discount rate at the beginning of the Great Depression did not stop the capital flight but intensified that flight and was interpreted as a signal that further flight would lead to devaluation. At the same time, the discount-rate rise served to heighten deflationary pressures on the domestic economy. The gold standard was thus charged with having contributed to the instability of the world economic system after 1929.

Professional support of a paper standard to replace the gold standard gained ground in the 1930s. This support, however, was tempered by the belief that unrestrained, a paper standard would encourage beggar-thy-neighbor policies. The Bretton Woods system embodied the views and experience of the 1930s. It was widely believed that pegged exchange rates were essential to prevent chaos in international financial and trade transactions, but national economies should be free to restrict capital flows and to devalue the international value of their currency whenever necessary. This would make it possible to avoid deflating domestic prices when there was a balance of payments deficit in current account. Under the Bretton Woods system, the objectionable feature of pegged rates that forced governments to implement monetary changes that conflicted with goals of full employment or price stability would be removed, and at the same time stable conditions in foreign exchange markets would be assured.

Resource Costs Associated with Maintaining the Gold Standard. For prices to remain stable under a gold standard, the monetary gold stock must increase at the same rate as the demand for money rises in response to real income growth plus or minus any change in the ratio of GNP to the money stock (a change in velocity). A well-known estimate for the United States by Milton Friedman (1951, p.

210) was that something over a 4 percent per year increase in the monetary gold stock would have been required to maintain price stability under a gold standard from 1900 to 1950. "Something over 4 percent" was derived as the sum of an average rate of growth of real income of 3 percent per year plus an average decline in velocity of 1 percent per year. With the money stock about half the size of national income, neglecting the change in velocity, about 1.5 percent of the national income would have to be devoted to the increase in monetary gold in order to maintain stable prices.

The world's monetary gold stock before 1929 did not grow at a constant 4 percent annual rate of increase. It grew by much smaller amounts (1 percent in the 1880s, 3 percent in the 1890s, 3.8 percent in the 1900s, 3 percent in the 1910s, 2 percent in the 1920s). In these decades, nongold money substitutes, however, increased at a rate far exceeding the rate of increase in monetary gold.

The resource cost of a gold standard has not played a significant role in current discussions (Cagan 1984). The issue has either been ignored or dismissed except by gold standard proponents. To them, high resource costs are a positive value of the gold standard since gold is regarded as having intrinsic value. It is difficult to reconcile this argument with the historical trend toward increasing use of substitutes for gold in circulation and in reserves. The market appears to seek means to achieve lower resources costs.

Political Manipulation. Under a fully functioning gold standard, government intervention in the determination of the price level and the overall level of economic activity is limited. How closely did the historical gold standard approximate the ideal?

There were two kinds of intervention: in the gold mining industry and in the required short-term adjustments of prices and incomes to maintain fixed exchanges rates.

Since the demand for gold was perfectly elastic with respect to its nominal price under the historical gold standard, government actions to stimulate gold mining during periods of falling prices and low real output would be stabilizing (Rockoff 1984). It is possible to interpret the legalization of hydraulic mining in California in 1893 in this light. Farmers had earlier succeeded in closing down hydraulic mines because debris from the mines ruined farmland downstream. The act authorizing the restoration of such mining was intended to stimulate a depressed industry as well as to expand the money supply. Possibly the extension of the railroad network into gold mining areas in the United States and Mexico also represented government support for the industry. There is also evidence of government regulation of the gold mining industry by means of direct and indirect taxation, as in South Africa.

Government intervention in gold mining, however, was not necessarily stabilizing. Profits in gold mining decline when prices in general (costs) rise. Government aid to the industry at times of inflation would inhibit an equilibrating decline in gold output. Recent actions by the Soviet Union and South Africa apparently to take advantage of the strategic role of gold have disregarded possibly destabilizing consequences.

Political conflict has obviously played a part in affecting the world's gold supply. Gold production declined during the Latin American wars of independence in 1815 and in the twentieth century during the Mexican and Russian revolutions. However, most gold output under the historic gold standard came from politically stable parts of the world, so wars and revolutions did not significantly affect world production. For example, although the Boer War interrupted gold production in South Africa, the effect on the total supply of gold in the world was limited.

There is disagreement about the amount of intervention by monetary authorities before 1914 in the operation of the gold standard. Some scholars deny that intervention was possible or that authorities ever exercised such an option; they believe international arbitrage in the commodity and capital markets operated quickly to equalize prices and interest rates worldwide without the need or opportunity for intervention by monetary authorities. Others interpret selected actions by monetary authorities as discretionary and interventionist. However, the gold standard could function effectively even if the kind of response by monetary authorities required by the gold standard was delayed. Though there was leeway in reducing monetary growth when gold or capital movements were decreasing the domestic monetary base, ultimately, given fixed exchange rates, monetary growth had to be reduced. Also, though there was leeway in accelerating monetary growth, if such action was not ultimately taken, the system would be undermined by maldistribution of gold and unequal burdens of adjustment across countries.

In the post–World War I period, intervention was indeed exercised by the monetary authorities. For example, from 1923 to 1929 the Federal Reserve System offset inflows of gold by open market sales of government securities and outflows by open market purchases. Federal Reserve credit moved inversely with movements in the gold stock. France also did not permit gold inflows to affect its money stock and prices after returning to the gold standard in 1928 at a parity that undervalued the franc. Similarly, gold standard requirements were ignored by the Federal Reserve System in 1929–31, when gold inflows were not matched by an expansion of the U.S. money stock and the quantity of money was even permitted to decline. After 1934, both inflows and outflows of gold were not permitted to affect monetary growth and the performance of the economy. When gold reserve ratios applicable to Federal Reserve deposits and notes approached the minimum legal requirement, the minimum was lowered and eventually abolished. Gold became a symbol rather than an effective constraint on the monetary authorities.

The Bretton Woods system had no provision requiring the internal supply of a country's currency to be governed by its gold holdings, as was the case before 1914, nor was there a requirement that a country had to undergo deflation or inflation to balance its external accounts. Although fixed exchange rates carried over to the post–World War II world, they were fundamentally divorced from gold standard restraints. The monetary system was fully subject to political control.

Conditions for the Restoration of the Gold Standard

A variety of proposals exists to restore the use of gold in some form in monetary arrangements. Here we limit consideration to two proposals: that the United States should unilaterally return to a domestic gold standard or alternatively that the industrialized countries should collectively agree to establish an international gold standard.

To achieve long-run price stability, advocates of a restoration of a domestic gold standard recommend that the government establish a new official fixed price of gold (by defining the dollar by its weight in gold) and maintain this price by buying and selling gold freely. The government would also maintain a ratio, possibly with upper and lower bounds, of the stock of gold to the total amount of Federal Reserve notes in circulation (or the monetary base); the Federal Reserve System would be required to reduce its monetary liabilities consisting of Federal Reserve notes (or the monetary base) when the reserve ratio declined and expand them when it rose. Legal tender gold coins, denominated in dollars, would be issued to serve both as hand-to-hand currency and as legal reserves for commercial and other bank deposits. No restrictions would apply to ownership of gold coin or bullion. Nongold currency would be convertible into gold on demand.

Under the alternative proposal for an international gold standard, the United States would fix the price of gold and then maintain fixed exchange rates with other countries after they defined the amount of gold in their monetary unit. Such a standard could be achieved either by international agreement or by evolution—the United States could be the first to reinstitute the fixed price of gold and other countries would follow suit. International payments imbalances would be settled by gold flows or by flows of dollars or dollar assets convertible into gold at the fixed price. The monetary base and the money supply would vary with gold flows.

To implement a restoration of either a domestic or international gold standard in the United States requires the solution of a series of interlocking problems.

Choosing the Price of Gold. A basic problem is called the *reentry problem*: how to determine the right fixed price at which to resume the convertibility of the dollar into gold. In the past, when a country reinstituted the gold standard, there was an old official price that was once again restored or that served as the base for revaluation or devaluation. The last official price of an ounce of gold, $42.22, is so out of line with current market prices of gold that it provides no guidance. The risk involved in choosing the wrong price is great. An incorrect price might lead to a huge inflow of gold and inflation if it were too high, or a huge outflow and economic contraction if it were too low.

There are three principal proposals to solve the reentry problem:

1. Arthur Laffer (1980) proposes that an announcement be made by the government that at a date some months hence a dollar unit of the monetary base of the Federal Reserve System would be linked to a fixed quantity of gold at that day's average transaction price in the London gold market. That would become the official price of gold in terms of dollars henceforth. If the price were too high or too low, the proposal recommends suspension of convertibility. The procedure would then be repeated, with a new announcement that convertibility would be reinstated at a future date at the price then prevailing in the market. Unfortunately, the proposal could result in instability in the price of gold as speculators bid up the price before the end of the first announcement period. Then if convertibility were suspended because the price was too high, speculators would unload gold and the price of gold would probably fall very low before the end of the second announcement period. Prospects for suspension of convertibility would be destabilizing and would probably undermine confidence in the system.

2. Another way to arrive at an equilibrium price of gold is to follow the approach of Robert Aliber (1982). He takes the price of $35 per

63

ounce in 1961, a year when the United States had virtual price stability, as an initial equilibrium price. Assuming no other factors have affected the real price of gold, since 1961 the nominal price should have increased to the same extent as the U.S. price level plus a return equal to the real rate of interest. The U.S. consumer price index tripled between 1961 and 1980; hence for that reason alone the nominal price of gold should have been $105 in 1980. With the change in the world consumer price index, the price should have been $155.

Other factors have affected the real price of gold in addition to the increase in the general price level. If world real income elasticity of industrial demand for gold is assumed to be 1.85 (based on econometric results for 1950–80), and the increase in world income is approximately 83 percent (based on an index of world real GNP), the demand for gold would have increased 154 percent (83 percent of 185) from 1961 to 1980. During the same period, the total world gold stock increased 35 percent. Thus the excess demand for gold amounted to about 120 percent (154 − 35 = 119). The real price would also have increased about 120 percent if we assume that the price elasticity of industrial demand for gold is −1 (that is, the percentage increase in the quantity demanded is just equal to the percentage decrease in the price) and that the price elasticity of supply is close to zero. Based on this estimate, the equilibrium price of gold in 1980 would have been between $230 and $340 (105 × 2.2 = 231 and 155 × 2.2 = 341). This calculation assumes that factors affecting the net asset demand for gold are transitory and would vanish once price stability under a gold standard is restored.

Assume that a gold standard is restored with the price per ounce of gold set within the calculated range of $230 to $340. In the current free market, a monetary demand essentially does not exist. Under a reinstituted gold standard, a monetary demand for gold would recur because the government must satisfy all demands for gold at that price. Only after the monetary demand for gold had been accommodated would the nonmonetary demand for gold be satisfied. Thus econometric results for the asset demand relationship for 1969–80 of a 1 to 2 percent real income elasticity would no longer be relevant. The supply equation, however, would presumably be unaffected by a return to the gold standard. The question then resolves itself into the adequacy of the supply relative to the prospective monetary and nonmonetary demand for gold.

3. A third approach to the problem of the price at which to reinstitute the gold standard seizes on the opportunity the selection offers to adopt simultaneously a 100 percent gold reserve against the money supply. The price of an ounce of gold is to be determined, under

this scheme, by dividing a money aggregate, such as the M1 measure of the U.S. money supply, by the number of ounces of gold held by the Treasury. One such calculation yielded a price of $1,500 per ounce. A variant of this approach divides the world dollar GNP by the world stock of monetary gold, yielding a price of $3,500 per ounce. Under either variant, a massive inflation would probably result. Because of the increase in the price of gold, production of gold would be very profitable, and the output of gold would be increased. This would increase the supply of money and the prices of goods and services until prices rose sufficiently to bring an end to the exceptional profits from gold mining.

Profits of Gold Devaluation. When the price of gold is raised, one dollar is equal to a smaller quantity of gold. This is called *gold devaluation*. All holders of gold profit when the price is raised. Assuming that the profits received by the Federal Reserve banks or the U.S. Treasury from a rise in the price of gold (gold devaluation) were sterilized in some fashion, would other central banks in the rest of the world also sterilize the gold devaluation? If not, the United States would be open to the transmission of inflation from foreign economies that chose to monetize the profits of revaluation. The reserve deposits of commercial banks at a foreign central bank that did not sterilize the gold devaluation would increase, and this would increase the money supply and prices in that country.

Pegging the Gold Price. Once a presumably correct price of gold had been determined, the principal central banks would then have to peg it. To prevent a rise in the price of gold, central banks would have to sell gold from existing stocks. To support the price, central banks would have to engage in open market purchases, with possible inflationary consequences. The pegging operation might conceivably be successful; responsibility for intervention in the gold market might be managed as it was under the Gold Pool of 1961 when the Bank of England acted as agent for the members of the pool. To be successful, all countries would have to support the effort, and there must be no changes in the exchange rate of any country. If a country changed its exchange rate, this would constitute a change in the price of gold in that country. Changes in the price of gold would encourage speculation in gold markets.

Linking the Domestic Money Supply to Gold Reserves. Once a pegged price of gold was established, a next step for reinstatement of the gold standard would be to link the domestic money supply to the country's gold reserves. The immediate problem would be to determine the conditions for convertibility of paper currency into gold.

Under a limited U.S. gold standard with convertibility between gold and the dollar available only to residents of the United States, the problem of how to enforce the limitation of convertibility appears intractable. Residents might be required to declare under oath that they were acting for themselves or for other residents, but not for foreigners, when demanding gold or supplying gold at the gold window. Alternatively, gold imports and exports might be embargoed. Opportunities for profitable violation would arise whenever there were discrepancies between the U.S. fixed price and the world market price of gold.

Restoring an international gold standard would involve restoring convertibility to dollar claims of foreign governments and central banks, not to mention private institutions and individuals in foreign countries. Such claims could affect the monetary base and thus the money supply in the United States, regardless of payments flows.

If we assume that convertibility can be arranged without creating serious problems, countries would then be required to give up the discretion that they currently exercise in determining the level and growth rate of their domestic money supplies; under a gold standard, they must accept the effects on their money supply that changing gold reserves would dictate. This is the key issue raised by the proposal to return to the gold standard.

Adequacy of Gold Output. It is arguable that if velocity were to increase at a rate of 3 to 4 percent per year, as was true of the ratio of GNP to the sum of currency plus demand deposits from 1960 to 1980, and real output growth were to remain on average at 3 percent per year, a constant money supply would be optimal. No increase in the monetary gold stock to support a growing demand for money balances would be needed since the upward trend in velocity would accomplish an equivalent expansion of the use of money in economic activity. Under such conditions, a return to the gold standard would involve no resource cost in mining gold for monetary use. An implicit stock resource cost, however, would still exist. Countries maintaining gold reserves could avoid this resource cost by selling their gold for nonmonetary use and putting the proceeds in earning asets.

If velocity failed to grow at a rate matching real income growth, returning to a gold standard would require a policy to assure adequate monetary growth. That would involve an adequate increase in the supply of gold. World gold reserves above and below ground may seem more than adequate when quoted in billions of ounces, but gold production responds sluggishly to changes in market price and since the 1960s has responded perversely. The trend of gold output, holding the real price of gold constant, has declined, generally 1 to 2 percent per year. Forecasts of gold output for the rest of the century in the market economies with known gold reserves are pessimistic. The inadequacy of the projected increase in supply might be offset by discovery of new mines or mining processes, changing patterns of industrial demand for gold, or shifts from current investment stocks. Reinstatement of the gold standard nevertheless poses a risk of long-run deflation of the economy. The political unrest in the United States during the deflation before 1896 was halted only by the upturn in prices when gold in ample quantities became available. Because of the change in social climate and the more activist role of government, a long and uncertain lag in the response of the gold supply to the changing demand for money would probably create greater problems today than in the nineteenth century.

The fact that the bulk of current world output of gold is from South Africa and the Soviet Union adds to the uncertainty of future gold supplies. Shocks in the gold market at home or abroad might also arise from changes in the demand for gold for investment and, on the supply side, from gold discoveries. Such shocks would make it difficult for one country alone to return to the gold standard because it would bear unilaterally the adjustment costs—inflation or deflation—imposed by the shocks.

Fixing Exchange Rates. The objective of a unilateral return to a gold standard by the United States would be to preserve flexible exchange rates and yet constrain domestic monetary growth by having a gold reserve requirement. Under such an arrangement, however, a shift from a foreign currency into gold by an American investor would impose the whole burden of adjustment on the exchange rate between the foreign currency and the dollar since the dollar price of gold would not change. A shift to gold from the pound, for example, would tend to lower the price of the pound in terms of dollars. If there were significant portfolio shifts by Americans between foreign currencies and gold, exchange rates would tend (all other things equal) to become more variable than they are under the present floating system. A major question is how such gold transactions (or possible purchases or sales of gold by other countries) would affect domestic monetary policy.

If all industrial countries returned to the gold standard, each country would adopt par rates of exchange for its currency relative to the dollar or other currencies. Under the pre-1914 gold standard, the official rate of exchange expressed an equilibrium that had gradually evolved among national price levels. At the present time, par rates of exchange would have to be arbitrarily chosen. The mistakes made in the choice of exchange rates when European countries resumed the gold standard in the 1920s and again under the Bretton Woods arrangements are not reassuring.

In 1925, for example, Great Britain returned to the gold standard at an unrealistically high gold price for the pound. In 1947, it repeated that mistake. In the first attempt, it struggled for six years in a vain attempt to deflate the economy to make the gold price viable in the face of gold outflows. The pound was then freed to float. In the second attempt, after two years the pound was devalued. In 1928, France returned to the gold standard at an unrealistically low gold price for the franc. Gold inflows into France (and U.S. sterilization of its gold inflow) destabilized the system.

A multilateral return to the gold standard would require international agreement and amendment of the International Monetary Fund rules. Yet there is no evidence that other countries are interested in reinstating the gold standard. The views they have expressed, in fact, are negative with respect to the desirability or feasibility of a return to the gold standard.

Summary

The historical gold standard before 1914 was a monetary regime in which there was a commitment by governments to buy and sell gold at a fixed price; there were fixed gold requirements for the issue of national currencies that were convertible into gold. Governments were restrained from issuing unlimited amounts of their national currencies by the obligation to pay gold on demand. Fixed exchange rates between different national currencies, each linked to gold, united countries in an international system.

These features of the gold standard were not set in concrete. They varied over space and time, particularly after 1914. Some central banks substituted for gold holdings interest-earning assets denominated in other national currencies and did not invariably respond promptly to increases or decreases in reserves by expanding or contracting the domestic money supply. Progressively, convertibility of nongold money into gold coin was withdrawn and replaced by convertibility into much heavier minimum weight units of gold bars, a right that was in turn withdrawn from domestic moneyholders and restricted to official institutions. The gold restraint on national money issues was ended with the abandonment of gold reserve requirements. The link was broken between alterations of a country's domestic money supply and deficits or surpluses in its international payments account. Fixed exchange rates under the Bretton Woods system evolved into adjustable pegged exchange rates. The system collapsed in the early 1970s, when confidence eroded in the gold convertibility of the U.S. dollar, the dominant reserve currency. Thereafter no significant role for gold remained in domestic and international monetary systems.

How satisfactory was the historical gold standard as a monetary regime? The key virtue that advocates claim for the gold standard is that it provided price stability. Yet price movements before World War I and during the interwar period were characterized by short-term variability and trends. The main benefit of the gold standard was long-term price predictability. Market participants undertook long-term contracts acting on the tendency for the price level ultimately to revert to its initial level. Although output growth was not smooth under the gold standard, cyclical changes may have reflected instability in money growth associated with the peculiarities of the U.S. banking system rather than with the character of the gold standard.

However, to the extent that cyclical changes occurred because of foreign monetary and nonmonetary disturbances that were transmitted by fixed exchange rates, fluctuations in output indeed were related to the monetary regime. Maintaining the gold standard also imposed resource costs on the economy. The stock of monetary gold could have been used for nonmonetary purposes and so deprived the economy of the yield from that alternative use. Furthermore, the costs of mining additions to the monetary gold stock to match increases in demand must be taken into account. Resource costs are acceptable to gold standard advocates but not to its detractors. Finally, although a fully functioning gold standard would be free of political intervention, increasingly governments and monetary authorities intervened to avoid the discipline the gold standard was designed to achieve.

Having given up the discipline of the gold standard, the world turned to a discretionary fiat money regime with managed flexible exchange rates. The record under the present regime has been one of high and variable inflation and interest rates, low productivity growth, and unstable foreign exchange rates, so the subject has been opened up of returning to the gold standard as a way of improving the record. Is it currently feasible to restore the gold standard regime? Serious technical problems would be encountered in an attempt to restore the gold standard. These include choosing the right price of gold, deciding what to do with the profits of gold devaluation, arranging for the pegging of the new gold price, linking the domestic money supply to gold reserves, assuring the adequacy of gold output, and fixing sustainable foreign exchange rates. These are technical issues. The solution to the difficulties each of these requirements poses would still not guarantee that the restored gold standard would provide a viable monetary regime. For that outcome, more than the solution of technical difficulties is required. Essentially, there must be precommitment by governments and their constituencies to the gold standard.

The gold standard can survive in a world in which countries allow gold to move freely; gold does not accumulate in any country, and gold does not drain away from any country without being allowed to exercise an expansionary or contractionary effect, respectively, on the level of prices; major disequilibria in price levels and financial conditions among countries are not endured. The forces that caused the breakdown of the Bretton Woods system were unleashed by actions of countries with a persistent deficit or surplus in their balance of payments. Those actions were taken to delay or resist changes in prices and costs expressed in national currencies. Under fixed exchange rates, convergence of national economic policies is essential for the system to be viable. The European Monetary System presupposes such behavior. Yet since 1979, when the system was established, member countries have repeatedly preferred to alter the relation between national price and cost levels by exchange-rate changes. This is not a good augury for restoration of an international gold standard.

Under the pre–World War I gold standard, governments in peacetime did not undertake expenditures that were financed by the printing press. (The gold standard collapsed when countries were engulfed by war or revolution.) In some gold standard countries, government was not divorced from business, and social insurance was accepted policy. Government participation in economic activity, however, was restrained by concern to preserve the integrity of the national currency and to maintain its domestic and external value. These concerns receded after 1929 as governments extended their activities to finance stabilization policies in response to interest groups wielding political influence.

The question then arises whether governments will reverse their course, returning to a more limited role, as in the pre–World War I era.[1] Of course, a limited role of the state is not in itself a guarantee of a viable international monetary system since in earlier eras international monetary affairs were often in disarray, even with limited states (Dam 1982, p. 38). The fundamental hurdle to a successful return to the gold standard is the resistance of political authorities and of modern democracies to precommitment and to forswearing of discretion. That hurdle is also a problem for a fiat money regime governed by a rule.[2]

The gold standard flourished before World War I possibly because of the special position of sterling and London. That position was threatened even before World War I when Paris and Berlin became important rivals of London. Thereafter, London's predominance was never reestablished. Under the Bretton Woods system, the dollar and the United States were in a special position. As the convertibility of the U.S. dollar into gold crumbled, the system collapsed. An important aspect of the successful operation of a gold-centered monetary system is an unshakable confidence that the reserve currency of a dominant country will always be converted into gold on demand. What country is willing to be the candidate for such a role in a future gold standard? The failure of the U.S. Gold Commission in 1982 to endorse a larger, if not central, role for gold in monetary arrangements bespeaks the absence of the necessary commitment to adherence to gold standard rules in the United States.

REFERENCES

Aliber, Robert Z. "Inflationary Expectations and the Price of Gold." In *The Gold Problem: Economic Perspectives*, Alberto Quadrio-Curzio, ed. Oxford: Oxford University Press for the Banca Nationale del Lavoro and Nomisma, 1982. Pp. 151–61.

Barro, Robert J. "Comment." In *A Retrospective on the Classical Gold Standard, 1821–1931*, Michael D. Bordo and Anna J. Schwartz, eds. Chicago: University of Chicago Press, 1984. Pp. 644–46.

1. Schumpeter's (1950, p. 451) verdict, referring to post–World War I developments, was that "no return to prewar policies proved possible even where it was attempted. This has been strikingly verified by England's gold policy and its ultimate failure. In a world that was no longer the world of free enterprise, the gold standard—the naughty child that keeps on telling unpleasant truths—ceased to work."

2. Compare this conclusion with that in the recent study of the gold standard by Flood and Garber (1984, p. 90): "Even a well-designed commodity money scheme is a foolproof inflation guard only when the scheme's permanence is guaranteed. Permanence may possibly be guaranteed by an underlying political economy that abhors inflation, but merely enactment of a new ephemeral rule does not ensure permanence."

Bordo, Michael D. "The Classical Gold Standard: Some Lessons for Today." *Federal Reserve Bank of St. Louis Review* 63 (May 1981), 2–17.

Cagan, Phillip. "The Report of the Gold Commission (1982)." In *Monetary and Fiscal Policies and Their Application*, Karl Brunner and Allan H. Meltzer, eds. Carnegie Rochester Conference Series on Public Policy, vol. 20. Amsterdam: North-Holland, 1984. Pp. 247–67.

Cooper, Richard N. "The Gold Standard: Historical Facts and Future Prospects." *Brookings Papers on Economic Activity* 13 (1982), 1–45.

Dam, Kenneth W. *The Rules of the Game*. Chicago: University of Chicago Press, 1982.

Fisher, Irving. "A Compensated Dollar." *Quarterly Journal of Economics* 27 (February 1913), 213–35, 385–97.

Flood, Robert P., and Peter M. Garber. "Gold Monetization and Gold Discipline." *Journal of Political Economy* 92 (February 1984), 90–107.

Friedman, Milton. "Commodity-Reserve Currency." *Journal of Political Economy* 59 (June 1951), 203–32.

Jevons, W. Stanley. "A Serious Fall in the Value of Gold Ascertained and Its Social Effects Set Forth." In *Investigations in Currency and Finance*, H. S. Foxwell, ed. London: Macmillan, 1884. Pp. 13–118.

———. "An Ideally Perfect System of Currency." In *Investigations in Currency and Finance*, H.S. Foxwell, ed. London: Macmillan, 1884. Pp. 297–302.

Laffer, Arthur B. *Reinstatement of the Dollar: The Blueprint*. Rolling Hills Estates, Cal.: A.B. Laffer Associates, 1980.

Marshall, Alfred. *Memorials of Alfred Marshall*, Arthur C. Pigou, ed. London: Macmillan, 1925.

Report to the Congress of the Commission on the Role of Gold in the Domestic and International Monetary Systems, Vols. 1 and 2. Washington, D.C.: The Secretary of the Treasury, March 1982.

Reynolds, Alan. "Why Gold?" *Cato Journal* 3 (Spring 1983), 211–32.

Rockoff, Hugh. "Some Evidence on the Real Price of Gold, Its Cost of Production, and Commodity Prices." In *A Retrospective on the Classical Gold Standard, 1821–1931*, Michael D. Bordo and Anna J. Schwartz, eds. Chicago: University of Chicago Press, 1984. Pp. 613–40.

Schumpeter, Joseph A. "The March into Socialism." *American Economic Review, Papers and Proceedings* 40 (May 1950), 446–56.

Schwartz, Anna J. "Introduction." In *A Retrospective on the Classical Gold Standard, 1821–1931*, Michael D. Bordo and Anna J. Schwartz, eds. Chicago: University of Chicago Press, 1984. Pp. 1–20.

Beyond the Historical Gold Standard

J. HUSTON McCULLOCH

THE DESCRIPTION of the gold standard by Schwartz shares a fundamental misconception with much of the literature on this subject: it conceives of the gold standard as a "commitment by government to buy and sell gold at a fixed price."[1] In fact, a gold standard is a monetary system in which gold coins, or demand claims on gold, circulate as money. There is no necessary reason why the government should take any direct part in such a monetary system, nor is there any reason to believe that nationalizing such a monetary system would be desirable.

If, for example, the government undertook to peg the price of wheat at $4 per bushel, we would not call this a wheat standard but merely government meddling in the wheat market. A paper money standard in which the government pegs the price of gold at its pleasure is a mere parody of a gold standard.

Schwartz does raise a number of important potential problems with a gold standard:

1. The amount of gold in a monetary unit must be decided.
2. A gold standard would be costly in terms of real resources.
3. A gold standard would not really guarantee long-run price stability.
4. In the past, a gold standard has been associated with greater short-run price instability than modern paper money standards.
5. A gold standard can be cast aside by the government as easily as a monetary growth rule.
6. The transition from the present monetary system to a gold standard must be determined.

The following comments address these and other aspects of a gold standard.

Units

Under a gold standard, gold coins circulate by weight, and money substitutes are obligations to pay a certain weight of gold on demand.

1. See also Chapter 4 by Meltzer, and Bordo (1981).

There is no reason to make up a new unit of weight for this purpose; the only choice is between the gram and the ounce.[2]

The relation between the paper dollar and gold is a purely transitional one, which I will deal with later. However, there is no question of the government pegging the weight of either the gram or the ounce under a gold standard.

Resource Costs

Many outspoken advocates of a gold standard do insist that both hand-to-hand currency and transaction deposits be either gold or backed 100 percent with gold.[3] This would indeed be a very costly system, as Schwartz's calculations show.

However, under a gold standard with a completely deregulated banking system, relatively little gold would actually need to be used, either to back deposits or to serve as currency. Interest-bearing deposits would be much more attractive than non-interest-bearing deposits. We have seen that money market fund shares function very well as transaction balances. Since these are run-proof and require only a very small inventory of clearing balances, they would probably be the dominant form of checking account in the absence of federal deposit insurance. The assets of gold standard money market funds would be short-term, negotiable, gold-denominated obligations, predominantly of finance companies, which would make less liquid, though equally short-term, commercial and personal loans.

Under complete banking deregulation, interest-bearing currency would be feasible and would probably tend to dominate gold coin for most transactions. However, this interest should not be paid, as Hall suggests in Chapter 6, by crediting the account of each customer who withdraws cash. Hall's method would not encourage the depositor to hold the bill unless the serial number of each bill were also laboriously recorded and flagged when it was cashed. Nor would it

2. I personally prefer the gram: the gram is standard in most of the world and is already quite familiar in the United States. The ounce, on the other hand, is not even an ounce; an ounce of gold is traditionally a troy ounce of 31.1 grams, whereas an ounce of almost anything else is an avoirdupois ounce of 28.3 grams. A troy ounce convention would mean either that special scales would have to be available just for weighing gold or else that odd conversion factors would have to be memorized by everyone in commerce. Unfortunately, large quantities of troy ounce gold coins are already in circulation, so we may be stuck with the troy ounce.

3. See, for example, von Mises (1953, pp. 438, 448).

give subsequent holders of the bill any incentive to hold the bill, since they would not be receiving the interest on it.

Nor should interest be paid by redeeming the note with interest from its date of issue, as was done with the original Bank of England notes in 1694.[4] This procedure would mean that notes in circulation would not be worth their face value and that interest would have to be calculated every time a note changed hands.

Rather, interest would most efficiently be paid through a lottery on the serial numbers. For example, a weekly drawing of a four-digit number that is to be compared to the last four digits of the serial number, and that paid ten times the face value of the note, would be equivalent to 5.2 percent annual interest. All bills in circulation would be worth just face value; winners would be instantly removed from circulation.

It should be noted that under a completely deregulated banking system, with interest-bearing private currency, some sort of a commodity link such as gold would be necessary to determine the price level. If the quantity of a zero-interest fiat money base were held constant, while the demand for it shrank to zero as people substituted interest-bearing alternatives, the price level would tend toward infinity. On the other hand, if the quantity of M1 were held constant by reducing the stock of standard fiat base money, while the demand for (mostly interest-bearing) M1 grew almost without limit as its opportunity cost fell toward zero, the price level would tend instead toward zero. A gold link would eliminate this indeterminacy and achieve Friedman's (1969) "optimum quantity of money" without the inconvenience of deflation.

It is true that under even a gold standard with deregulated banking, many risk-averse people would derive expected utility from actually being paid in gold, or from having a 100 percent reserve checking account. This would represent a resource cost of the gold standard, but it would not be a welfare loss, any more than the very real resource cost of the life and casualty insurance industries represents a welfare loss.

Schwartz suggests that fractional reserves "accentuate" the effects of gold flows on the quantity of money. I view this the other way around: gold flows do not drive the quantity of money. Rather, shifts in the demand for money induce gold flows. Fractional reserves therefore serve to reduce the gold flow necessary to accommodate a given shift in money demand.

4. See Richards (1929/1965, p. 156, n. 5).

Long-run Price Stability

Sophisticated gold standard advocates recognize that gold does not have a constant purchasing power and may be subject to substantial fluctuations over the decades.[5] However, this just means that under a gold standard, shrewd borrowers and lenders should simply link long-term debt contracts to an acceptable price index. Indeed, early advocates of indexation such as Jevons and Fisher had in mind the long-run vagaries of gold, not paper.

I had thought that it was nevertheless generally agreed that gold is more predictable in purchasing power over the long run than is paper money, the opposite of Meltzer's conclusion in Chapter 4. I do not eactly understand his calculations, but I find it very hard to believe that gold does not have a greater degree of long-run stability and predictability than does paper. Meltzer's equation is based on the brief period 1890–1914, which may be part of the problem. The United States was on a de facto gold standard from 1834 to 1861 and a legal one from 1879 to 1933. The U.S. wholesale price index was around 29 (1972 = 100) in 1834, 1861, 1879, and again at the outbreak of World War I in 1914.[6] The dollar price level could easily be converted into a gold price level for the years 1862–78, giving a much longer eighty-year time series from 1834 to 1914 that would show much more mean-reversion. It should be remembered that the gold dollar was in the wings during the de facto silver standard years 1792–1834 and was worth only about 5 percent more than silver, so the time series could be carried back even farther. In 1792, before the global inflation of the Napoleonic War era (the pound was suspended from 1797 to 1819), the gold price level was again in the vicinity of 29.

Short-run Price Stability

The price level apparently showed much greater short-run variability during the 1879–1914 gold standard than it has under the postwar paper money standard, though Cooper's evidence cited by Schwartz

5. See, for example, von Mises (1953).
6. Note that in March 1933, after the World War I inflationary episode had been completely liquidated, the price level was again back to about 29. This suggests that at that time the price level, if not the rest of the economy, was finally back in the vicinity of equilibrium.

in Table 2–1 shows hardly any difference for the United States, and actually greater postwar variability for the United Kingdom.[7]

However, even assuming there was greater short-run price volatility under the historical gold standard, it is not clear whether this was the fault of gold per se or simply of the banking system that happened to be in place: if one wished to devise a banking system for a highly seasonal agricultural economy that was guaranteed to have an annual liquidity crisis, a good start would be to impose a three times greater gold reserve requirement on deposits at banks in the largest cities than on deposits at country banks.[8] In order to prevent banks from diversifying either their assets or their deposit bases, one could further prohibit interstate banking or, better yet, require unit banking in most states. And to bring about unnecessary suspensions, one could prevent banks from dipping into their abundant required reserves to pay off depositors.

As for the currency, in order to prevent it from responding to either the seasonal variation or the secular growth in trade, one could tie it rigidly to a declining national debt. If one wished to guarantee that the currency department of the note-issuing banks would have a permanent liquidity problem, one could require that the notes be backed by long-term bonds rather than by short-term bills of exchange. And in order to prevent the states from coming up with a better currency system, one should not forget to slap a prohibitive tax on state bank notes.

Schwartz does mention flaws in the banking system as a possible source of short-run industrial fluctuations, if not price fluctuations, but the only flaw she identifies is the lack of government deposit insurance.

Even the best-designed denationalized gold standard might be subject to unavoidable short-run shocks, stemming from the erratic monetary policies of foreign governments. However, it is not clear that this is what we are seeing in simple historical comparisons.

7. I am at a loss as to why Cooper would base this calculation on the residuals of the nonsense equation, $ln\ P_t = a\ ln\ P_{t-1}$, or why Schwartz would cite these figures. Meltzer's calculations do show more short-run risk to the price level under the historical gold standard, though I must admit I do not understand his calculations.

8. Deposits at central reserve city banks were backed 25 percent by gold and other lawful money, whereas deposits at country banks could be backed by as little as 7.4 percent in ultimate reserves. Country banks had a 15 percent reserve requirement, but three-quarters of this could be on deposit at a reserve city bank. The reserve city banks had a 25 percent reserve requirement, but half of this could be on deposit with a central reserve city bank: $0.4(0.15) + (0.6)(0.15)(0.25)(0.5 + 0.5(0.25)) = 0.074$.

The Vulnerability of a Gold Standard

A gold standard is allegedly as easy to cast aside as a monetary growth rule. This is certainly true of a Bretton Woods–type system in which government paper money is legal tender and the government simply diddles at its pleasure in the gold market. Such a system would be hardly worth the trouble. Under a denationalized gold standard, however, the government would have no monetary obligations to declare legal tender. Its only role would be as a third party, enforcing contracts, auctioning the assets of defaulted banks, protecting copyrights on bills and coins, and prosecuting the emitters of counterfeit coins and fraudulent balance sheets.

With great effort, the government can overthrow a gold standard. The United States did in 1862 and again in 1933. In the former case, however, it felt compelled to return to gold after the fiscal emergency, perhaps because it had not dared to seize the gold coins in circulation. In the latter case, it was able to seize the public's gold through a ruse, but it had already insinuated its way much more deeply into the monetary system than it had in 1862. It is questionable whether the public would fall for the same trick again.

According to von Mises, "The excellence of the gold standard is to be seen in the fact that it renders the determination of the monetary unit's purchasing power independent of the policies of governments and political parties" (1953, p. 416). Why then would the government cooperate in setting one up, as Schwartz asks in her concluding paragraph? The answer is that administrations change. Only one sympathetic administration is necessary to burn the paper bridges that lead to inflationary finance. These bridges can, it is true, be rebuilt by subsequent administrations, but only at great cost and never perfectly, given the possibility of a substantial underground circulation of gold coins once these are in general use.[9]

A gold standard, with gold coins in circulation and readily available to the public, makes inflationary finance much more difficult than it would otherwise be. It provides a "mechanism for binding the

9. Another, less tangible obstacle to the overthrow of a gold standard once in place is the relation between law and public opinion. As Dicey (1963) noted in 1914, the law is molded by public opinion, but public opinion is equally molded by the law. If a gold standard once exists and is recognized in law, it will come to be regarded as just even if it is the pinnacle of inequity, and any effort to dislodge it will be considered outrageous. On the other hand, the general public would scarcely be aware of a monetary growth rule or of deviations from it until (too late) inflation became rampant (if then). Unfortunately, Dicey's rule works against the overthrow of a paper money standard as well.

policymaker's hands in advance," and such a mechanism would, as Barro points out in Chapter 1, have many desirable macroeconomic implications.

Many economists take it for granted that any counterinflationary restraints on the money supply should be suspended during wartime. Von Mises, however, writing in 1924, regarded war as the one inflation-financed government expenditure that it is particularly desirable to obstruct with a gold standard. In *The Theory of Money and Credit* (pp. 394–95), he actually charges that before World War I the powers deliberately "weaned" the public away from the use of gold coins in order to facilitate wartime finance.

Transition

An important set of public policy problems that would need to be resolved in even the most denationalized of gold standards is what to do with the present monetary system. What should be the relation, if any, of the existing money supply, both monetary base and deposits in private banks, to gold? What should be done with the existing monetary gold stock? And how should existing nonmonetary dollar-denominated debts be paid off?

A particularly draconian option would be simply to allow the dollar to hyperinflate as money demand switches to stable gold and away from inflationary dollars. At the other extreme, but almost equally harsh, the government could require all dollar-denominated debts to be paid in gold at the current price of gold—or at $42.22, or even $20.67, an ounce.

Intermediately, the government could redeem its own monetary base for gold at the current gold price and then declare private debts to be payable in gold with purchasing power equal to the purchasing power of the dollar on the conversion date, adjusted for an inflation factor presumably built into nominal interest rates as of the conversion date.

Ironically, in 1980 the price of gold was so high and the demand for real cash balances so low that the government could have paid off every dollar of currency and bank reserves in gold at the market price of gold with its monetary gold reserves and still have had some to spare. This situation existed, however, only because of the high inflationary expectations at the time. It is difficult to predict what would have happened to the price level (in terms of gold) if such a conversion had taken place. On the one hand, if the public perceived gold as more stable in value than the paper dollar, the demand for real cash balances would have risen sharply, resulting in a deflation of gold prices. On the other hand, the introduction of money substitutes, including interest-bearing currency, by a deregulated banking system could have reversed this tendency and led to an even higher gold price level.

I do not know the answers to these transitional questions, but it should be kept in mind that they are secondary to that of the basic desirability or undesirability of a permanent gold standard. Surely the issue of how to dispose of the government's existing wheat stocks, and at what price, should be secondary to the issue of whether wheat storage is best left to the market or to the government.

One particularly difficult transitional problem is whether the government should give any push at all in the direction of a gold standard per se, or whether the market should be left to decide this for itself. Indeed, this brings us to an even deeper issue, namely, whether a metallic standard should necessarily even be based on gold. The appeal of a gold standard is really for a monetary system based on a convenient, and therefore probably metallic, commodity. Historically, the world's metallic money has been primarily silver, not gold, from Roman times to at least the eighteenth century. Indeed, the dollar itself was originally a Spanish silver coin. The world ended up on gold only through a series of bungled government efforts to supplement silver with gold. The international gold standard itself lasted barely one generation, a mere flash in the pan of history.

In 1975, Hans F. Sennholz edited a book entitled *Gold Is Money*, the implication being that from time immemorial, gold has been the primary monetary commodity. Ironically, if this title were translated into French and back, it would become *Gold Is Silver!*[10]

Because of the geographical dispersion of silver deposits—and the geographical concentration of gold deposits—the supply of silver is likely to be much more steady and much less prone to political intervention than is the supply of gold (McCulloch 1982, pp. 76–77). Furthermore, silver is much more convenient for small transactions than is gold.[11]

Nor should one overlook the possibility of a voluntarily adopted bimetallic standard, that is, one with no legally imposed legal tender status of one metal in payment of debts contracted in terms of the

10. An all-too-common misconception is that the German word *Geld* is related to *gold*. In fact, *Geld* derives from Old High German *geltan*, "to pay", which is related to English *guild* and *yield*. *Gold* on the other hand, derives from the color of the metal and is cognate with *gelb* and *yellow*. Note that Germany was in fact an historical stronghold of the *silver* standard.

11. I am cynical enough to believe that Bismarck's replacement of silver with gold in Germany was itself a scheme to wean the public away from the use of standard money coins and to pave the way for inflationary finance.

other, but in which both gold and silver coins circulate and debts are customarily contracted with a bimetallic clause at a conventional ratio.[12]

In summary, it is wrong to view the gold standard, as Schwartz and many others do, as a return to the historical gold standard. Certainly we have much to learn from the historical gold standard, but to turn the old phrase around, those who study and even admire history need not be condemned to repeat all the mistakes of the past.

REFERENCES

Bordo, Michael D. "The Classical Gold Standard: Some Lessons for Today." *Federal Reserve Bank of St. Louis Review* 63 (May 1981), 2–17.

Dicey, Albert V. *Lectures on the Relation between Law and Public Opinion in England during the Nineteenth Century*, 2nd ed. London: Macmillan, 1963.

Friedman, Milton. *The Optimum Quantity of Money and Other Essays*. Chicago: Aldine Publishing Co., 1969.

Greenfield, Robert L., and Leland B. Yeager. "A Laissez-Faire Approach to Monetary Stability." *Journal of Money, Credit and Banking* 15 (August 1983), 302–15.

Hall, Robert E. "Explorations in the Gold Standard and Related Policies for Stabilizing the Dollar." In *Inflation: Causes and Effects*, Robert E. Hall, ed. Chicago: University of Chicago Press for the National Bureau of Economic Research, 1982. Pp. 111–22.

Hayek, Friedrich A. *Denationalisation of Money*, 2nd ed. London: Institute of Economic Affairs, 1978.

McCulloch, J. Huston. *Money and Inflation: A Monetarist Approach*, 2nd ed. New York: Academic Press, 1982.

Richards, Richard D. *The Early History of Banking in England*. London: P. S. King & Son, Ltd., 1929; Reprint ed., New York: Kelley, 1965.

Sennholz, Hans F., ed. *Gold Is Money*. Westport, Conn.: Greenwood Press, 1975.

von Mises, Ludwig. *The Theory of Money and Credit*, H. E. Batson, trans. New Haven: Yale University Press, 1953.

12. A price-level indexed monetary system such as that proposed by Hayek (1978) and the ammonium nitrate-copper-aluminum-plywood standard suggested by Hall (1982) has considerable appeal but does lack the tangibility of a metallic coin standard. See also Greenfield and Yeager (1983).

Market Discipline of the Monetary System

J. RICHARD ZECHER

IN DISCUSSIONS of the gold standard, an important question is, Would it currently be feasible to restore the gold standard mechanism? Schwartz notes that serious technical problems would be encountered in an attempt to restore the gold standard. These include choosing the right price at which to resume the gold standard, arranging for the pegging of the new gold price, and linking output and prices through multilateral exchange rates. Schwartz's general view of the gold standard comes across as very negative, too negative in my opinion, given the fact that we spent so much of our history on the gold standard despite the problems she enumerates.

A more important question than the technical problems of returning to the gold standard is, Isn't it naive to expect the government to give up the great discretionary power it now has over money creation? What lessons can we draw from history concerning the role of government in the money supply process?

Let us start by going back even further than the nineteenth century, to before the Revolutionary War. It is fair to characterize the system in the colonies during that period as the pure market system of money creation. That is, the colonies imported money or exported money, depending on domestic financial conditions, as needed. If the economy were growing faster than the rest of the world, the colonies would run a balance-of-payments surplus and import money so that they could maintain the same price level-interest rate structure that is consistent with the rest of the world. The money supply process for the colonial United States was like the money supply process today for Panama, a country without a central bank. It proceeded quite well in the sense that the private sector determined the stock of money without the intervention of any active monetary authority. There were monetary authorities other places, of course, and that was important. But from the point of view of the colonies, it was basically a pure private sector system determining the money supply.

Looking at later periods, we find that one of the trends over time is that the role of government in the process of determining money supply increases in each period, not evenly over time, but it does increase with each stage. By the post–Civil War period, as Friedman and Schwartz (1963) pointed out, there is fairly active Treasury management of the money supply. In the Federal Reserve period there was a much more active policy. And then the Bretton Woods system set the stage where holding gold by individuals is not permitted— international transactions in gold are not permitted on the part of individuals—and the discipline on the system that can be imposed by the private sector was constrained a great deal. And then one finally comes to the current system. I do not know what effect the private sector now has on the money supply process directly other than through bank borrowings at the Federal Reserve banks; that is the part of the money supply process, in a sense, determined by the private sector.

That progression of increasing government control of the money supply process is really a very key, critical development for us to examine in considering a return to a more market-disciplined type of system like the gold standard.

A very specific criticism of the account of the gold standard by Schwartz has to do with the interpretation of the activities of the Federal Reserve in the 1920s. Schwartz observes that specie flows and domestic credit creation tended to move in opposite directions, and this is attributed to an offsetting policy by the Federal Reserve. I would read these numbers just the other way around to say the Federal Reserve was increasing and decreasing domestic credit for a variety of reasons, and the balance of payments was operating like a shock absorber, as it had in the original period, to offset these shocks and bring domestic money supply into balance with money demand.

On the more general theme, an important topic is the role of the private sector in the current period and the private sector's response to this period. Let me begin by setting up two assumptions. One is that this is a very risky period in terms of volatility of prices, interest rates, and exchange rates. The second is that the role of the private sector in providing any independent discipline to the money supply process is very minimal, if it exists at all, in this period. How has the market responded to these conditions?

One response has been an explosive development in knowledge: knowledge of financial risk, of understanding how to measure it and how to manage it. At least part of the rapid development of new theories of financial risk management can be attributed to the existence of much more financial risk to deal with. Over this period, since the end of Bretton Woods basically, portfolio theory, capital asset pricing theory, options pricing theory, and efficient market theory have developed rapidly. And they led to phenomenal development of new risk-management instruments: options, futures, and all kinds of financial instruments. Today these are not small markets, yet none of them existed before 1971. Equally notable is the fact that corporations and other private sector entities are devoting not only more but much higher quality resources to managing financial risk. But these developments are widely in response to a much riskier environment that the private sector cannot do very much about, except in political terms, and so it has decided to deal with it by insulating itself from this risk.

Most of the things mentioned deal with very short-run financial risk. Most of these markets go out only a year to a year and a half. They do not deal directly with the long-term problem. It would appear that many people still prefer to make long-term bets on the price level in terms of going into very long-term fixed nominal contracts. Now that is not a bet on a stable price level but a bet on a predictable price level: 25-year, 30-year mortgages, corporate securities, government securities. People want to buy and sell these securities, and they are willing to do it in very large amounts. As often mentioned, people tend to prefer fixed nominal contracts. At the same time, another big market has developed, which basically allows purchasers of securities, at their discretion, if their preferences change, to transform these long-term commitments into short-term commitments. This SWAPS market, which has become so important, also is not a small market. It started only in 1982; no one knows for sure, but I would guess that U.S. interest-rate SWAPS are now over a $50 billion business at an annual rate. So the private market has learned to manage financial risk since the monetary system has become so volatile.

The basic question to me is not, Should we return to the gold standard? The basic question is rather, Should we expand the role of the market place in determining the money supply in ways that will discipline the monetary system and make it more stable?

My answer is that we should.

REFERENCE

Friedman, Milton, and Anna J. Schwartz. *A Monetary History of the United States, 1867–1960.* Princeton: Princeton University Press, 1963.

THREE

A Monetary System Based on
Fixed Exchange Rates

RICHARD N. COOPER

THIS PAPER addresses the use of fixed exchange rates as a system of domestic monetary management. It begins by sketching briefly the historical reliance on fixed exchange rates among national currencies. That is followed by a discussion of the implications of fixed exchange rates for monetary and fiscal policies in a country. The third section then addresses fixed exchange rates from a global perspective and points out that fixing exchange rates cannot by itself determine the global monetary system. The fourth section discusses the merits of fixed exchange rates for a single country in light of its circumstances and its economic objectives. The fifth section addresses how the adjustment process works under fixed exchange rates. The final section concludes with some general observations on fixed as opposed to flexible exchange rates. It raises some questions about the adequacy of present economic knowledge and analysis on this crucial choice that countries must make in today's permissive environment with respect to exchange rate arrangements.

A Brief History

Most of the world has had fixed exchange rates most of the time. Fixed exchange rates among the circulating media of different countries have been the dominant form of monetary arrangement, against which 1973–85 has been an aberrant period of floating exchange rates. For centuries money was commodity money, generally gold and silver, and while different states struck coins of differing weight and gold or silver content, the coins circulated widely outside the minting state and for significant transactions traded at their metallic value. (Spanish silver coins circulated widely in the American colonies of Britain, for example.) In this sense, foreign money and domestic money were indistinguishable.

Beginning in the eighteenth century, paper money began to sup-

85

plement metallic coins as a medium of circulation. So long as the bank notes were readily and fully convertible into money metals, this addition did not alter the fixity of exchange rates between monies, although it did lay the basis for a clear differentiation among national monies, since the bank notes were typically not acceptable abroad and indeed were often not acceptable far from their bank of issue even within the same country.

The situation changed fundamentally when the convertibility of bank notes into gold or silver was suspended or when the physical export of metallic money was prohibited. Such developments were usually associated with wars or severe civil unrest, as when American and French paper currency depreciated against gold (and the pound sterling) during the American and French revolutions, respectively (on the latter, see Harris 1930), when the British suspended gold convertibility and gold export during the Napoleonic Wars and the pound depreciated against the U.S. dollar, or, again, when the U.S. greenbacks depreciated against European currencies during the U.S. Civil War until resumption of gold convertibility (specie payment) in 1879.

Even convertibility into metallic money was not by itself enough to assure nearly fixed exchange rates. When the age-old ratio of exchange between gold and silver was abandoned in the 1870s, and several major countries moved onto the pure gold standard, silver depreciated sharply against gold, and countries whose monetary system was tied to silver (most importantly, India and China) found their currencies with fluctuating exchange rates against those of gold standard countries.[1] The Indian rupee depreciated so sharply that Americans complained in the 1890s of competition in European markets from cheap Indian grain exports. But these episodes mark exceptions to a general rule of (almost) fixed exchange rates among national currencies until World War II, with brief episodes of floating exchange rates in 1914–25 and 1931–36.

Exchange rates were only almost fixed because the commitment of each government was to mint gold or silver coins (into which bank notes were convertible) at a fixed weight and fineness that served as legal tender. Melting down, shipping, insuring, and reminting gold involved real costs, and these costs prevented a literal fixity of exchange rates between national currencies. In the 1880s, the range of variation in the exchange rate between the British pound and the U.S. dollar

1. J.M. Keynes's (1913) early professional work was on the problem of Indian currency under the silver standard.

was 1.3 percent, reflecting those costs of gold arbitrage, very little of which actually took place (Morgenstern 1959, p. 177).

It would be a mistake to assume that exchange rates were rigidly fixed even within a nation. Bank notes traded at a discount far away from the issuing bank within the United States, and in periods of financial uncertainty these discounts became as high as 35 percent.

After World War II, most countries adhered to the Bretton Woods agreement, under which they undertook inter alia to fix their currencies to gold or to some currency convertible into gold, with a range of variation not to exceed 2 percent around the declared par value. Thus the world continued, with exceptions such as Canada during 1950–62, on a system of almost fixed exchange rates. But there was a fundamental difference between this Bretton Woods system and the prewar gold or gold exchange standards. Under the latter, exchange rates were expected to be irrevocably fixed (except in periods of great turbulence such as those noted), whereas under the Bretton Woods adjustable peg system, exchange rates were expected to be altered if necessary to correct a fundamental disequilibrium in international payments, and in particular if there seemed to be a sharp conflict between maintaining balanced international payments and domestic full employment.

This difference may seem of no importance much of the time, but in fact it alters crucially the expectational environment in which investment decisions are made. Under fixed exchange rates, the government is committed to alter its policies as much as necessary to maintain the exchange rate, whereas under pseudo–fixed exchange rates, as Corden (1972) has called them, the government pursues its desired economic objectives and if necessary alters the exchange rate to accommodate the requirements of equilibrium in international payments.

The exchange rate features of the Bretton Woods system broke down in March 1973, and since then the world has frequently been described as being a system of dirty floating. In fact, however, fewer than 20 percent of the currencies of the world are allowed to float, even under management. Most currencies are pegged to some other currency or basket of currencies, as shown in Table 3–1. Only five major currencies—the U.S. dollar, the Canadian dollar, the British pound, the Japanese yen, and the Swiss franc—really float, and most of them are managed from time to time. So the world remains, by and large, with fixed exchange rates, although the importance of those currencies that float is so great that every country feels the impact of floating rates.

Table 3-1. Exchange Rate Arrangements, 1983, as Reported to
the International Monetary Fund

Declared arrangement		Number of currencies
Currency fixed to		
U.S. dollar		35
French franc		13
Special drawing right (SDR)		12
European currency unit (Ecu)		8
Other		31
Currency adjusted according to indicators		5
Floating currencies		39
of which, multiple currency practices	13	
		143

SOURCE: International Monetary Fund, *IMF Survey*, November 7, 1983, p. 353.

Monetary and Fiscal Policy under Fixed Exchange Rates

The key point about a commitment to fix exchange rates is that monetary policy, as usually conceived, ceases to be a discretionary instrument of policy. The money supply on any meaningful definition must be altered if necessary to preserve the exchange rate. The qualification in the first sentence is necessary because monetary policy in reality is not a single-dimensioned variable. For instance, it includes the terms and conditions under which the central bank will lend money to other banks, the limits it may wish to place on the interest rates to be paid on certain kinds of deposits, the limits it may wish to place on certain kinds of credit (for example, stock market margins), and so on, as well as the direct purchase and sale of domestic securities (conventional open-market operations). These instruments of policy are not all individually hostage to the fixed exchange rate, but some combination of them is.

Fixing the exchange rate in the absence of direct controls over international transactions entails a willingness by the central bank to buy or sell on demand at the stipulated price local currency in exchange for the foreign currency to which the home currency is fixed in value or, alternatively, to enter the foreign exchange market as a seller or buyer of the foreign currency in exchange for domestic currency so as to maintain market exchange rates within the permissible range of variation around the fixed rate. Under the market-based alternative, the central bank engages in open-market operations in foreign currency, in effect exchanging holdings of marketable foreign-currency securities for marketable domestic-currency securities. The actual transactions are somewhat more complicated, since the central bank typically holds marketable, interest-bearing securities, which it must sell for foreign-currency deposit claims, which in turn it sells for domestic-currency bank claims, which in turn are used to purchase domestic-currency securities. In other countries, the central bank actually makes the market between the home and foreign currency.

In either case, the central bank is strongly committed to a particular course of action with domestic monetary consequences. It can often neutralize the domestic monetary impact of its transactions for a period by undertaking other actions that offset them. For example, if it is selling foreign exchange, its purchase of local currency contracts the money supply and, in some economies, tends to raise interest rates on short-term domestic securities. This effect can be undone by a conventional open-market purchase of domestic securities in equivalent amount, thus "sterilizing" the foreign exchange intervention. But if the exchange market pressure continues, the country will sooner or later face the prospect of exhausting its holdings of foreign currency as well as its borrowing capacity in that currency and will have to follow a restrictive monetary policy to relieve the pressures.

While a country with fixed exchange rates has some scope for independent monetary action (it may control the structure of financial claims and liabilities within the country, and within limits perhaps even control overall monetary conditions), this scope is likely to be highly circumscribed, the more so the closer the substitutability of domestic for foreign securities in portfolios both at home and abroad. To a first approximation, it can be said that monetary policy in any period longer than several months is determined by the commitment to fix the exchange rate. For a brief review of empirical estimates of offset coefficients—the extent to which a given open-market operation is offset by an opposite foreign-exchange transaction—for industrial countries based on fixed exchange rates during the 1960s, see Goldstein (1980, p. 38).

There is considerably more scope for independent fiscal action than for independent monetary policy, provided there is a market for the government's securities so that monetary and fiscal policy are not inextricably linked, as they are in many less developed countries. A government can raise expenditures or cut taxes so long as it can find buyers at home or abroad for its securities. If its securities are good substitutes (under credibly fixed exchange rates) for foreign securities, it will be able to find foreign buyers. Any budget deficit will be financed from the rest of the world, thus strengthening the balance of payments, perhaps to the point at which the central bank must buy foreign securities as a partial offset.

If domestic government securities are not good substitutes for foreign securities, domestic interest rates must rise enough to make them sufficiently attractive for foreigners to hold, and that may crowd out some domestic private investment to induce domestic residents to hold them as well. In this case, a given reduction in taxes will offer less economic stimulus than in the former case, but except in the limiting case of complete crowding out, the government is left with some room for macroeconomic maneuver through fiscal action. It is only in those countries that cannot borrow abroad and have no domestic market for securities that a commitment to fix exchange rates also sharply circumscribes the independence of fiscal policy. In these circumstances, fiscal deficits are financed by the central bank, fiscal and monetary policies are fused into one, and autonomous monetary and fiscal expansion cannot be reconciled with the fixed exchange rate.

In sum, a commitment to fix the exchange rate is a commitment to a particular rule for monetary policy, a rule that involves fixing a particular price; beyond certain limits both interest rates and monetary magnitudes become determined by this commitment and cannot be determined independently.

Fixed Exchange Rates and the Global Monetary System

While a commitment to fix its exchange rate can represent a monetary regime for a single country, a general agreement to fix exchange rates cannot represent a monetary regime for the world as a whole. This is a crucial point. With n currencies, there are only $n-1$ independent exchange rates, leaving one degree of freedom. Fixing exchange rates all around leaves open how world monetary stability is to be achieved; it determines the price level of each country in relation to the others, but it does not determine the world price level. The world price level was determined in the nineteenth century by tying currencies to gold. Under the Bretton Woods system, it was determined de facto by tying currencies to the monetary policy of the United States, although until 1968 the United States retained a formal link to gold.

Indeed, the implicit bargain under the Bretton Woods agreement, nowhere found in the formal commitments, was that other countries would tie their currencies to the U.S. dollar, and the United States would pursue a domestic policy conducive to economic stability. In this bargain, the United States gained some room for financial maneuver with respect to its balance of payments—indeed, the very meaning of a deficit in the U.S. balance of payments is unclear under this system, although that did not prevent the Commerce Department from publishing a measure of the "deficit" for years—and the rest of the world imported economic stability and enjoyed a certain degree of export-led growth as a result of an overvaluation of the dollar relative to other currencies, as compared with alternative monetary regimes.

On this view of the Bretton Woods system, the United States violated its part of the bargain in the late 1960s with its excessive fiscal and monetary expansion as a result of the Vietnam War and the Great Society programs. Some Europeans contended that there was excessive expansion in the United States in the early 1960s, but they would have found much less agreement from Americans on that view. Indeed, one of the problems with this alleged bargain is the potentiality for disagreement over what exactly is economically stabilizing behavior by the United States. But excessive expansion by the United States was in any case only the proximate cause of the breakdown of the Bretton Woods exchange rate system; it contained an intrinsic flaw, discussed next, that sooner or later would have led to a breakdown.

The global monetary system under fixed exchange rates need not rely only on gold or on the monetary policy of its largest nation to determine world monetary conditions. One could imagine, for instance, all exchange rates tied to a synthetic monetary unit such as special drawing rights (SDRs) maintained by market intervention in SDRs. World monetary conditions would be determined by the issuance of SDRs, which in turn could be under a firm rule or decided on a discretionary basis.

The fact that a system of fixed exchange rates leaves open the question of global monetary conditions poses a special problem for the United States. While it is meaningful for any other country to fix the value of its currency in terms of some other currency—the pound, the yen, or the U.S. dollar—the same issue applied to the United States raises the question, to what should the U.S. dollar be fixed? The most obvious answer is to the German Deutsche mark (DM), which in turn is linked to other European currencies in the European Currency Unit (Ecu). But to what is the DM/Ecu fixed? Is the United States to let the Bundesbank govern U.S. monetary conditions? The United States could, of course, fix the dollar to a weighted average "basket" of currencies, such as the DM, the yen, and the pound. But that would only obscure the problem without solving it. We must still ask, What determines monetary conditions for the group as a whole? McKinnon (1984) has offered a solution to this problem (in the context of managed flexibility rather than fixed exchange rates) by suggesting that the United States, West Germany, and Japan should strive for a steady growth in the sum of their money supplies.

The point is that under a system of fixed exchange rates this important question—how world monetary conditions are determined—remains open and requires resolution. With this unresolved issue in the background, we can go on to discuss fixed exchange rates as a monetary regime for any small or medium-sized country.

Fixed Exchange Rates for a Single Country

An evaluation of fixed exchange rates from the point of view of a country considering whether to adopt them turns out to be exceptionally complex and, at the present state of economic science, not at all definitive. A net assessment of the pros and cons depends both on the objectives of the country and on its circumstances. The latter in turn involve the structure of its economy, the nature of the exogenous disturbances to which it is likely to be subjected, and a judgment about its own ability to execute successfully any course of policy action that it might choose to adopt.

There is a rapidly growing professional literature on optimal exchange rate policy, with a bewildering array of results. This literature is highly technical. But the flavor of its diversity and complexity can be conveyed by discussing in succession the possible objectives, the differences in structure, the diverse disturbances to which national economies may be subjected, and the interaction of these three factors to determine optimal exchange market intervention policy, of which fixing the exchange rate represents one possibility. Then we address the question of the ability of governments to execute an optimal policy, the closely related question of policy "discipline," and the role of fixed exchange rates in reducing subjective uncertainty.

Objectives. Various national economic objectives have been postulated for the purpose of evaluating alternative exchange rate regimes. The most commonly used is stabilization of output and the closely related objective of stabilization of employment. These two objectives are usually assumed to be identical, although they are not if the country's system of production is subjected to shocks, such as weather in an agricultural society, that alter the relationship between output and employment. Some studies postulate stabilization of consumption as the objective. This is also closely related to output, but it may not be identical to output if there are changes in the international terms of trade. A difference may also result by altering the net asset position of the country with respect to the rest of the world, either through private capital transactions or through changes in the country's international reserves.

Price stability has been suggested as a national objective, a variable whose importance has been reinforced by reliance on what is called the *Lucas supply function*, whereby variations in output arise solely from a deviation of actual from expected prices, plus an independently distributed random variable such as the weather. In the presence of this kind of supply function, minimizing unexpected price variability (price forecasting errors) is the same as minimizing ex ante output variability. Various combinations of these and other specific objectives may, of course, play a role in the overall national objectives. A frequent proposal as a national objective is a weighted average of output and price variability around some desired value. A background assumption of all of these objectives is that the society desires a high living standard and hence wants to use its resources as efficiently as possible.

Objectives that have not been postulated in formal models, but that might be important to government authorities, are economic growth stimulated by a deliberately undervalued currency, or revenue stability when taxes on imports and/or exports are an important source of government revenue, as they are in many developing countries.

The national objective function is likely to be complex, at best. In addition, however, governments and the public typically do not know precisely what their objectives are, so their pursuit of objectives tends to be somewhat unstable. A national objective function is an analytical abstraction, more useful for clarifying concepts than for guiding policy choices or even choices among policy regimes.

Economic Structure. The economic structure of a national economy also influences its performance under alternative exchange rate arrangements. One important characteristic of a country is simply its size relative to the world economy. This determines how much feedback it gets from the rest of the world with respect to its own disturbances and actions. Most analytical work assumes that the economy is small and need not be concerned with its influence on the rest of the world, and therefore can take as (stochastically) given the characteristics of the rest of the world, including interest rates, prices, and aggregate demand. At the other extreme is a country so large that it cannot ignore its impact on the rest of the world, including policy reactions there. This has been illustrated in the formal literature by two-country interactive models.[2] In between are medium-sized countries, such as the major European countries, Japan, and some developing countries, that cannot take the price of their foreign trade goods as given but are not sufficiently large to influence perceptively the overall tone of the world economy by acting alone.

A second important characteristic of a country is the relative size of its tradable goods sector, that is, those goods and services that are subject to the influences of international competition. While the ratio of merchandise exports to a country's gross national product varies among countries from under 10 percent to over 50 percent, the variation in tradable goods is not so great, perhaps ranging from 30 to 60 percent for market economies, and is as wide as it is largely because of governmental barriers to trade that insulate certain potential tradables from international competition. The larger the tradable sector, the more likely it is that disturbances originating abroad will impinge on the home economy and that disturbances originating at home will be diffused abroad.

A third important structural feature of a country is the degree of capital mobility between it and the rest of the world, taking capital mobility to encompass two different features: the tendency of capital movements to respond to economic variables such as interest rates, and the ability of capital to move. Insulation from the rest of the world through policy is much more extensive with respect to capital movements than with respect to trade. Capital mobility determines the extent to which home financial markets are integrated with those abroad, and this in turn can be both a source of disturbance to the domestic economy and an outlet for diffusing and thus attenuating domestic disturbances and policy actions.

Other aspects of the economic structure of a country that are important are the degree of price stickiness, the extent to which nominal or real wages are unresponsive to conditions in the labor market, the degree of responsiveness of savings and spending to changes in the real interest rate, and the responsiveness of exports and imports to changes in their relative prices. For instance, fixed

2. See, for example, Canzoneri (1982); Buiter and Eaton (1985); and Carlozzi and Taylor (1985).

exchange rates for a small economy will lead to less domestic price variability in response to a change in the external terms of trade if the demand for imports is price-inelastic, but more if the demand for imports is price-elastic (Black 1976, p. 10). Similarly, the presence of wage contracts that cannot be altered within their term can under some circumstances lead to a preference for strong intervention in exchange markets to reduce the movement of exchange rates (Canzoneri and Underwood 1985).

Dynamic structure is also important—response lags (wage contracts provide one example), changes in price elasticities over time (leading, for example, to J-curve effects in the response of a trade balance to a change in foreign trade prices), and timing of the availability of information to various economic agents. For instance, when financial markets have superior information on contemporary shocks to the economy, a freely fluctuating exchange rate may provide useful (national welfare-improving) information to the producers who must make decisions about output and employment (Flood and Hodrick 1985).

Nature of Disturbances. Economies are moved away from desired or satisfactory positions by a wide variety of possible disturbances, and the nature of these disturbances can influence the optimum foreign exchange rate arrangements. Disturbances can arise domestically in the demand for goods and services (either tradables or nontradables) and in the demand for money. They can arise in the supply of goods and services. They can arise in shifts in foreign demand for the country's goods or securities or in the external terms of trade.

It used to be thought that if disturbances were primarily domestic in origin, a country should elect fixed exchange rates; if they were predominantly foreign in origin, it should elect flexible exchange rates. The argument was that rate flexibility would stop foreign disturbances at the border by absorbing them largely or wholly in movements of the exchange rate. Fixed exchange rates, by similar reasoning, would help transmit domestic disturbances to the rest of the world, and thus reduce their impact on home output, employment, and prices.

It is now recognized that the situation is much more complex, that no generalizations as sweeping as this are likely to be valid, and indeed that few generalizations are possible at all. One of the few on which there seems to be general agreement is that if the national objective involves stability in the real side of the economy, this can best be achieved against switches in portfolio preferences across national currencies by fixing the exchange rate, so in effect central bank action offsets the private realignment of portfolios.

One problem with the typical modeling of disturbances is the (analytically convenient) assumption of independence among them. In reality, a common disturbance often hits many economies at once (for example, the worldwide oil price increases of 1974 and 1979–80), so that several different types of external shocks—both primary and secondary—hit a single country at about the same time; or the disturbances are clearly correlated, as when the foreign public switches out of foreign bonds into our goods, producing a financial disturbance and a real disturbance at the same time—indeed, they involve the same action, and separation is artificial. Canzoneri (1982) treats disturbances in pairs to reflect this general phenomenon.

Interactions. The interaction among objectives, economic structure, and the nature of disturbances is strong. A given set of disturbances will usually call for different optimum exchange rate arrangements for different objectives and different economic structures. For instance, in a small open economy confronting domestic supply disturbances, fixed exchange rates offer a superior regime if the objective is to stabilize prices, whereas flexible exchange rates are superior if the objective is to stabilize output (Turnovsky 1983). Many models suggest that flexible exchange rates are superior to fixed in insulating an economy from foreign monetary disturbances (Black 1976; Frenkel and Aizenman 1982). Yet with high capital mobility a shift in foreign demand from money to bonds will induce a realignment of portfolios between foreign and domestic bonds. That in turn will affect domestic output under flexible exchange rates, but the impact can be reduced or eliminated under fixed exchange rates.

Most recent work by economists is rather clinical in nature—formal modeling on specific assumptions about economic structure and objectives, with little effort to test the models, either formally or informally, against the realism of the assumptions. The general result is that the optimal exchange rate policy involves official intervention in exchange markets to influence the exchange rate, with the optimal rules of intervention depending intimately on the particular choice of objectives and economic structure, where the latter includes the information that is currently available to the monetary authorities. Free floating is almost never optimal, and fixing the exchange rate is optimal only under special circumstances, although heavy intervention—close to fixing—is appropriate in a wide range of circumstances. However, not all optimal intervention has the effect of reducing exchange rate fluctuations as compared with freely flexible rates; in some circumstances, the authorities should lean with the wind—sell domestic currency when it is depreciating—and thereby increase exchange rate variability in the interest of stabilizing output.[3]

One form of interaction has received much attention outside of technical journals: the possibility that a vicious circle will develop under flexible exchange rates. Journalistic discussion of vicious circles was frequent in the second half of the 1970s. Much of it was impressionistic and had little structure, but the key idea was that the exchange rate itself could become a source of disturbance, going beyond the initiating disturbance. A depreciation of the currency will raise local currency prices of imported goods, and this in turn will stimulate increases in home goods prices and in wages, the extent depending on elasticities of substitution and on the extent of real wage rigidity (due, for example, to indexation of wages to the consumer price index). These price and wage increases in turn would trigger a further depreciation of the currency, with a further stimulus to price and wage increases, and so on in a vicious circle.

Critics have argued that the process must sooner or later come to a stop if not met by monetary accommodation since the real value of money balances will fall. But that may put too much weight on real balance effects, and it offers cold comfort if it requires a period of inflation slowly reduced by growing unemployment to offset a disturbance transmitted by the exchange rate that might have little or nothing to do with policy actions by the country in question.[4]

Furthermore, the exchange rate may take on its own dynamic, initially independent of the prospects for greater inflation. Currencies have something of the quality of assets, whose current value is determined by expectations about future value. This makes flexible exchange rates subject to high short-run volatility in response to "news" that, however imperfect or incomplete, may have some bearing on future values. Much of this "news" contains a lot of noise and will be quickly reversed. But if expectations are fragile, as they are in a period of general uncertainty, asset markets can become dominated for a time by their own dynamic, with a depreciation of the currency, for instance, taken to signal a further depreciation; currency traders jump on the bandwagon, their eyes on other traders rather than on the fundamentals (Tobin 1982). This process can go on so long as the prospect for further gain outweighs the probability of reversal. Theorists have lately discovered this phenomenon, long known to practitioners, and have called it a *bubble*. Bubbles burst sooner or later, but perhaps

3. See Turnovsky (1983) and Buiter and Eaton (1985).
4. For a discussion of the vicious circle and counterarguments, see Goldstein (1980, pp. 18–29).

not before they have done damage to the real economy, or even become self-fulfilling by affecting the price and wage fundamentals via the process described.

An argument for fixing the exchange rate is that it would stop the vicious circle before it can get started and prevent the emergence of bubbles in the foreign exchange market.

Ability to Execute Optimal Policy. It was observed that most formal modeling on the subject leads to the conclusion that optimal exchange rate policy involves some flexibility but less than full flexibility. Intervention in the exchange market is generally desirable. But the rules for optimal intervention vary considerably with the particular objectives and circumstances, even within these models, and the models themselves fall far short of capturing the complexities in any real situation. Even if the models did capture reality adequately, execution of the optimal rules would require a high degree of talent and great subtlety in managing the foreign exchange market. This stiff requirement, plus the artificial precision of the models themselves, suggests that inevitably authorities would have to rely heavily on rough rules of thumb, such as leaning against the wind. If objectives and economic structure suggested a rule of leaning heavily against the wind, the corresponding rule of thumb might well be to fix the exchange rate, at least tentatively, although the two are by no means the same.

Another aspect supports fixing the exchange rate: domestic government policy itself might be a major source of disturbance. Governments may be tempted, for short-run political reasons, to engage in excessively expansionist economic policies, for instance. Or they may simply be prone to make mistakes. If the currency is floating, this represents a safety valve for the errors in policy. Proponents of fixed exchange rates argue that the commitment to a given exchange rate imposes a discipline on economic policy—and even on wage bargaining and price setting by major firms—that would be absent under a regime of floating exchange rates. The commitment to a given rate avoids macroeconomic disturbances that would otherwise take place and leads to quick offsetting action when they do take place. Haberler (1964), who on balance favors floating rates, considers this disciplining effect on weak governments to be the strongest argument in favor of fixed exchange rates.

The effect on discipline is not decisive. Under fixed exchange rates a government may still purchase some short-run expansion by running down its foreign exchange reserves, even without public knowledge for a time. Under flexible exchange rates, the consequences of the government's actions are manifest more immediately. But restoration of reserves (unless they were very large at the outset) is a more compelling national objective than is restoration of a particular exchange rate under a regime of floating rates, so the disciplining effect may well be larger under a regime of fixed exchange rates and errors in policy more likely to be reversed. (This judgment assumes that the commitment to a given exchange rate—such as parity with another currency—is a strong one, not easily or costlessly changed as some countries did under the adjustable peg system.) And governments themselves may find fixed exchange rates not only easier to pursue technically but also useful as a defense against various political pressures to which they are subjected.

Fixing the exchange rate poses its own technical problems, however, in a world of floating currencies. The country must decide exactly what it should fix its currency to: another currency (and if so, to which one?) or to a weighted average of currencies. In the latter case, there are difficult but not insuperable technical problems of intervention in a system that relies on an exchange market since the actual intervention must take place against some particular currency, not an abstract basket of currencies.

The question of which currencies a country should tie its own currency to has been analyzed by several authors (Black 1976; Canzoneri 1982). It is closely related to the question of the choice of partners in forming a currency union (Marston 1985). Unfortunately, but not surprisingly, the results of the analysis are complex and depend not only on the numerous factors that have been discussed but also on the relationship among the foreign currencies under consideration, and in particular on their covariances. Moreover, fixing the rate between two currencies under some circumstances will stabilize variables of interest within the union but destabilize the same variables in third countries, or may stabilize variables of interest to one partner but destabilize them to the other, assuming they are of comparable size. In general, optimal exchange rate policy for all countries must involve agreement among all countries on the rules of intervention (Jones 1982). Of course, this issue need not concern a single, small country trying to choose the best arrangement for itself; it need only look at the best currency or combination of currencies against which to intervene.

Reducing Subjective Uncertainty. While the relationship between exchange rate movements and the movements of such important economic quantities as output and the price level is highly complex and carries the possibility that (under some circumstances) greater

99

flexibility in exchange rates can reduce variability in output or prices, there seems to be little doubt that flexible exchange rates increase the subjective (i.e., perceived) uncertainty of many economic agents. Traders and investors feel that variations in exchange rates, for reasons that are entirely unclear to them, introduce a new and even somewhat mysterious element of uncertainty into their decisions.

It is clear that floating exchange rates do not vary solely in response to differentials in national inflation rates or even in response to cyclical divergences in economic activity among nations, although both factors do influence exchange rate movements. Especially when capital is highly mobile, short- and even medium-run exchange rate movements are strongly influenced by the factors that determine capital movements, and those in turn involve an unfathomable combination of economic, political, and psychological factors. While traders and producers have some feeling for the blend of these factors in their own product markets, they rarely have any feeling for them in the world of international finance; for them it represents an increase in the general uncertainty in their background environment.

This uncertainty can be reduced by hedging any particular transaction, so long as it does not cover too long a period of time. But as Kindleberger (1970) pointed out, the economic activity cannot be hedged; if uncertainty rises in production for external markets, that is likely to reduce investment in those activities. Moreover, while any particular transaction can be hedged, that offers small comfort when forward exchange rates are themselves highly variable, as they have been, since a trader or producer cannot have any certainty about what the forward rate will be when that person wants to hedge in the forward market. It is probable that flexible exchange rates have discouraged both trade and investment, although our ability to sort out the impact is greatly complicated by the fact that flexible exchange rates have prevailed during a decade in which turbulence was caused by other sources as well, notably discontinuous jumps in oil prices and higher rates of inflation in many countries, with unpredictable and divergent national reactions to them.

In reality, economic agents who make decisions with respect to production and trade typically do not know whether movements currently observed in exchange rates are temporary or permanent, and they do not know the underlying structure of the economy in which they are operating. Expectations can be very fragile and highly variable, especially if agents have recently lived through a turbulent period. Under the circumstances, the most important contribution of credibly fixed exchange rates may be to stabilize expectations and thereby to inhibit erratic changes in behavior in response to noisy news that shifts expectations around a lot. Weakly held expectations in turn reinforce jittery feelings, increase uncertainty, discourage real investment and trade, and generally worsen economic performance in the present and in the future. The assumption of rational expectations characteristically used in formal modeling of exchange rate intervention policies cannot capture this effect since it assumes full knowledge both of the nonstochastic economic structure and of the probability distributions of disturbances, neither of which is known with any confidence.

To stabilize expectations, exchange rates would have to be credibly fixed, and that is where past history and the reputation of governments (as well as current economic circumstances) play a crucial role. A system of pseudo–fixed exchange rates, with expectations of frequent change, often surrounded by financial turbulence, cannot perform that service.

Adjustment under Fixed Exchange Rates

Suppose a country chooses to fix its exchange rate. How does adjustment take place if there is an exogenous switch in world demand away from one of the country's exports? Under flexible exchange rates, at least in theory, which is to some extent borne out by experience, adjustment is achieved via a depreciation of the currency, which raises local currency prices of import goods and their local substitutes and thereby reduces real wages. This in turn increases the profitability of producing importables and potential exports, and the trade balance is gradually corrected while employment and output are maintained, at least after a brief recessionary transition period. A cutback in domestic spending is at the same time induced by the decline in real money balances, and this helps directly to reduce the trade deficit and to release resources for further improvement in the trade balance. What is the analogous process under fixed exchange rates?

Several possibilities, not mutually exclusive, were discussed extensively during the late days of the Bretton Woods system.[5] In the first instance, unemployment of labor and capital will occur in the export industry from which demand has shifted. The resulting decline in income will help correct the new trade deficit except insofar as residents borrow abroad or run down their claims on foreigners to maintain their consumption. Insofar as wages are responsive to

5. See Fellner, Machlup and Triffin (1966); Whitman (1967); and Cooper (1968), especially Chapter 7.

unemployment, wages will fall (or rise less than they otherwise would in a growing economy), and that will increase the competitiveness of local substitutes for imports and of potential exports. Insofar as migration is possible and socially acceptable, labor may move to localities where demand is stronger, thus reducing local unemployment and increasing receipts from remittances, which help to brake the fall in output and employment in the region from which demand has shifted.

If the country is part of a larger association, such as the European Community, there may be compensatory fiscal transfers among the members of the region, and these too will help to brake the decline in output and employment by maintaining local purchasing power. Such fiscal transfers take place routinely among the regions of a single country, as tax payments to the central government fall from the region from which demand has shifted and rise from the regions toward which demand has shifted. This readjustment of tax burden is typically reinforced through direct payments, such as for unemployment compensation or public works expenditures.

This mechanism does not work among nations that have no common budgetary expenditures and no mechanism for fiscal transfers. But fiscal action within the country from which demand has shifted can often help smooth the adjustment, in two quite different ways. First, the government can borrow abroad to cover the trade deficit and to maintain demand at home. If the expenditures are for productive investments, preferably in or related to the tradable goods sectors, the borrowing can go on for a long time—this possibility has been emphasized by Ingram (1962) drawing on the experience of Puerto Rico. If too much of the investment is in the nontradable sector (which includes much traditional public works), then future debt-servicing requirements will necessitate a decline in the relative domestic prices of tradable goods, and that will create its own adjustment problems if prices are not flexible (Cooper and Sachs 1985).

Second, the government can alter the burden of domestic taxation by shifting taxes from factors of production that are mobile to those that are immobile, in order to attract from abroad the mobile factors. In practice, this is likely to entail reducing taxes on capital and (insofar as government expenditures are maintained) increasing taxes on land and labor. The mechanisms can be highly varied—for example, by providing tax holidays for new investment or public financing of infrastructure that is cost-reducing for new investments. The net effect is to reduce the after-tax real wage of immobile factors, and that can improve the international competitiveness of the country's potential exports and thus restore the trade balance (Cooper 1974).

The two fiscal mechanisms can be combined whereby the country offers tax relief to attract foreign investment and borrows in the international capital market to cover the temporary shortfall of revenue. One form of assistance frequently observed within the United States is for state governments to borrow in order to relend to commercial enterprises through industrial development bonds. This technique of subsidization is made especially attractive in the United States because of the exemption of state and municipal bonds from federal taxation, but sovereign governments often can borrow on the international market at somewhat lower rates than many private firms can.

Both of these fiscal approaches to facilitating adjustment to a decline in external demand for a country's products—the most difficult kind of disturbance to deal with under fixed exchange rates—presuppose that fiscal policy is in fact flexible. They also presuppose a high international mobility of capital, including enterprise capital. A system of fixed rates is likely to work much more smoothly with high international capital mobility than without.

Although adjustment to real disturbances under a system of fixed exchange rates may take place smoothly, it may also be prolonged and costly, a possibility often characterized pejoratively as a gold standard type of adjustment, through deflation. Whether it is relatively smooth or relatively painful depends on the structural characteristics of the country and of the world economy in which it is embedded, and in particular on the responsiveness of real wages to slack in the labor market and to the degree of integration of the world capital market.

It was concern about this central issue, and the possibility of conflicts between the domestic and balance-of-payments objectives of policy to which it gives rise, that led the architects of the Bretton Woods system to rely on discrete changes in fixed exchange rates as a final recourse, not to be undertaken lightly but to be undertaken (with international approval) if absolutely necessary to correct a fundamental disequilibrium in a country's international payments position. The step devaluation could, it was assumed, bring about the reduction in real wages necessary to preserve payments (trade) balance with full employment of resources.

Of course, this mechanism presupposed that real wages could in fact be reduced by raising import prices; to the extent that real wages are sticky or that workers demand wage adjustments to cover price increases, the reconciliation of external and internal objectives is thwarted. (The statement that money illusion is required for the system to work is not correct—at least insofar as that phrase implies that workers cannot distinguish clearly between nominal and real magnitudes. Workers may have no illusions at all and still be willing to accept a decline in real wages brought about by a rise in the price level, leaving the wage structure unchanged, and not be willing to accept piecemeal reductions in nominal wages that are likely to alter the wage structure.)

The difficulty with the Bretton Woods system of fixed but adjustable exchange rates is that it also presupposed a low international mobility of capital. By the time a disequilibrium was evidently fundamental in nature, it would be clear to everyone who was paying attention, and that in turn created a one-way speculative option for holders of funds to move out of a currency soon to be devalued (or into one soon to be revalued) at no risk of loss beyond transactions costs. Thus as the international money and capital markets revived during the 1960s, the speculative movement of funds became huge (greatly complicating domestic monetary management), and the fixed but adjustable rate system became untenable except under conditions of economic management that would rule out the need for exchange rate adjustment—a move toward a true fixed rate system. Instead, the system broke down with the move to generalized floating in 1973. The fixed but adjustable exchange rate system fostered a very different expectational environment from what would prevail under a system of credibly fixed rates. High capital mobility is a source of disturbance under an adjustable peg system; as noted, it can facilitate adjustment under a fixed exchange rate system.

The disturbing nature of capital movements from time to time under an adjustable peg system, sometimes even forcing exchange rate alterations that the authorities (rightly or wrongly) would prefer to avoid, raises the question whether maintaining controls on capital movements might not restore the viability of a system of fixed but adjustable exchange rates. It is not accidental that countries that fix the external value of their currencies also maintain controls of varying degrees of severity over the movement of funds into or out of the currency. Nor is it merely coincidental that the basic articles of the Bretton Woods agreement condone controls over capital movements while at the same time prohibiting restrictions on current payments. Capital controls were not formally mandated, but they were required by the logic of the fixed but adjustable exchange rate system.

With the passage of time, it has become more and more difficult to maintain effective controls over capital movements, especially for the major industrial countries. This is partly because the nature of trade has altered so that it is impossible to make a sharp distinction between current and capital transactions in principle—to be effective capital controls would have to cover long-term trade transactions as well—and partly because the number of channels through which capital transactions can take place has multiplied so greatly, especially via direct investments, where international transactions take place within individual firms.

Nonetheless, determined controllers could still control bank flows, which account for the bulk of short-term capital movements, and it would be possible to inhibit other short-term portfolio movements that typically go through banks or other regulated financial institutions. Such actions would make an adjustable peg system less vulnerable to speculative attack, and they would reduce disturbances to the real side of national economies under a system of flexible exchange rates. They would be unnecessary and on balance harmful under a system of credibly fixed exchange rates.

Some Concluding Observations

The foregoing analysis has pointed out that a system of fixed exchange rates does not by itself offer a full monetary system as an alternative to the gold standard or to a world of countries following money-growth rules. It leaves open what determines monetary conditions for the world as a whole. To fix the exchange rate of its currency with respect to some other currency does, however, represent a practical monetary rule for a single country, and many countries have followed this rule even in a world in which several major currencies are free to float with respect to one another. The important point is that for a single country, fixing the exchange rate does represent choice of a particular monetary rule, and having done it, the country is not then free to select some other course for its monetary policy. The main thrust of monetary policy is determined by the commitment to the exchange rate, although that is not inconsistent with considerable scope for variation in the structure of monetary policy and even for deviation from its main thrust for short periods of time, provided the country is willing to allow corresponding movements in its international reserves.

Is it advisable for a country to fix its exchange rate? That is a complex question. It depends on many factors and does not lend itself to a simple answer. The formal analysis of optimum exchange rate arrangements suggests that some form of managed flexibility is typically optimum, with fixed exchange rates being optimal in only a few (improbable) circumstances. This analysis always takes the nature of disturbances as given, beyond the influence of the hypothetical country under examination.

But if some form of managed flexibility is optimal, why do economists not recommend it for New Hampshire, or even for Hanover? Can we have too much of a good thing? Is it desirable (from Hanover's point of view, or New Hampshire's) to be embedded in a fixed exchange rate currency area with the rest of the United States? And if it is desirable for New Hampshire, why not for Canada—or even for Europe and Japan? Several reasons have been suggested why the formal analysis may not tell the whole story. One is that a commitment to a fixed exchange rate imposes a certain discipline on national economic policy and thus may eliminate or reduce one source of economic disturbance compared with a regime of exchange rate flexibility.

A second reason, not unrelated to the first, is that a fixed exchange rate helps to stabilize the expectational environment in which business decisions are made. It reduces subjective uncertainty that can arise if government policy is not disciplined or if real exchange rates move in ways that seem arbitrary to businessmen—for example, due to rapid and unpredictable shifts in portfolio preferences among the world's asset holders, affected both by new (if often irrelevant) information and by exchange market dynamics.

If the value of a currency becomes too unpredictable, residents of a country will denominate their transactions in another currency and will hold that currency as a short-term store of value, as McKinnon (1963) pointed out. But the experience of some countries suggests that conditions must become very bad for this to happen on any scale, particularly against the resistance of the country's monetary authorities (in recent years the residents of Mexico, Israel, and Argentina have moved in varying degrees toward dollarization). At a minimum, such a switch deprives the residents collectively of the seigniorage gains from having their own currency. Again, is this important enough to warrant New Hampshire having its own currency?

The issue may be far deeper than economists have explored and may reside in our still very imperfect understanding of the role of money in a modern economy. Curiously, in formal economic modeling, money is still primitively treated as an asset to hold, with unexplained demand for it, and all functions are assumed to be homogeneous of degree zero in nominal variables. That is, in making the perfectly sensible assumption that units of measurement do not matter for real variables, economists also assume that rapid parallel variations in all nominal variables do not matter. In short, money, a nominal variable, plays no essential role when prices can vary freely. So long as economists treat money in this way, they will not understand well the true costs either of inflation or of flexible exchange rates.

A final observation concerns the role of market-determined exchange rates as a source of contemporaneous information. The theory of rational expectations with its assumptions of forward-looking economic behavior, places a great deal of emphasis on the information that is available to decisionmakers when they make their decisions. A market-determined exchange rate is one of the few kinds of information that is available on a daily—indeed, on an hourly—basis. Is it important for private decisionmakers to have this information? If so, will not fixing the exchange rate (or even influencing it through official intervention) deprive these decisionmakers of information that will help them make socially wiser decisions?

This raises the more fundamental question of how much information, and in what forms, it is optimal to make available. I was one of those who felt it was a mistake during the 1960s for the U.S. Department of Commerce to publish its measure of the balance-of-payments deficit every quarter, with monthly estimates sometimes being offered. I did not object to publication of the detailed balance-of-payments statistics. The argument for the former (which has since been dropped because the notion of a balance-of-payments deficit for the United States has become even less meaningful than it was then) was that politicians, journalists, and the public could not be expected to analyze the detailed tables. They needed some summary statistic to let them know whether things were going well or badly.

This argument carried the day until 1976, when it was dropped. But what does it tell us about information processing and the formation of expectations? Information processing by decisionmakers is a time-consuming and uncertain matter, and the results are often not believed with high confidence, but they are acted on anyway. The publication of a summary statistic provides a rallying point around which expectations can form. This is often desirable, if the resulting path of the economy is itself a desirable one. But if it sets the economy on a suboptimal but "rational" (self-fulfilling) path, it is undesirable. The burden of proof is shifted to analysts to make the case that the conventional wisdom is wrong. In practice this can be done only with a lag, sometimes a long one. In the meantime, real but avoidable costs may have been incurred.

A key question, therefore, is what kind of information should be collected, collated, and made available and when. Do we really lose economically useful information by controlling the exchange rate, keeping in mind that some variability will take place within the intervention bands? I am skeptical, but if further analysis shows this judgment to be wrong, the same information can be conveyed by publishing daily changes in official reserves under a fixed exchange rate system.

REFERENCES

Bhandari, Jagdeep S., ed. *Exchange Rate Management under Uncertainty*. Cambridge: MIT Press, 1985.

Bhandari, Jagdeep S., and Bluford H. Putnam, eds. *Economic Interdependence and Flexible Exchange Rates*. Cambridge: MIT Press, 1983.

Black, Stanley W. *Exchange Policies for Less Developed Countries in a World of Floating Rates*. Essays in International Finance, no. 119. Princeton: Princeton University, December 1976.

Buiter, Willem H., and Jonathan Eaton. "Policy Decentralization and Exchange Rate Management in Interdependent Economies." In *Exchange Rate Management under Uncertainty*, Jagdeep S. Bhandari, ed. Cambridge: MIT Press, 1985. Pp. 31–54.

Canzoneri, Matthew B. "Exchange Intervention Policy in a Multiple Country World." *Journal of International Economics* 13 (November 1982), 267–89.

Canzoneri, Matthew B., and John M. Underwood. "Wage Contracting, Exchange Rate Volatility, and Exchange Intervention Policy." In *Exchange Rate Management under Uncertainty*, Jagdeep S. Bhandari, ed. Cambridge: MIT Press, 1985. Pp. 247–71.

Carlozzi, Nicholas, and John B. Taylor. "International Capital Mobility and the Coordination of Monetary Rules." In *Exchange Rate Management under Uncertainty*, Jagdeep S. Bhandari, ed. Cambridge: MIT Press, 1985. Pp. 186–211.

Cooper, Richard N. *The Economics of Interdependence*. New York: McGraw-Hill, 1968.

———. *Economic Mobility and National Economic Policy*. Stockholm: Almquist and Wiksell, 1974.

———. "Monetary Theory and Policy in an Open Economy." *Scandinavian Journal of Economics* 78 (1976), 146–63.

Cooper, Richard N., and Jeffrey D. Sachs. "Borrowing Abroad: The Debtor's Perspective." In *International Debt and the Developing Countries*, Gordon Smith and John Cuddington, eds. Washington, D.C.: World Bank, 1985. Pp. 21–60.

Corden, W. Max. *Monetary Integration*. Essays in International Finance, no. 93. Princeton: Princeton University, April 1972.

Fellner, William, Fritz Machlup, and Robert Triffin, eds. *Maintaining and Restoring Balance in International Payments*. Princeton: Princeton University Press, 1966.

Flood, Robert P., and Robert J. Hodrick. "Central Bank Intervention in a Rational Open Economy: A Model with Asymmetric Information." In *Exchange Rate Management under Uncertainty*, Jagdeep S. Bhandari, ed. Cambridge: MIT Press, 1985. Pp. 154–85.

Frenkel, Jacob A., and Joshua Aizenman. "Aspects of the Optimal Management of Exchange Rates." *Journal of International Economics* 13 (November 1982), 231–56.

Goldstein, Morris. *Have Flexible Exchange Rates Handicapped Macroeconomic Policy?* Special Papers in International Economics. Princeton: Princeton University, June 1980.

Haberler, Gottfried. "Integration and Growth of the World Economy in Historical Perspective." *American Economic Review* 54 (March 1964), 1–22.

Harris, Seymour E. *The Assignats*. Cambridge: Harvard University Press, 1930.

Ingram, James C. *Regional Payments Mechanisms: The Case of Puerto Rico*. Chapel Hill: University of North Carolina Press, 1962.

Jones, Michael. " 'Automatic' Output Stability and the Exchange Arrangement: A Multi-Country Analysis." *Review of Economic Studies* 49 (1982), 91–107.

Keynes, John Maynard. *Indian Currency and Finance*. London: Macmillan, 1913.

Kindleberger, Charles P. "The Case for Fixed Exchange Rates, 1969." In *The International Adjustment Mechanism*. Boston: Federal Reserve Bank of Boston, 1970. Pp. 93–108.

Marston, Richard C. "Financial Disturbances and the Effects of an Exchange Rate Union." In *Exchange Rate Management under Uncertainty*, Jagdeep S. Bhandari, ed. Cambridge: MIT Press, 1985. Pp. 272–91.

McKinnon, Ronald I. "Optimum Currency Areas." *American Economic Review* 53 (September 1963), 717–25.

———. *An International Standard for Monetary Stabilization*. Washington, D.C.: Institute for International Economics, 1984.

Morgenstern, Oskar. *International Financial Transactions and Business Cycles*. Princeton: Princeton University Press, 1959.

Mundell, Robert A. *International Economics*. New York: Macmillan, 1968.

Tobin, James. "The State of Exchange Rate Theory: Some Skeptical Observations." In *The International Monetary System under Flexible Exchange Rates: Global, Regional, and National*, Richard N. Cooper, Peter B. Kenen, Jorge Braga de Macedo, and Jacques van Ypersele, eds. Cambridge: Ballinger, 1982. Pp. 115–28.

Tower, Edward, and Thomas D. Willett. *The Theory of Optimum Currency Areas and Exchange-Rate Flexibility*. Special Papers in International Economics. Princeton: Princeton University, May 1976.

Turnovsky, Stephen J. "Exchange Market Intervention Policies in a Small Open Economy." In *Economic Interdependence and Flexible Exchange Rates*, Jagdeep S. Bhandari and Bluford H. Putnam, eds. Cambridge: MIT Press, 1983. Pp. 286–311.

Whitman, Marina. *International and Interregional Payments Adjustment: A Synthetic View*. Princeton Studies in International Finance, no. 19. Princeton: Princeton University, 1967.

Perspectives on Exchange Rate Regimes

KENNETH W. CLEMENTS

THE BOTTOM LINE of Cooper's discussion of fixed versus floating exchange rates is some cautious support for fixed rates. I first offer some perspectives on the choice of the exchange rate regime. I then discuss some difficulties for small countries that fix their exchange rates to the U.S. dollar. Finally I make some comments about Cooper's views on exchange rate policy.

The Choice of the Regime

Under fixed rates, domestic and foreign currencies are indistinguishable, as the central bank is always willing to buy or sell the two monies at the fixed exchange rate. As a result, over the longer term the country cannot have an independent monetary policy in that the central bank is unable to determine the money supply. The quantity of money is endogenous; it is determined by the domestic demand for money. If the authorities attempt to expand the money supply too rapidly, then the country loses international reserves. Also under fixed rates, arbitrage in capital and goods markets ensures that interest rates and inflation at home and abroad are equalized.

Under floating rates, the standard results of closed-economy monetary economics apply. Here, at least in principle, the supply of money can be controlled by the authorities. Excessive monetary growth generates higher inflation, and over the longer term, the exchange rate depreciates according to the inflation differential.

There is a fundamental duality between fixed and floating rates with respect to what bears the burden of the adjustment to shocks. For fixed rates, international reserves, a quantity, serve as the buffer stock, while under floating rates, the inflation rate and the exchange rate do the adjusting.

This perspective on the two regimes suggests that there are no compelling reasons to choose one system rather than another. Variations in international reserves that would be observed under fixed rates are more or less equivalent to variations in the value of the

110

currency when the rate is floating. These variations would reflect the evolution of the underlying fundamentals such as monetary growth, real growth at home and abroad, and most importantly, expectations.

I hasten to add that this view is incomplete, as countries are clearly not indifferent to the choice of the regime. It does nonetheless serve to highlight the importance of putting the two systems on an equal footing when carrying out a comparison. In particular, this analysis makes clear it is simply naive to argue against a fixed exchange rate on the basis that it is a distortion that involves price-fixing.

The decision to fix or float involves a choice about the domain of the currency; the domain increases with fixed rates as foreign and domestic monies become for all intents and purposes perfect substitutes. As a result, the benefits of using one form of money (in terms of reduced transaction costs and increased certainty about the store of value function of money) would point in the direction of fixing the exchange rate.

To be balanced against this argument in favor of fixed rates is the problem that countries having fixed rates give up the option of having an independent monetary policy, as well as the discretionary use of the inflation tax. These costs and benefits of fixed rates are analyzed in the literature on optimal currency areas, originally due to Mundell (1961).

As the choice of a fixed rate involves giving up independent policy options and tying monetary conditions at home with those abroad, an important consideration in making this decision is the confidence one has in government, both at home and abroad. Some persons no doubt view the national currency and an independent monetary policy as a right to assert the worth of the nation (along with national airlines, the national car, and other monuments). Others, more skeptical of government, would argue that this right is more likely to be abused than properly exercised. These persons would emphasize the propensity of governments to make mistakes and thus argue against the use of discretionary monetary policy and favor fixed rates.

This argument for fixed rates is that we should have more faith in the government of the country to which we peg than in our own government. This view has validity for many small countries today. It seems that these countries can and do benefit from tying their financial conditions to those in larger countries by fixing their exchange rates. Some of the inherent volatility of small, narrowly based economies can be avoided by having fixed rates.

At the same time, we should not be under any illusion about the inherent difficulties associated with fixed exchange rates. As fixed rates involve countries sharing common monetary conditions, international pressures and conflicts always arise. These conflicts between countries tend to be more frequent and more difficult to settle than those that arise within countries. The experience of the United Nations does not inspire great confidence in the ability of countries to agree on international policy coordination.

Some New Problems of Fixed Rates

There can be an externality problem in today's mixed system of fixed and floating rates. In this system, the currencies of many small countries are fixed to major currencies, with the latter floating more or less freely. The basic problem is that this system can induce great financial instability for the small countries that fix their exchange rates.

Consider the following simple model. Let the small country's exchange rate be fixed rigidly to the U.S. dollar. Let interest rate parity hold, so that nominal interest rates within the small country are the same as those on comparable securities in the United States; interest rates would be equalized, provided there is unrestricted international capital mobility. Now let the U.S. dollar sharply appreciate relative to the other major currencies. This means that the dollar price of many of the small country's traded goods (exports, imports, and close substitutes) will decline sharply. As traded goods account for a relatively large part of small economies, the decline in their price would cause strong deflationary pressures—not only for the traded goods but probably also for quite a wide spectrum of other commodities (via substitution).

What happens to nominal interest rates in the small country depends entirely on what happens to rates in the United States because interest rates in both countries are pegged to each other via interest parity. For simplicity, let us take U.S. interest rates to be fixed (if they rise, as seems likely when the dollar appreciates, then my conclusions are strengthened). As a result of the appreciation of the dollar vis-à-vis the other major currencies, nominal interest rates in the small country are fixed and inflation falls. Accordingly, realized (or ex post) real interest rates rise with the appreciation of the dollar.

The internal prices of traded goods may therefore move differently from what would be indicated by the country's exchange rate behavior and by world prices. Moreover, inflation in the small country will probably be substantially below that in the United States. The appreciation of the dollar will not bring down U.S. inflation as powerfully and as quickly, simply because traded goods in the United States account for a smaller fraction of the overall economy. Thus there is an important difference between the structure of small countries and the United States—the relative size of the traded goods sector, which generates the asymmetry regarding the effects of the exchange rate on prices.

This analysis has been used by Sjaastad (1985) to explain the evolution of Chile and Uruguay, which have gone from boom to bust in almost perfect step with the strength of the dollar. The financial sectors of these economies became highly integrated with the world capital market during the 1970s, while maintaining some form of a fixed exchange rate with the dollar. Table 3–2 shows the prices of traded goods and real interest rates in Chile from 1977 to 1982. Although Chile was fixing to the dollar, inflation for the traded goods was unrelated in the short run to U.S. inflation. Moreover, real interest rates increased by about 30 percentage points from 1979–80, when the dollar was weak, to 1981–82, when the dollar appreciated sharply.

Specific Comments on Cooper's Analysis

Expectations and Uncertainty of Floating Rates. Cooper emphasizes the volatility of floating rates due to fragile expectations and bandwagon effects of speculators; he then argues that all of this can be avoided by fixing the rate. This argument is basically about destabilizing speculation and, as such, ignores the old point due to Friedman (1953) that destabilizing speculation is unlikely to last, as it is

Table 3–2. Prices and Real Interest Rates in Chile

| Year | Percentage per annum | |
	Change in prices of Chilean traded goods	Real short-term bank deposit rate
1977	5.1	19.6
1978	6.1	26.2
1979	26.8	5.4
1980	16.6	5.4
1981	−5.5	29.1
1982	−8.6	36.9

SOURCE: Larry A. Sjaastad, "Exchange Rate Regimes and the Real Rate of Interest," in *The Economics of the Caribbean Basin*, Michael B. Connolly and John McDermott, eds. (New York: Praeger, 1985), p. 135. Change in prices based on Jose Gil-Diaz, "Del Ajuste a la Deflacion: La Politica Economica Entre 1977 y 1981 (Chile)," November 1983 (mimeographed).

unprofitable. Such speculation involves selling when the price is low (which drives the rate lower) and buying when it is high (which causes it to go even higher); obviously the speculators lose money. As a result, there is at least some presumption that this type of speculation will not continue.

Cooper states that "there seems to be little doubt that flexible exchange rates increase the subjective (i.e., perceived) uncertainty of many economic agents." I would argue that exchange rate variability reflects the variability of the underlying fundamentals, including expectations and news. Consequently, it is not clear that the increased uncertainty is due to flexible exchange rates per se but rather to the volatility of their determinants. I am not convinced that the choice of the actual regime affects the overall uncertainty of the economic environment to the extent that Cooper does.

Fixed Exchange Rates as a Discipline on Policymakers. The discipline aspect of fixed rates, emphasized by Cooper, raises the question regarding what is endogenous to what. Does behavior (including policy) adjust to given institutions, or do institutions adjust to behavior? Or, to put it another way, do we simply get the institutions we deserve?

The Role of the United States. The fundamental questions not adequately addressed by Cooper are, What is the appropriate exchange rate regime for the United States and what should be its role in the world monetary system? A related question is, If we have a return to fixed rates for the major currencies, can the dollar be trusted to act as a reserve currency?

Cooper (1984) has elsewhere proposed a world currency under the control of a Super Fed. What he seems to have in mind is a system whereby all major countries, including the United States, replace their national currencies with Super Money that circulates freely internationally. This solution to problems associated with fluctuating exchange rates is to eliminate exchange rates altogether. In other words, Cooper views the world as an optimal currency area. The difficulties with this proposal are the problems of fixed exchange rates: the problems of achieving international policy agreement and coordination.

REFERENCES

Cooper, Richard N. "Is There a Need for Reform?" In *The International Monetary System: Forty Years after Bretton Woods*, Conference Series

No. 28. Boston: Federal Reserve Bank of Boston, May 1984. Pp. 21–39.

Friedman, Milton. "The Case for Flexible Exchange Rates." In *Essays in Positive Economics*. Chicago: University of Chicago Press, 1953. Pp. 157–203.

Mundell, Robert A. "A Theory of Optimum Currency Areas." *American Economic Review* 51 (November 1961), 509–17.

Sjaastad, Larry A. "Exchange Rate Regimes and the Real Rate of Interest." In *The Economics of the Caribbean Basin*, Michael B. Connolly and John McDermott, eds. New York: Praeger, 1985. Pp. 135–64.

Fixed Exchange Rates and the Rate of Inflation

ROBERT Z. ALIBER

RICHARD COOPER highlights the fact that the prevailing exchange market arrangements differ sharply from those before the early 1970s—starting in the eighteenth century, most currencies were pegged most of the time. The reliance on floating exchange rates since the early 1970s is an historical anomaly. Cooper also reminds us that many more currencies are pegged than float; thus smaller countries peg their currencies while larger countries permit their currencies to float; few small countries permit their currencies to float, and no large country now pegs its currency. An additional stylized fact is that national decisions to stop pegging currencies are usually associated with inflation or, much less frequently, with deflation.

Thus, before the current episode with floating exchange rates, the link between the British pound and gold was broken at the time of the Napoleonic Wars, World War I and its immediate aftermath (1914–25), and between the Great Depression and World War II (1931–39). Similarly, the link between the U.S. dollar and gold was broken during the Civil War and its aftermath (1863–78) and during a ten-month interval in 1933–34. Episodes of pervasive worldwide inflation and floating exchange rate regimes are highly correlated, as in the post–World War I period and the 1970s. The converse is that very few countries have permitted their currencies to float when their own inflation rates and those of their associated metropoles have been low.

These stylized facts about exchange market arrangements can be integrated with the search for the monetary regime most likely to lead to economic stability. One inference is that most countries have acted as if their national economic self-interest is served better by adherence to fixed or pegged exchange rates, except in those episodes when their own inflation rates differ significantly from those of their major trading partners. The move from fixed or pegged to floating exchange rates by medium-sized and large countries reflects an effort by their national monetary authorities to gain greater control over

116

domestic money supply growth, either to inflate to finance wartime expenditures or to avoid importing an inflation from abroad.

The breaks in the link between the U.S. dollar and gold during the Civil War, and between the British pound and gold during World War I, were initiated to obtain greater control over the growth of domestic money, in both cases to facilitate wartime finance. In contrast, in February 1973, Germany stopped pegging the mark in the belief that greater control over its own money supply and its price level was preferable to control over the exchange rate. In 1950 and again in 1970, Canada stopped pegging its dollar to the U.S. dollar in an attempt to insulate its price level more fully from changes in the U.S. price level.

These observations lead to three questions about the relation between the exchange rate regime and monetary stability. The key question is why a fixed exchange rate system appears associated with relative price stability while a floating exchange rate system is associated with inflation. Is this relationship causal or merely one of association? A second question involves the locus of monetary management and control over the price level when each national money is pegged. The third question involves the relationship between contractual regimes designed to achieve monetary stability and emergency episodes like wars and great depressions.

Fixed Exchange Rates and Monetary Stability

The system of fixed exchange rates initially was implicit in the gold standard; as long as each country adhered to its gold parity, the cross-mint parities established a system of fixed exchange rates. The dominant reason one asset rather than another evolved into a money was its promise as a stable store of value and its relative convenience or ease in exchange. The promise of future stability usually was based on performance. Gold's natural attributes provided greater price stability than most other commodities, and so gold became the dominant money (Hicks 1969). Even in the sixteenth century, when the import of gold from the New World to the Old World led to an increase of the world price level by a factor of four or five, the annual increase in the price levels in Europe averaged 2 percent a year (Jastram 1977).

Initially, paper monies were acceptable largely because of the money-back guarantee in terms of gold; the producer of the paper or fiat money promised to buy it back in exchange for gold at a fixed price. The domain of particular fiat monies expanded as their promise of stable price-level performance increased and contracted as this promise appeared less credible. The expansion of the roles of the U.S. dollar in the world economy after both World War I and again after World War II reflected that the U.S. dollar appeared more likely to maintain its value in terms of gold than did the British pound. While the association between fixed exchange rates and monetary stability appears compelling, a system of fixed exchange rates is no assurance that countries will pursue stable monetary policies.

Thus, the Bretton Woods system of fixed exchange rates broke down in the early 1970s because the countries with the payments surpluses and the countries with the payments deficits (primarily the United States) were unwilling to pursue the domestic monetary policies necessary to maintain the viability of the exchange-rate regime. Moreover, most of the surplus countries also were reluctant to revalue their currencies or to permit them to float, while the United States was unwilling to devalue.

In other cases, countries have suspended their commitments to fixed exchange rates because they wished to pursue very expansive monetary policies in a period of dire emergency associated with a war; the decision to inflate represents a policy of taxing wealth holders. The retention of the parity would have enabled some wealth holders to escape the tax.

The conservative argument for fixed exchange rates is that if countries have the monetary independence afforded by the floating exchange rate regime, they are likely to abuse it and pursue policies that prove to be inflationary (Viner 1956). The need to maintain the parity may have constrained countries from following policies that would otherwise have proven inflationary. The adherence to a parity is not a guarantee that a country will not pursue inflationary policies, but the likelihood of these policies may be reduced because they would involve the explicit violation or suspension of a commitment. Some countries, faced with the need to finance a surge in expenditures, suspended the constraint and then pursued policies that proved inflationary. In the late 1960s, on the other hand, the United States was able to pursue expansive monetary policies without being subject to the constraint normally associated with the fixed exchange rate because of the reserve-currency role of the U.S. dollar.

The Locus of Monetary Management

The historical record suggests that most countries fix or peg their currencies to an external money. Before World War II, the national currencies were pegged to gold. Changes in aggregate holdings of monetary gold were determined by accidents of gold discoveries. The apparently serendipitous result was that there were accommodating discoveries of gold and of new techniques for refining gold ores, so that during a period when the demand for money increased, the supply of gold increased, with the result that the average annual change in the world price level was modest, much below that since 1965.

Reliance on a system of fixed exchange rates means that no country can inflate substantially more rapidly than its trading partners. The tendency toward monetary expansion in some countries would be constrained by the more conservative policies elsewhere. The system of fixed exchange rates in the global monetary context would lead to a low inflation rate only if there were some mechanism to constrain the growth of money or reserves in the countries following the more conservative policies. Nature's niggardliness provided this constraint from the sixteenth to the nineteenth century.

A system of fixed exchange rates based on gold, on some other commodity money, or on a fiat asset like the U.S. dollar, the British pound, or the special drawing right, is not guaranteed to be inflation-proof. If some historical accident had led to massive gold discoveries at the end of the nineteenth century with the consequence of massive inflation, it is probable that investors would have sought a more stable money—but only after the real value of their gold holdings had declined sharply.

After World War II, many countries pegged their currencies to the U.S. dollar to meet the Bretton Woods commitments. From the early 1920s on, the United States sought to insulate changes in the domestic money supply from changes in domestic gold holdings. One exception occurred in the early 1930s, when the gold outflow forced a U.S. monetary contraction. In the 1960s, in contrast, the U.S. monetary authorities reacted to the decline in domestic gold holdings with a wide array of progressively more severe restrictions on payments abroad by U.S. residents. Whether the U.S. monetary expansion reflected a dire national emergency is arguable, but the external constraint did not prevent the adoption of policies which proved inflationary.

A system of fixed exchange rates needs a locus of monetary management—an agent that will manage the rate of money supply growth. The selection of the agent is likely to be based on previous performance. The risk is that at some future time, various exigencies may lead the agent to pursue policies that prove to be inflationary.

Robert Z. Aliber

Shocks and Monetary Regimes

The theme of this book is the search for a monetary regime that will provide monetary stability. The gold standard provided comparative long-run price stability. For fifteen years, the Bretton Woods system of pegged exchange rates also provided stability. Both systems, however, broke down.

The decisions of the United States and Great Britain to break the link between their currencies and gold in the nineteenth century and again in the twentieth century point to the limits on the reliance on fixed exchange rates. When perceived national needs became pressing, the authorities either suspended the commitment to fixed exchange rates or else inflated and then broke the commitment. In two of these four cases, the emergency involved the needs associated with financing large wars. At other times, the concerns that led the authorities to alter their commitments were high levels of unemployment, especially in tradable goods. In each of these instances, the decision to suspend gold convertibility involved circumvention or abrogation of domestic legislation. Moreover, in one instance the United States violated its international treaty commitments under the Bretton Woods agreements.

The review of the experience with fixed exchange rates and their breakdown suggests that one important aspect of any regime designed to achieve monetary stability is the elasticity of monetary rules or arrangements in response to wars and other emergencies. Many monetary arrangements are fair-weather friends; as long as the political environment is stable, these arrangements are likely to provide monetary stability because there is a strong demand for a relatively stable price level. From time to time, however, emergencies may arise; then the issue becomes whether the arrangement may be abandoned (an event like an extended bank holiday) or the monetary rule modified. Counterfactual history suggests that each regime might be tested by its implications for the behavior of the authorities in 1863, 1914, 1933, or 1971. Some analysts may prefer a rigid monetary constitution that would limit the ability of the authorities to inflate; they would then have to consider whether they would risk sacrificing the state to save the constitution.

REFERENCES

Hicks, John R. *A Theory of Economic History*. Oxford: Clarendon Press, 1969.

Jastram, Roy W. *The Golden Constant*. New York: John Wiley & Sons, 1977.
Viner, Jacob. "Some International Aspects of Economic Stabilization." In *The State of the Social Sciences*, Leonard D. White, ed. Chicago: University of Chicago Press, 1956. Pp. 283–98.

FOUR

Some Evidence on the Comparative Uncertainty Experienced under Different Monetary Regimes

ALLAN H. MELTZER

THE TWENTIETH century has produced diverse monetary experience. This experience can be organized in several different ways. One emphasizes the role of gold in international monetary arrangements. Early in the century, domestic monies of major trading countries were convertible into gold at a preestablished fixed price, and gold coins circulated. Currently, few governments set the price of gold, and there is no formal requirement on governments in major trading countries to exchange gold for currency or currency for gold. This is a relatively recent phenomenon, and some prefer to return to a fixed, guaranteed price of gold.[1] A second type of organization focuses on the arrangements for exchanging a country's currency for other currencies and particularly on the choice between fixed and fluctuating exchange rates. The choice of exchange regime permits

I AM INDEBTED to Robert J. Gordon for providing quarterly data, to Clemens Kool for providing Kalman filter forecasts and errors of forecast, and to Debu Purohit for his assistance with the empirical work. Parts of this paper appeared earlier as "Monetary Reform in an Uncertain Environment," *Cato Journal* 3 (May 1983). I am grateful to the Cato Institute for permission to reproduce some of the material used here. Much of the material is new, however, and I have modified some of the previous material to reflect developments of my thinking and discussions with Karl Brunner and Alex Cukierman. Carl Christ and Stanley Fischer made helpful comments on an earlier version.

1. Some writers want to restrict the use of the term *gold standard* to refer to a relation between the number of ounces (or grams) of gold and the unit of account; for example, one guinea is one ounce of gold. Here, the guinea is a unit of account, that is, a convention for expressing values. The convention tells us nothing about money prices or about the relation of gold to money prices or the price level. For gold to affect the price level, there must be a connection between ounces of gold and money prices. This requires more than the choice of a unit of account. Fixing the price of gold, by agreeing to buy and sell ounces of gold at a fixed price, establishes a link and opens the possibility of stabilizing the price level by buying and selling gold. I see no point to "reform" the unit of account. One unit, even an abstract unit, is as useful as any other.

a country to seek internal or external stability in the value of its currency. Major trading countries now either permit exchange rates to be determined by market forces or adjust the rates frequently to reflect market forces. Most do not achieve either internal or external stability.

A third method of organizing experience focuses on the role of governments or central banks in the monetary system. Under either a gold standard or a regime of fixed currency exchange rates, the government sets a price and agrees to buy and sell its money at that price. The decision to control the price or exchange rate leaves the determination of the quantity of money and the internal price level to market forces. A decision to control the quantity of money perforce requires that the prices of gold and other currencies be permitted to change relative to the home currency; external stability is sacrificed, or its provision is left to others.

Experience with various monetary arrangements has served to heighten awareness of the disadvantages of each. The interwar gold standard helped to transmit the price deflation and contraction of the early 1930s and contributed to the depth and extent of the Great Depression. The postwar international system known as Bretton Woods established fixed, but adjustable, exchange rates and, after more than a decade, increased welfare by establishing convertibility for major currencies. The price of gold was fixed, but gold had a minor role, and its role diminished as the system matured. The Bretton Woods system avoided deflation but transmitted inflation. When the system ended, major trading countries moved toward a loose system of domestic monetary control with fluctuating or adjustable exchange rates and preannounced targets for growth of one or more monetary aggregates. This system is often criticized for its "excessive" volatility. McKinnon (1984) has a recent statement of the argument.

Some main problems with the current arrangement are well known. Most countries have not avoided inflation; costs of disinflation have been higher than generally anticipated; and in many countries, monetary targets have not been achieved with enough regularity to make the announcements of planned money growth credible. Consequently, expectations about growth of monetary aggregates are volatile at times, and there is widespread skepticism about the intention of central banks to provide noninflationary money growth. Since 1979, interest rates (at all maturities) in the United States and many other countries have been higher (after adjusting for inflation) and more volatile than formerly. Real rates now incorporate a risk premium to compensate for increased monetary variability (Mascaro and Meltzer 1983). The rise in real rates to compensate holders for bearing greater risk shifts resources from investment to consumption and lowers future output. The concurrent increase in the variability of interest rates and money under current arrangements suggests that the present system is inefficient; central banks may be able to reduce variability in both money growth and interest rates and in exchange rates also. Consequently, the variability of prices and output may be reduced.

Monetary management, at the discretion of central banks or governments, based on forecasts of future economic activity and inflation has not eliminated recessions as some economists expected. Experience has shown that the errors in economists' forecasts of quarterly changes in real output often exceed the average change.[2] Further, government fiscal actions are less stabilizing than many economists and public officials once believed.

Research based on rational expectations has shown that every policy is a choice of rule; the only purely discretionary policy is a purely random or a haphazard policy. Hence, the rational choice of policy is a choice between rules. Policy rules may differ in a variety of ways, including complexity, formal statement, prescribed flexibility, responsiveness to relative and absolute changes in supply and demand for goods and services, and the uncertainty that they engender about the future. The more frequent are changes in the policy rule, the less certain is the actual or perceived adherence to the rule. The flexibility that permits government to change policy rules has a cost: anticipations about the future conduct of policy are altered, and uncertainty about the future conduct of policy increases (Kydland and Prescott 1977; Barro and Gordon, August 1983; Cukierman and Meltzer 1986).

The main objectives of this chapter are to compare the levels of uncertainty experienced under the different monetary regimes in the United States during the twentieth century and to begin an empirical

2. McNees (1981) gives several measures of the errors of forecast by forecast horizon for sixteen separate forecasters from 1976 to 1980. The average absolute error in sixteen forecasts of the growth of real GNP made during the same quarter is 2.7 percent. (Eight forecasts made after the middle of the quarter are only slightly more accurate. Their error is 2.4 percent.) The mean error of forecasts of real growth made four quarters ahead is 1 percent for the same period. For inflation, the mean errors are about 1 percent for both the current and the four quarter ahead forecasts. Webb (1983) reports similar data on the median error of forecast computed from a large sample for the years 1971–82. For both real growth and inflation four quarters ahead, the averages of the median errors for the twelve years are the same, 1.7 percent. For the shorter period most closely corresponding to the McNees data, the average of the annual median errors is 0.8 percent for real growth and 1.3 percent for inflation.

evaluation of the effects of risk or uncertainty on economic perform-ance. An accurate assessment of different regimes requires separa-tion of the variability induced by policy actions or social arrangements from the variability induced by nature. If nature is benign, a partic-ular period may be relatively stable despite policy action or a policy regime that increases variability. At the other extreme, nature may introduce substantial variability in prices and output that is damped by the policy regime but is not damped enough to reduce variability relative to other periods. To compare across regimes, care must be used to separate nature and policy institutions. This chapter is, at best, a first step.

Comparisons of this kind are subject to some important caveats. Small errors in data can have a relatively large effect on computed measures of variability used in the measurement of risk and uncer-tainty. Data for the early years of the twentieth century, and for the latter part of the nineteenth century, have been constructed from related series long after the period ended. Gordon (1982) has a brief description of the data. Whether, or perhaps when, data collection smoothed or amplified fluctuations and variability is unclear.

There are benefits that compensate for some of the severe limi-tations of the data. Comparisons of the gold standard, other com-modity standards, monetary rules and discretionary monetary policy, based on formal analyses, have not proved conclusive. Much of this work ignores variability, risk, and uncertainty. Conclusions of work incorporating variability often depend on the parameters and models used. Fischer's (1977) path-breaking paper assumes that the level of output is independent of the exchange rate regime, imposes pur-chasing power parity, and ignores capital mobility and inflation—the principal reasons for exchange rate changes. Even with these abstractions, comparison of the effects of fixed and fluctuating exchange rate systems on the variability of prices and consumption depends on the slope of the Phillips curve, the correlation of shocks across countries, and the types of shocks that occur. Flood (1979) permits capital mobility and chooses price stability as his criterion. He shows that his conclusions about the relative merits of fixed and floating rates depend on such parameters of the model as the response of spending to interest rates and the size of real balance or wealth effects.

Removing abstractions by including the resource costs of the alter-native regimes, differences in fiscal rules, the extent to which an economy is open to trade or to capital flows, and perhaps differences in relative size is unlikely to render the conclusions of formal analyses less qualified or conditional. A general conclusion about the superiority of fixed or fluctuating exchange rates is not likely to be reached deductively.

In the following section, I discuss proposals for monetary reform, compare a commodity standard to a monetary rule, and suggest why empirical evidence is required to evaluate the outcomes under different monetary regimes. Next I distinguish between risk and uncertainty and discuss the procedure used here to measure risk and uncertainty. Then I compare the risk and uncertainty experienced under six monetary regimes during this century. The concluding section offers a proposal for monetary reform.

Proposals for monetary reform usually assume that the public prefers a noninflationary rate of money growth. This may be true, but it has not been demonstrated that voters in democratic countries prefer the monetary regime that best maintains price stability. Nor has it been shown that the rate of inflation that maximizes wealth, or the utility of wealth and private consumption, is identically zero. More likely, the costs and net benefit of price stability depend on the choice of institutional arrangements (or policy rules) used to achieve stability. Institutional arrangements that reduce risks and uncertainty lower the cost of achieving any chosen rate of inflation or deflation, including zero.

I avoid discussing the optimal rate of inflation and assume throughout that price stability is preferred. A monetary rule is as capable of producing one average rate of money growth as another; for a monetary rule, the issue can be resolved once the decision is made to control money and allow exchange rates to change. Proposals that permit market forces to determine the rate of money growth cannot ensure price stability. Money growth is endogenous, and its average rate of change depends on costs of production of the commodity used as money, alternative uses of the commodity, and other real factors. Those who favor a fixed exchange rate regime urge, not always explicitly, some alternative to a stable average price level or an optimal (average) rate of inflation as a means of maximizing welfare. Exchange rate stability is not an end in itself. It is a means to other ends: higher individual welfare and reduced uncertainty.

Types of Monetary Reform

Experience with fluctuating exchange rates has stimulated interest in monetary reform. Three types of reform, each with many variants, are advocated. The first is a return to some type of gold or commodity standard under which the central bank would be obligated to buy and sell gold, or some other commodity or basket of commodities, at a preannounced price. This reform seeks greater external monetary stability. The second, a monetary rule, emphasizes internal stability. This reform keeps the growth rate of money on a prescribed path that is either fixed or contingent on observable events. The third proposal, associated with the work of Friedrich Hayek (1978), eliminates the government and the central bank from the monetary system. Proposals for competitive, unregulated banking—often called *free banking*—leave control of money growth to the decisions of the public. Wealth-maximizing bankers produce the quantity and type of money that the public demands. This proposal attempts to avoid government monopoly over the quantity of money and government fixing of price or exchange rate. I have discussed this reform previously (Meltzer 1983).[3]

This brief comparison of proposed monetary reforms suggests two reasons why analysis has not resolved the issues or prescribed a unique optimal standard. First, gold or commodity standards avoid the requirement of monopoly by increasing the resource cost of the monetary regime. Monetary rules avoid price control by establishing a government monopoly. General economic reasoning does not support price (exchange rate) control and does not support the grant of monopoly power, even limited power, except under specific circumstances (see Vaubel 1984). Second, in countries that import most of their consumables, the relevant price of consumption is the world market price. For this reason, size of country and extent of openness to trade are often suggested as main reasons for choosing between fixed and fluctuating exchange rates.

The distinguishing feature of a gold or commodity standard is that the government or central bank makes an enduring commitment to control one set of prices and to accept the monetary and economic consequences that are consistent with that set. Friedman (1951) has a thorough analysis of the benefits and costs of commodity reserve currencies under the assumption that the level of output is independent of the choice of policy. The assumption of independence is restrictive, however. The choice of a monetary system determines the types of risk and uncertainty that society bears. When there is risk aversion, risk or uncertainty is costly; further, uncertainty affects the distribution of spending between consumption and investment and thus the size of the capital stock. The assumption that output (or consumption) is independent of the choice of monetary standard

---

3. Examples of free banking are rare. The evidence in later sections of this chapter sheds no light on the degree to which free banking affects uncertainty.

should be relaxed. Fischer (1977) addresses part of the problem by fixing output but allowing consumption to change.

The most familiar version of a quantity rule—Milton Friedman's monetary rule—requires the central bank to keep a broad or inclusive measure of money growth at a rate equal to the long-term average rate of growth of real output. Several alternative rules do not require constant money growth; they provide for systematic changes in the growth rate of money that are contingent on prescribed events. Some of these rules require the central bank to vary money growth in the direction opposite to the short-run changes in the current or recent average rate of inflation or to the current or average rate of change in the price of a basket of commodities. These rules are a type of commodity-price stabilization scheme, but they avoid the cost of buying, selling, and storing commodities. The government sells securities to reduce money growth when the prescribed index rises and buys securities to increase money growth when the prescribed index falls.

Another type of monetary rule, proposed by Friedman (1948), requires a cyclically balanced budget, a fixed tax structure, and fixed rules for tax and transfer payments. Exchange rates fluctuate freely. The stock of money grows on average, at the rate of growth of government spending. The latter is equal to the maintained (identical) average rates of growth of taxes and output, so the average rate of money growth is equal to the average rate of growth of output. The budget deficit or surplus fluctuates cyclically; this permits money growth to rise relative to trend during recessions and deflations and to fall relative to trend during booms or inflation. Other contingent rules make the money stock depend on the level or the rate of change of output or income. A rule that reduces fluctuations in prices and exchange rates is suggested in the conclusion of this chapter.

A credible monetary rule reduces uncertainty about money growth but does not eliminate all short- or long-term changes in prices or the rate of inflation. Changes in output, in the terms of trade, or in excise taxes often affect the price level and the measured rate of price change. These changes are permanent changes in level but transitory for rates of price change. Productivity shocks that change the growth rate of output must be followed by changes in the growth of money to avoid long-term inflation or deflation. Under a monetary rule, the risks borne by the public depend, therefore, on the type of monetary rule that is adopted, on the type of shocks that occur, on the distribution of shocks between aggregate demand and supply, on the contingencies specified by the rule, and on the errors that policymakers make when applying the rule. Generally, permanent and transitory changes in the level or growth rate of output or of demand cannot be predicted in advance or instantly identified as they occur. A contingent rule that requires the central bank to respond to events involves some unavoidable errors. In effect, the public trades the gain from a more prompt response to a permanent change, properly identified, with the loss or cost of response to a transitory change that is misperceived as permanent.

Most analyses of monetary rules fail to distinguish between permanent and transitory changes (e.g., Friedman 1948; Fischer 1977; and Flood 1979). Transitory, random shocks do not require a response. At the opposite pole, permanent changes in the growth rate of output require an adjustment of money growth if price stability, on average, is an objective. The general belief seems to be that the maintained long-term growth rate of output in the United States has varied little, so permanent changes in output growth can be neglected. Experience in Japan, postwar Europe, Brazil, parts of Asia, and elsewhere suggests, however, that relatively large changes in maintained growth rates occur. Failure to adjust money growth to observed changes in real growth means that prices are not stable on average.

If policymakers could promptly identify permanent changes in productivity growth, the size of the change in growth would be irrelevant for the policy rule. The reason is that, in this case, price level stability could be increased by changing money growth in response to changes in productivity growth or other changes in real growth. This suggests that the proper criterion for choosing to respond to these changes is not the size of the change in growth rate; it is the cost of mistaking transitory changes as permanent—the cost of excessive activism— compared to the cost of treating permanent changes as transitory— the cost of excessive passivity. These costs depend on the ability of the monetary authority to identify permanent changes in real growth. Related costs arise with respect to identifying demand and supply shocks under some monetary rules.

A rule setting the growth rate of money has two clear advantages over a rule setting the exchange rate. First, the resource costs of the monetary rule are lower, since less real output is stored as a monetary reserve (Friedman 1951). Second, the monetary rule avoids the costs of operating a gold or commodity standard unilaterally and the costs of organizing and maintaining a multilateral standard. On the other side, costs of monitoring are higher for the quantity rule. The central bank or government often has incentives to deviate from noninflationary money growth, as emphasized in Barro and Gordon (August 1983) and Cukierman and Meltzer (1986).

Friedman (1951) estimated the annual resource cost of a commodity reserve currency to be as much as half of the average growth rate of annual output, using data for the late 1940s and assuming that, on average, there is no inflation. A similar computation, using the current ratio of money to income in the United States as a reference, reduces the cost to about 16 percent of the average growth rate of annual output. Unless there is a reason to anticipate a dramatic decline in average cash balances, the resource cost of a full commodity standard remains high.

The resource cost of an international standard is probably higher than the estimates for the United States. The ratio of money to income in much of the world is above the U.S. ratio, so that a larger fraction of world commodity stocks would have to be held as monetary reserves, and a larger fraction of the growth rate of output would be added to the reserves on average. If gold and other metals are exhaustible resources, their prices will rise over time relative to the prices of reproducible commodities. The rise in price encourages private holding of gold (or commodity money) instead of productive capital but also lowers the resource cost of increasing monetary gold stocks.[4]

It is difficult to estimate the likely rate of increase of the gold price. We cannot reliably separate, or hold constant, the policies of the principal governments that control most gold production so as to obtain an estimate of returns to scale in gold production. The crude data in the report of the Commission on the Role of Gold (*Report* 1982) and Fellner (1981) do not show evidence of constant returns to scale in gold production. Fellner (1981) notes that the price elasticity of the supply of gold has been low, and possibly negative, since the 1940s.

A further complication in evaluating the costs of a gold standard arises from changes in the demand for industrial and commercial uses of gold. Growth in these demands is absorbing much of the new production, but, again, it is difficult to separate the effect of expected inflation on the demand for jewelry from other determinants of the demand for gold (see *Report* 1982, pp. 176–78).

A gold or commodity standard is costly to operate unilaterally. Even if they use all available information, people may be slow to distinguish relative from absolute changes or permanent from transitory changes. Unless price levels adjust instantly, all the real and monetary shocks that change the world demand for gold (or whatever

4. With constant returns, all of the additional gold is provided by new production and with totally inelastic supply by a rise in the price of gold relative to commodities. Between these extremes, the amount of additional resources used for gold production depends on the elasticity of supply.

commodity is used as money) affect prices and output in the country that maintains the standard. For example, under a unilateral gold standard, whenever wars, revolutions, increases in inflation abroad, or other unanticipated events increase foreigners' demand for gold, the domestic stock of money falls and the home price level falls until the rise in the relative price of gold restores equilibrium in the gold market. The agreement to supply gold at a fixed nominal price means that every unanticipated event that affects the gold market leaves its mark on real income and prices in the home country, except in the extreme case when foreign prices adjust instantly to foreign shocks and absorb the entire adjustment.

A unilateral gold standard is a service to the world. The cost of providing the service is borne by the public in the home country. Income and prices are more variable; if variability or uncertainty lowers the capital stock, future income and wealth are lower as a result.

A further advantage of a fixed growth monetary rule arises from the constancy of money growth. Suppose that money growth is set at a rate that achieves price stability on average, so that expected and actual money growth change only when there is a maintained change in the growth rate of real output or the growth rate of velocity. If the rule is specified in terms of the monetary base, constant growth of the base implies that there is no correlation between base money growth and base velocity growth, so the variance of nominal output growth equals the variance of velocity growth. The variance of velocity growth is, in this case, equal to the variance of inflation, plus the variance of the growth rate of real output, plus or minus any effect of correlation (covariance) between inflation and real growth.[5] If the government or central bank stabilizes the growth rate of a more broadly defined money stock—for example, M1 defined as currency and checking deposits—there are some additional sources of variability. The quality of monetary control can reduce or increase the variability arising from these sources.

Fixed exchange rates are inconsistent with the stable growth of money; money growth is endogenous. The variance of the growth rate of nominal output in a fixed exchange rate regime is equal to the sum of the variances of money growth and velocity growth plus or minus the effect of interaction (covariance) between the growth

5. Let m, v, y, and p be the rates of change of money, velocity, real output, and prices, and let V be a variance and C a covariance. Then

$$V(m) + V(v) + 2C(m,v) = V(y) + V(p) + 2C(y,p).$$

The monetary rule sets $V(m)$ to zero, so $C(v,m)$ is zero also. The expected rate of price change is zero, but prices change, so $V(p)$ is not zero.

rates of money and velocity. The latter can be positive or negative, depending on the type of shocks that occur, the frequency with which supply and demand shocks occur, and the location at which they occur—at home or abroad. I see no way to decide in advance whether money growth and velocity growth are positively or negatively correlated. Indeed, the correlation may change if variances and covariances are not constant. In fact, money growth and velocity growth typically move together cyclically but not always secularly, so there is at least some evidence that the correlation depends on the length of the period used as a unit of observation.

One of two conditions is required for lower variability of nominal output or its rate of growth under fixed exchange rates. The growth rate of velocity must be less variable by an amount that compensates for the variability of money growth and any positive correlation between variability of the growth of money and velocity. Or a negative correlation between velocity growth and money growth must be large enough to compensate for the variance of money growth.[6]

This static comparison ignores the effect of regime change on velocity and on the variability of velocity growth. One potential source of change arises from differences in the expected rate of inflation. Flexible exchange rates and monetary control are capable of keeping the average and expected rates of inflation at zero, although policymakers may not do so. There is nothing in the rules of the gold standard to keep inflation at zero, and experience under the gold standard shows decades with rising and decades with falling prices.

Another source of difference in the behavior of velocity arises from the variability of exchange rates. With fixed exchange rates, foreigners may hold larger balances in key currencies, lowering the demand for domestic money and raising the demand for the key currencies. Differences in population growth, or income growth between countries, then affect the distribution of money balances and the rate of change of velocity and its variability. Under a monetary rule, differences between expected and actual exchange rates affect interest rates, the demand for money, and velocity. This source of variability is dampened, however, by the operation of forward markets and the close relation between changes in spot and forward rates (see Mussa 1979).

A study of annual velocity growth from 1869 to 1949 using a broad

6. Using the notation in note 5, the first condition states that $V(v)$ must be smaller under fixed exchange rates by more than $V(m) + C(m,v)$. The second condition restricts $C(m,v)$ to be negative and restricts $|C(m,v)| - V(m)$ in relation to the difference in $V(v)$ under the gold standard and the monetary rule.

definition of money, and from 1915 to 1949 using a narrow definition of money, shows a weak contemporaneous positive relation between money growth and velocity growth (Gould, Miller, Nelson, and Upton 1978). On average, changes in money growth were positively related to changes in velocity growth under the pre–World War I and interwar gold standard. A shift from the gold standard to a regime of fluctuating exchange rates and constant money growth would have eliminated the variability of income arising from the positive covariance and from the variability of money growth.

The rate of change of base velocity and monetary velocity was considerably more variable under the gold standard than under the Bretton Woods system or during the 1971–80 period of fluctuating exchange rates. Calculations reported in Brunner and Meltzer (1983) for the 1970s show that the variances of the quarterly rates of growth of base and M1 velocity were about 2 percent and 4 percent, respectively, at annual rates. The variance of base velocity growth during this decade of fluctuating rates is less than half of the variance of base velocity growth under the gold standard, and the variance of monetary velocity in the 1970s is a fraction of the variance of monetary velocity (M2) for 1869–1949 (or M1) for 1915–49 (shown in Gould et al. 1978).

These data suggest that the variability of velocity has been lower under the fluctuating exchange rates of the 1970s and 1980s than under the gold standard. The evidence is far from conclusive, however. The data make no allowance for differences in permanent and transitory changes, so they do not distinguish between purely random fluctuations around a firmly held expectation and persistent changes that alter expectations and lead to revision of investment and consumption plans. To go beyond the evidence in these preliminary findings, we must separate the sources of variability, introduce an operational definition of uncertainty, and distinguish between risk and uncertainty.

Uncertainty and Risk: Definition and Measurement

My definitions of *risk* and *uncertainty* follow the definitions used by Knight (1921) and Keynes (1921, 1936).[7] *Risk* refers to the known distributions of outcomes. These are of two kinds. People may know the probability of an event, for example, the toss of an unbiased coin, or they may classify events based on experience or subjective

---

7. Meltzer (1982) compares Knight and Keynes and distinguishes their view of expectations from current versions of rational expectations.

belief. Following Knight (1921, pp. 224–25), we may identify the first with mathematical probability and the second with empirical probability.

Uncertainty refers to events for which the distribution of outcomes is unknown and the basis for classification is tenuous. An example, used by Keynes (1937), is the probability that capitalism would survive until 1970. Wars, atomic explosions, and various political decisions affecting tax rates or regulation are best described as uncertain as to timing and often as to occurrence. Changes in taste, technology, or political arrangements induce permanent changes in the level or growth rate of prices and output that cannot be predicted reliably. Recent events, including changes in the price of oil, in the relative size of government, or the permanence of the decline in world inflation and the stability of political regimes in the Middle East are illustrative. For events of this kind, there is no reliable way to classify times of occurrence into distributions or to compute the expected time of occurrence for a particular event.

The choice of policy regime affects the ability to classify events. A credible system of fixed exchange rates lowers risk and uncertainty about the exchange rate but increases the risk and uncertainty about money growth. A credible monetary rule lowers the risk and uncertainty about future money growth but increases the risk and uncertainty about future exchange rates and interest rates. In principle, each regime generates different expected responses of prices and output and different variability of prices and output.

Diversification, pooling, and hedging are examples of market arrangements that reduce risk and the cost of risk-bearing. The development of each of these arrangements depends on someone's ability to classify events into probability distributions and compute expected values. Costs of risk-bearing differ with the degree of risk, as measured by the parameters describing the, often subjective, distribution of outcomes. The cost of risk bearing is likely to be smaller than the costs of uncertainty. The reason is that uncertain events cannot be readily classified, so costs cannot be reduced by market arrangements that convert risky outcomes into smaller and more certain costs.

Individuals can reduce the cost of uncertainty, under any monetary or fiscal regime, by holding relatively safe assets, including foreign assets, in place of risky assets. Private decisions of this kind do not lower the social cost of uncertainty. Countries with a history of political or economic instability generally have less capital per person, and less durable capital, than countries with stable governments. The reason is that people shift wealth to assets with values that are less dependent on policy decisions, including foreign assets and precious metals. The stock of domestic real capital remains low, and the marginal product of capital is relatively high. The high marginal product compensates owners of capital for bearing the uncertainty generated by the policy environment.

The costs of bearing avoidable uncertainty fall on present and future generations. Domestic and foreign lenders demand a premium to compensate for the additional uncertainty, so real rates of interest are higher than the rates in more certain environments.[8] Real investment is lower; the capital stock is smaller. Future real income and consumption are reduced below the level that could be achieved in a less uncertain environment.

Monetary reform cannot compensate for all shocks arising from political instability, tax and spending policies, or other sources of uncertainty.[9] But differences in monetary arrangements damp or augment particular shocks and change the ways in which the shocks are felt. An example is the difference in the effect of an unanticipated change in the size of a fiscal deficit. A rule requiring constant money growth prevents the deficit from being financed by money creation. A monetary rule that requires money growth to rise and fall in fixed relation to budget deficits and surpluses increases the money stock during recessions, when prices and output fall, and reduces the money stock when prices and output rise cyclically. Even if the two monetary rules are accompanied by the same restriction on the growth of government spending and the same tax arrangements, they differ in the degree to which they reduce monetary variability.

If all shocks are temporary, cyclical changes in aggregate demand, the two monetary rules generate indistinguishable steady-state outcomes but different short-term outcomes. With constant money growth, deficits are financed by selling bonds, and surpluses are financed by retiring bonds. Under a rule requiring countercyclical issues of money, an unanticipated change in money finances part of an unanticipated deficit. Money is more variable, and debt is less variable, under the countercyclical monetary rule, but there is no differential uncertainty about future budgets or money growth under the two rules. People planning consumption anticipate the same tax rates, size of government, and price level if either rule is strictly observed.

Suppose that, in addition to transitory or cyclical shocks to aggre-

8. For evidence of the effect of monetary uncertainty on interest rates, see Bomhoff (1983) and Mascaro and Meltzer (1983).

9. This is recognized in proposals for reform by, inter alia, Simons (1948), Friedman (1948), and Brennan and Buchanan (1980). Recent work by Brunner and Meltzer (1972), Christ (1979), McCallum (1984), and many others shows that some combinations of fiscal and monetary policy are unstable.

gate demand, there are permanent and transitory shocks to output. Technical innovations, fluctuations in weather, political disturbances, and variations in tariffs and cartels are examples. Before World War I, plagues or diseases that killed a significant fraction of the labor force would have had a prominent place in a list of output shocks. Agriculture was more important, so that changes in weather patterns had a larger effect on aggregate output. When there are persistent changes in the growth rate of output or the level of ouput, there is uncertainty about future prices and rates of price change. This uncertainty is reflected in interest rates, in exchange rates and, therefore, in portfolios and in the allocation of real resources. Since the two monetary rules require different responses of debt and money to finance any budget deficit or surplus that occurs, there are differences in uncertainty about the size and duration of the budget deficit and about the stocks of money and debt that will follow any shock. In principle, this uncertainty is reflected in future prices and interest rates also.

To measure risk and uncertainty, I compute the variance of one-period-ahead forecasts for both log levels and rates of change of the variables used in the empirical work. The forecasts are the values predicted for period $t + 1$ using a multistate Kalman filter and values of the individual series through period t. By assumption, each error term consists of three statistically independent terms: a transitory change in the log level, a permanent change in the log level or, equivalently, a transitory change in the rate of change, and a permanent change in the rate of change. If x_t is the logarithm of the level of one of the series, following Bomhoff and Kool (1983),

$$x_t = \bar{x}_t + \varepsilon_t; \tag{1a}$$

$$\bar{x}_t = \bar{x}_{t-1} + \hat{x}_t + \gamma_t; \tag{1b}$$

$$\hat{x}_t = \hat{x}_{t-1} + \rho_t; \tag{1c}$$

so that

$$x_t = \hat{x}_{t-1} + \bar{x}_{t-1} + \rho_t + \gamma_t + \varepsilon_t. \tag{1d}$$

Here, $\bar{x}_t$ is the expected (log) level of x at time t; $\hat{x}_t$ is the expected rate of change, and ε_t, γ_t, and ρ_t are, respectively, serially uncorrelated, statistically independent disturbances affecting current values of x, $\bar{x}$, and $\hat{x}$. By assumption, the disturbances have zero mean and nonzero variance. Transitory shocks to the (log) level are given by ε_t; γ_t is a permanent change in the level of the series, and ρ_t is a permanent change in the growth rate.

As shown in equation (1d), people can observe x_t, but they cannot observe either the (log) level of the expected (or permanent) component, $\bar{x}_t$ or the expected (or permanent) rate of change, $\hat{x}_t$. The multistate Kalman filter is a way of estimating the unobserved values of $\bar{x}$ and $\hat{x}_t$ using the knowledge that the permanent level, $\bar{x}$, is a random walk with stochastic drift, as shown in (1b), and $\hat{x}$ is a random walk (1c).

The three error terms or disturbances are divided into "normal" errors and outliers by initially setting prior probabilities on the distribution of errors so as to classify 95 percent of the errors as normal and 5 percent as outliers. The initial prior probability for each error is specified in advance. Posterior probabilities are calculated after observing the current error and are used to revise the prior probabilities. People learn about changes as they occur, but they cannot be certain whether any change is transitory or permanent. As time passes, people learn more about past shocks and use this information to revise their estimates of the variances of the permanent and transitory shocks. Persistent changes that are large or small relative to past experience induce changes in the relative weights (probabilities) assigned to the permanent and transitory components and change the parameters of the statistical model used to forecast the future.[10]

The data were analyzed in (log) levels and in rates of change. For the analysis of rates of change, there are no transitory changes in level. There are only transitory and permanent changes in the rate of change. Transitory changes are, in this case, observations around a given expected rate of change, and permanent changes are changes in the growth rate.

Using all the information available from the past, people can forecast the next period or as far ahead as they choose to look. If all

10. The algorithm is described more fully in Bomhoff and Kool (1983). Bomhoff (1982, p. 20) describes the procedure: The procedure "allows for feedback from the data to the forecasting algorithm. A number of separate fixed filters are applied to the data, and the forecasts are computed as a weighted average of the forecasts from the individual filters, with weights that are adjusted over time according to the success of each separate filter over the recent past. The composite forecasts therefore are both recursively determined and adapt to new information about the laws of motion. . . " Bomhoff and Kool (1983, p. 236) use as an example an ARIMA (0,2,2) model,

$$\Delta^2 x_t = (1 - Q_1 B - Q_2 B^2)a_t, \ a_t \sim N(0, \sigma_a^2)$$

where Δ is the difference operator, B is the lag operator, and a_t is the shock. The left-hand side can be written using equations (1a) to (1c) of the text, in terms of the shocks,

$$\Delta^2 x_t = \varepsilon_t - 2\varepsilon_{t-1} + \varepsilon_{t-2} + \gamma_t - \gamma_{t-1} + \rho_t.$$

The values of Q_1, and Q_2, and a_t change as new information arrives. The values of Q_1 and Q_2, reflect the probabilities assigned, and reassigned, to the three types of shock, ε, γ, and ρ. As the weights assigned to the various shocks change with new information, the values of Q change to reflect the new information.

137

errors are transitory changes in level—the errors denoted ε_t—forecasts for the distant future are no less reliable than forecasts for the next period. The reason is that ρ_t and γ_t are zero in this case and $\hat{x}_t$ is a constant, as can be seen in equations (1a) through (1d). The permanent level, $\bar{x}_t$, grows at a constant rate, $\hat{x}_t$, and the expected value of x grows at this same rate. Despite reliance on Bayesian procedures, this is a situation with risk but with no uncertainty. People neither revise their estimates of the future rate of change nor adjust their actions in the present as new information arrives. They act on the assumption that all changes are drawn from a distribution with a fixed mean rate of change.

At the opposite extreme, all variability is perceived as a permanent change in the rate of change, and none is perceived as a transitory change in level or growth rate: $\varepsilon_t = \gamma_t = 0$. The value of $\hat{x}_t$ changes with new information. From equation (1), it is easy to see that the variance of the forecast error depends on the variance of ρ. If ρ is relatively variable, levels in the distant future are highly uncertain. People adjust promptly to each change because they perceive the change as permanent, but they have little information about rates of change in the more distant future. I describe this circumstance as a situation with uncertainty but with no risk.

Computed probabilities are neither 0 nor 1. All observations are a mixture of risk and uncertainty. In the following computations, the computed probabilities of transitory and permanent changes are the weights used to distribute the computed variance of the forecast error between risk and uncertainty (see Bomhoff and Kool 1983 for the computation of the probabilities).

In a growing economy with stable prices, the levels of real income and money are expected to rise. For real (and nominal) income, and for money, it is often useful to restrict the term *uncertainty* to the variability of unforeseen changes in the rate of change. We can, however, discuss uncertainty about the level of income or money by combining the variance of permanent changes in level and the variance of permanent changes in the rate of change. Risk can refer to transitory changes in level, or if computations are restricted to rates of change, risk can refer to the variability of transitory changes in the rate of change of income or money. Price stability, on the other hand, refers to the level of prices, not to the rate of price change. Prices are stable and are expected to remain stable, if they vary randomly around a constant level. Unless otherwise noted, I restrict the terms *risk* and *uncertainty* to a single meaning. Uncertainty about the future price level, level of GNP, or money includes the variability of permanent changes in level and the variability of permanent changes in the rate of change. Risk refers to transitory changes in level.

Computed Measures of Risk and Uncertainty

Gordon (1982) compiled quarterly data on prices, output, and nominal GNP from 1890 through 1980, a total of 364 observations. Friedman and Schwartz (1963) provide quarterly data on M2 and M1 since 1907 and 1914, respectively. These series can be extended to 1980 using the *Federal Reserve Bulletin.*[11] In all, there are 290 quarterly observations for M2 and 264 quarterly observations for M1 in the data analyzed here.

After the data were processed using the multistate Kalman filter, I divided the observations into six periods representing the six monetary regimes in the United States from 1890 to 1980. In some cases, dates for the beginning and end of a regime are based on judgment. An example is the end of the Bretton Woods regime and the shift to fluctuating exchange rates. I chose the date on which President Nixon closed the gold window, third quarter of 1971, but cases can be made for either an earlier or a later date. Also, I ended the interwar gold standard with the departure of Britain (third quarter of 1931) rather than using the later date, first quarter of 1933, when the United States allowed the dollar to float. Table 4–1 describes the regimes and gives the relevant dates.

The six regimes differ considerably in the amount of variability experienced. Table 4–2 shows the variance of the levels of logarithms of the raw data by regime. There are notable differences. The variance of nominal GNP is highest under the classical gold standard and lowest in the period of pegged interest rates. The variance of real GNP has a similar pattern. The variance of the price level increased under pegged interest rates, but it is highest in the recent period of fluctuating exchange rates and relatively high inflation. The variances of the two measures of money growth do not show any consistent pattern. For M2, the variance is highest under Bretton Woods; for M1, the variance is relatively low under that regime and even lower under fluctuating exchange rates.

The variability of actual outcomes is less costly if forecasting accuracy is high. Forecasts made using the multistate Kalman filter rely only on past observations, so they are "true" forecasts that, in prin-

11. M1 is currency and demand deposits. M2 is M1 plus time deposits at commercial banks other than large denomination certificates of deposit. The change in definition of M2 does not permit this series to extend beyond the fourth quarter of 1979.

Table 4–1. Six Monetary Regimes, 1890–1980

Regime	Beginning	End	Description	Observations and comments
1	1890–I[a]	1914–IV	Gold standard without a central bank	100[b]
2	1915–I	1931–III	Gold exchange standard with a central bank	67 Ended when Britain left the gold standard
3	1931–IV	1941–IV	Mixed system, no clear standard	41 Ended when interest rates were pegged
4	1942–I	1951–I	Pegged interest rates	37
5	1951–II	1971–III	Bretton Woods	82 Ended when President Nixon closed the gold window
6	1971–IV	1980–IV	Fluctuating rates	37[c]

[a]Roman numeral denotes quarter.
[b]Thirty observations for M2; none for M1; one observation lost in computation.
[c]Thirty-three observations for M2.

Table 4–2. Variance of Log Levels of Actual Data

Regime	Nominal GNP	Price level	Real GNP	M2	M1
1	0.150	0.012	0.084	0.015	n.a.
2	0.066	0.024	0.024	0.084	0.042
3	0.058	0.004	0.033	0.043	0.071
4	0.033	0.031	0.007	0.063	0.057
5	0.123	0.020	0.044	0.098	0.030
6	0.072	0.035	0.007	0.043	0.028

ciple, could be used to predict quarterly values. The variances of the forecast errors for each period are shown in Table 4–3. Also shown is the percentage of the variability of the log levels (from Table 4–2) that remains after using the Kalman filter. The percentage is computed by dividing the variance of the forecast errors by the variance of the actual data and multiplying by 100.

The most striking feature of Table 4–3 is the postwar decline in the variances of the forecast errors both in absolute value and relative to the variances of the raw data. For real GNP and prices, the postwar variance of the forecast error is less than 10 percent of the lowest variance recorded before World War II, regimes 1 through 3. For

Table 4–3. Variance of the Forecast Error (times 100) for Log Levels, Computed
Values, Column 1, and Percentage of Measured Variance, Column 2

Regime	(1)	(2)	(1)	(2)
	Nominal GNP		Money (M2)	
1	0.298	1.99	0.026	1.73
2	0.180	2.73	0.020	0.24
3	0.564	9.72	0.163	3.79
4	0.067	0.49	0.020	0.32
5	0.013	0.10	0.003	0.03
6	0.013	0.18	0.004	0.09
	Price Level		Money (M1)	
1	0.025	2.08	n.a.	n.a.
2	0.060	2.50	0.026	0.62
3	0.024	6.00	0.043	0.61
4	0.060	1.94	0.031	0.54
5	0.002	0.10	0.005	0.17
6	0.002	0.06	0.009	0.32
	Real GNP			
1	0.283	3.37		
2	0.141	5.88		
3	0.402	12.18		
4	0.078	11.14		
5	0.011	0.25		
6	0.014	2.00		

the two definitions of money, postwar variances of the log level
forecasts are no more than one-third to one-fifth of the lowest prewar
variance. The variance of the error for prices and real GNP declined
relative to the variance for money. These findings cast doubt on the
notion that the time series data can be treated as if they had constant
variance, as is often done in econometric studies. Different regimes
appear to give rise to different variances of forecast errors.

The postwar decline in the variance of forecast errors relative to
the measured variance is, at times, larger than the decline in the
variance of the forecast error itself. The relative decline between
regimes 1 to 3 and the postwar era is most notable for prices and
nominal GNP. Money also shows a decline in relative variability in
the postwar period, but the relative decline in M1 is the smallest of
any variable. The principal reason appears to be that the variance
of forecast errors for M1 is not very large in any of the five regimes.

There are also differences among variables within a given regime.
Under the mixed standard of the 1930s (regime 3), the variance of
forecast errors for real and nominal income is three times its levels

under prior regimes, but the variance for prices is smaller. Under interest rate pegging, wartime price controls, and early postwar adjustment (regime 4), the variance of forecast errors for money and real and nominal income fell, but the variance rose for prices.

The Bretton Woods regime has the smallest variance of any regime for each of the variables, although the values are duplicated in regime 6 for nominal GNP and the price level. The shift to fluctuating exchange rates was accompanied by increased variance of forecast errors for money and real GNP, but the increase is small. By prewar standards, the period of fluctuating exchange rates has been remarkably stable, if stability is measured by short-term predictability (the variance of errors in quarterly forecasts).

An alternative measure of stability is the extent to which prices, income, and money are stationary over a longer term. Stationary prices have some attractive features, and possibly a stationary money stock is attractive also. Stationary real income implies that per capita income declines as population increases, so stationary income is not desirable.

To separate short- and long-term stability, I used the posterior probabilities computed to develop weights on the three errors, ε, γ, and ρ. The Kalman filter program computes these weights using past observations and an arbitrarily chosen set of initial (prior) probabilities assigned to each type of error. Each period the weights change, so the arbitrary initial values have little influence on the weights after a few periods. The change in the weights is largest when there are large forecast errors, but two consecutive errors are required to determine that an error is not transitory. A large probability of a permanent change implies that, when large errors are made, they tend to last for more than one period. Table 4–4 shows these probabilities. Normal and outlier changes are combined.

Column 1 shows the mean posterior probability of a transitory change in level. If this probability is close to 100, most forecast errors are pure random changes, or white noise. Forecast errors are randomly distributed around a stable level, so the future level of the variable is expected to be the same as the current level. When the value in column 1 is relatively small, errors in level or in growth rate persist. This is shown by relatively large probabilities in columns (2) or (3).

Under the classical gold standard (regime 1), the probability of transitory changes in level is much larger than in other regimes. The probability declines in regime 2, after the establishment of the Federal Reserve, but the lowest values are found in the postwar period. The postwar values imply that a relatively small part of the variance

142

Table 4–4. Posterior Probabilities* in Percentage

Regime	Transitory change in level (1)	Permanent change in level (2)	Permanent change in growth rate (3)	(1)	(2)	(3)
	Nominal GNP			Money (M2)		
1	19.7	37.4	42.9	16.8	34.8	48.4
2	2.9	38.5	58.6	2.3	8.8	88.9
3	3.7	47.5	48.8	9.0	12.3	78.7
4	3.5	30.7	65.8	11.6	31.9	56.5
5	0.3	10.0	89.7	0.9	14.7	84.4
6	1.4	61.4	37.2	0.2	18.4	81.4
	Prices			Money (M1)		
1	16.2	33.4	50.4	n.a.	n.a.	n.a.
2	10.8	27.2	62.0	8.6	19.0	72.4
3	5.5	52.7	41.8	0.8	8.0	91.2
4	0.5	35.1	64.4	2.8	22.0	75.2
5	1.1	59.1	39.8	0.8	23.9	75.3
6	0.2	62.8	37.0	0.1	14.2	85.7
	Real GNP					
1	21.4	41.3	37.3			
2	11.4	29.6	59.0			
3	3.2	37.3	59.5			
4	8.2	61.7	30.1			
5	1.2	28.9	69.9			
6	3.8	36.7	59.5			

*Columns 1, 2, and 3 sum to 100.

of forecast errors in the postwar regimes reflects risk; the postwar weight shifted toward greater relative uncertainty. For prices, the largest probability under fluctuating exchange rates is assigned to changes in level. This reflects the relatively high uncertainty about the future price level during the 1970s. The same is not true for the two measures of money stock. Principal weight is given to permanent changes in rates of change. For money, the data suggest, this is the typical allocation, common to each of the regimes.

Lower probabilities do not imply a reduction in risk or uncertainty. I measure risk and uncertainty by multiplying the probability of a particular error by the variance of the forecast error. This procedure treats the variance of the forecast error as a weighted sum with weights equal to the computed probabilities of the three types of error shown in Table 4–4. Since these probabilities sum to 1 (or 100), the sum of the measures of risk and uncertainty, in columns 1 to 3 in Table 4–5, is the variance of the forecast error shown in Table 4–3, column 1.

The measures of risk and uncertainty are shown in Table 4–5. Column 1 shows the variance of the transitory error, ε, the measure I have called *risk*. It is the product of the total variance of forecast error and the probability that the disturbance is transitory. Columns 2 and 3 are, respectively, the variance of changes in level and the variance of changes in the rate of change computed in an analogous way. The data in these columns are used to measure uncertainty about future values.

Risk practically vanishes in the postwar regimes for prices and money and is relatively small for real and nominal income. This implies that most postwar changes persist either in levels or in rates of change.

For prices, stability is a benefit. Under the gold standard, both

Table 4–5. Measures of Risk and Uncertainty*

Regime	Risk (1)	Uncertainty of level (2)	Uncertainty of growth rate (3)	(1)	(2)	(3)
		Nominal GNP			Money (M2)	
1	0.0587	0.1114	0.1278	0.0044	0.0090	0.0126
2	0.0052	0.0693	0.1055	0.0005	0.0018	0.0178
3	0.0209	0.2679	0.2752	0.0147	0.0200	0.1283
4	0.0023	0.0206	0.0441	0.0023	0.0064	0.0113
5	0.0000	0.0013	0.0117	0.0000	0.0004	0.0025
6	0.0002	0.0080	0.0048	0.0001	0.0007	0.0032
		Prices			Money (M1)	
1	0.0040	0.0084	0.0126	n.a.	n.a.	n.a.
2	0.0065	0.0163	0.0372	0.0022	0.0049	0.0188
3	0.0013	0.0126	0.0100	0.0003	0.0034	0.0392
4	0.0003	0.0211	0.0386	0.0009	0.0068	0.0233
5	0.0000	0.0012	0.0008	0.0000	0.0012	0.0038
6	0.0000	0.0012	0.0007	0.0000	0.0013	0.0077
		Real GNP				
1	0.0606	0.1169	0.1056			
2	0.0161	0.0417	0.0832			
3	0.0129	0.1499	0.2392			
4	0.0064	0.0481	0.0235			
5	0.0001	0.0032	0.0077			
6	0.0005	0.0051	0.0083			

*The sum is equal to the variance of forecast error shown in column 1, Table 4–3.

managed and classical, transitory errors in forecasting levels are larger than in later periods, particularly the postwar periods. The risk of short-term errors of price forecast is larger under the gold standard than under the Bretton Woods and fluctuating exchange rate regimes.

Not only was there more risk of price fluctuations under the gold standard, but there was more uncertainty also. This is seen by comparing the values in columns 2 and 3 for the prewar and postwar regimes. The sum of these columns is a measure of price level uncertainty.

The main reason that risk and uncertainty were higher under the gold standard is that errors of forecast were larger. Even after removing short-term transitory disturbances, the remaining variability—the sum of columns 2 and 3—is larger than the average error of forecast in the postwar years.

Reduced uncertainty about the future price level in the postwar years does not imply that the price level is less likely to change. The average rate of inflation was higher in the 1970s than in any of the decades covered in this study. The data do not deny that the price level is expected to rise and, with continued inflation, converge to infinity. The data suggest, instead, that forecast errors declined and the anticipated rate of change became less variable. Table 4–4 shows that since 1951 more weight has been assigned to the probability that observed errors of forecast are changes in the price level. In earlier regimes, greatest weight was assigned to permanent changes in the rate of price change. Relatively less weight was placed on changes in level, and relatively more weight on changes in rates of change.

The comparison of regimes suggests that, contrary to frequent claims, the gold standard did not provide greater long-term predictability of prices. The so-called automatic features of the gold standard limit the degree to which a single country can inflate or deflate relative to other countries. The various gold standards limited the range within which the future price changed more effectively than the current regime. These restrictions do not reduce uncertainty, however, if the range is wide and variability is relatively high. The data suggest that permanent shocks to the rate of price change were relatively large and frequent under the gold standard, so that forecasts of future price levels and rates of change were subject to large errors. The problem was most severe in the periods that include the two major wars (regimes 2 and 4), but uncertainty was relatively high also in the years of the classical gold standard.

The declines in uncertainty between regimes 1 to 3 and 5 and 6 are largest for real and nominal GNP. Under the gold standard, uncertainty about the rate of nominal GNP growth and its level were almost equal. In the postwar years, both measures of uncertainty decline, and in regime 5, uncertainty about the rate of change dominated. Uncertainty about the level of GNP became relatively small. Permanent changes in level are transitory changes in growth rate, so the relatively low weight suggests that the public did not expect recessions, or expansions, to have a lasting effect on the maintained rate of growth of GNP. Similar, but somewhat weaker, statements about comparative weights apply to real GNP. Even in regime 3, which includes the depression of the 1930s, the public gave considerable weight to uncertainty about the level of real GNP, although the dominant uncertainty is about the rate of change.[12]

Comparison of price and real GNP uncertainty shows the marked difference between the first four regimes and the postwar era. Within the first group, there is some evidence of a tradeoff; periods of increased uncertainty about the rate of price change have reduced levels of uncertainty about real GNP and conversely. Uncertainty about the level of real GNP declined in regime 2 and rose in regime 3, while uncertainty about the rate of price change rose in regime 2 and declined in regime 3. There is no evidence of a tradeoff in regimes 5 and 6. These regimes have lower uncertainty about both variables than the first four regimes. Further, during regime 6, price uncertainty remained almost unchanged relative to regime 5, while uncertainty about real GNP rose.

For money, risk is negligible in almost all periods; most of its variance is assigned to uncertainty. Uncertainty is lower in the postwar period but higher under fluctuating rates than under Bretton Woods. The reduction in uncertainty about money is consistent with the proposition that control of money has increased in the postwar period.

A major problem in using these data to compare monetary regimes is that lower variability of output or prices can result from greater stability in nature and trading arrangements or from greater stability in monetary and other policies or policy regimes. The policy regime can increase uncertainty, but if nature is sufficiently benign, variability and measured uncertainty may remain low. Conversely, the

12. Computations were made using rates of change (first differences of logarithms) as input. In this case, uncertainty means only changes in the rate of change. We can compare this measure of uncertainty to the data reported in column 3 of Table 4–5 and computed from log levels. The principal differences are for nominal and real GNP. A principal reason is that transitory errors are larger for the GNP variables and prices, particularly in the first regime. Forecasts based on rates of change omit the transitory changes in level. These differences aside, the general appearance is similar, and the reduction in uncertainty in regimes 5 and 6 remains.

benefits of a stable regime will be difficult to observe, and measured uncertainty may increase, if real shocks are sufficiently destabilizing.

The data suggest that uncertainty (the sum of columns 2 and 3) about real GNP and money are related. The rank correlation for uncertainty about M1 and real GNP is 0.9 for the five regimes, 2 to 6, with complete data. The correlation is significant at the 5 percent level. For M2 and real GNP uncertainty, the rank correlation is 1.0.

Further, the data suggest that the declines in monetary and income uncertainty are of similar order of magnitude. Table 4–6 shows the ratios of the variances attributable to uncertainty about money and real income in regimes 2 through 6, as computed from the data in Table 4–5.

Many explanations have been offered for the greater stability of income in the years after World War II. Reductions in the relative size of agriculture, greater fiscal activism, and built-in stabilizers are prominent among the explanations. Each of these may have contributed. The data in Tables 4–5 and 4–6 suggest, however, that changes in the monetary regime have had a prominent role that is often overlooked.

As a statistical matter, the differences in the probabilities between periods generally are not significant at the 5 percent level. The probability distributions overlap to a nonnegligible degree. As an economic matter, differences in the variance attributed to uncertainty are often consequential. As an example, consider the uncertainty about future real GNP. The lowest variance attributed to uncertainty is 0.1090 (0.0077 + 0.0032) in regime 5; the highest is 0.3891 (0.2392 + 0.1499) in regime 3. If we use two standard deviations to approximate the range within which the growth rate typically fluctuates from quarter to quarter, we have 0.66 for the lower value and 1.25 for the higher value. For the classical gold standard, the variance is 0.2225, so two standard deviations is 0.94; for fluctuating exchange

Table 4–6. Ratios of Variances Attributed to Uncertainty

Regime	M1/real income	M2/real income	M1/nominal income	M2/nominal income
2	0.23	0.13	0.18	0.10
3	0.16	0.46	0.14	0.39
4	1.00	0.44	0.52	0.23
5	0.57	0.29	0.33	0.17
6	0.44	0.16	1.60	0.60

rates, two standard deviations is 0.23, or less than one-fourth of the variability under the gold standard.

Conclusion

The right to own gold is a valuable right. The fact that many people choose to exercise the right is informative about the uncertainty or risks that people perceive. They may fear inflation or confiscation of their assets or some type of political restriction on property. They may fear default on the note issue following a wave of bank failures. Whatever the reason, ownership of gold or precious metals reduces the uncertainty that individuals perceive and bear but also reduces the demand for productive assets and the capital stock. Society is poorer because of the uncertainty that leads individuals to hold gold instead of productive capital.

The choice of a monetary regime is a decision to reduce some private risks by incurring costs that are borne by society as a whole. These costs include the resource cost of maintaining and operating the regime and the cost of bearing the risks that the monetary standard imposes. The basis for rational, economic choice between monetary standards, or the choice between so-called free competitive banking and a central bank, is relative efficiency. The most efficient monetary arrangement minimizes the cost and maximizes the benefits to individuals subject to the standard.

The efficiency criterion is more difficult to apply to the choice of monetary regime than to many other choices. An international commodity standard, based on gold or a commodity basket, requires a cartel agreement to keep the commodity's price at a set level. An international agreement to fix exchange rates is a decision to maintain the external stability of the value of money if necessary at the expense of domestic price stability. A monetary rule that fixes the growth rate of money, or that determines money growth as part of a contingent plan, depends for its execution on a central bank with monopoly power and on a commitment to let exchange rates fluctuate. A regime of this kind requires society to choose greater stability of the internal price level at the cost of greater fluctuation in exchange rates and in the prices of imported goods and services. Economic efficiency is rarely compatible with either price-fixing or monopoly arrangements. Yet, in the case of money, a central bank with monopoly power can be the most efficient method of producing money.

Among the principal ways that a central bank monopoly can increase efficiency are substituting inconvertible paper money for commodity money to reduce the resource cost, reducing some monitoring or enforcements costs that arise under a fixed exchange rate system, maintaining domestic price stability, and reducing uncertainty about expected future values. On the other hand, any rule limiting the issue of inconvertible paper money requires monitoring to prevent inflation or deflation. And a fluctuating exchange rate introduces risks of exchange rate changes in place of the risk of domestic price fluctuations inherent in a system of fixed exchange rates. Hence, no unique optimum is likely to be found analytically. The optimum, if one exists, depends on the relative costs and benefits of each regime.

For small countries that trade with the rest of the world, the cost of exchange rate fluctuations often exceeds any gain from controlling the price level of domestic commodities. Such countries can fix their exchange rates by pegging to the currency of a larger country that chooses a monetary rule. They benefit from price stability elsewhere by paying the cost of maintaining a fixed exchange rate and by incurring the risk of policy changes in the large country. A large country, with relatively little foreign trade, can increase the stability of its income, consumption, and prices, at least in principle, by choosing a quantity rule. Large and small countries may therefore have a symbiotic relation. All can gain if the large country chooses a regime that increases stability.

Pure monetary regimes have not occurred in practice, and few comparisons of actual monetary regimes have been made. This chapter compares measures of risk and uncertainty about levels and rates of change of money, prices, and GNP under six monetary regimes that governed the U.S. money stock in the twentieth century. A multistate Kalman filter provides an estimate of the variance of the one-quarter-ahead forecast, using information available at the time the forecast could have been made. Changes in each data series are divided into transitory and permanent changes in level and permanent changes in rates of change, based on prior probabilities of each type of change. The prior probabilities are revised as new information arrives. I used the computed posterior probabilities and the variances of forecast errors to compute measures of risk and uncertainty for each of the six monetary regimes.

The data suggest that, for prices and GNP, risk and uncertainty were greater under the gold standard, with or without a central bank, than under either the Bretton Woods regime or the current regime of fluctuating exchange rates. Risk and uncertainty about real GNP declined initially after the Federal Reserve was established, but the decline was relatively small and did not persist. The decline was accompanied by a rise in uncertainty about rates of price change.

A much larger decline in both risk and uncertainty about real GNP followed World War II, when the gold standard was replaced by the Bretton Woods regime and later by fluctuating exchange rates. For prices, differences in risk and uncertainty between the pre–Federal Reserve gold standard and the post–World War II period are somewhat smaller. The data place a higher probability that the long-term price level would remain constant under the gold standard than under either postwar monetary regime. Forecast errors were larger under the gold standard, however, so uncertainty about the future price level is higher under the gold standard than under the postwar regimes. Price level risk is higher under the gold standard also.

The rate of inflation has been higher in many of the postwar years than it was under the gold standard. People do not expect prices to be stable; they expect prices to rise without limit. The lower variance of forecast errors in the postwar years implies that the change in prices is more predictable now than under earlier regimes, even though the expected change is larger. This is the sense in which uncertainty about future prices has been reduced.

Many of my findings rely on computations of variances from quarterly forecasts. These findings can be heavily influenced by a few large outliers. The procedure used permits recomputation to omit the influence of outliers. None of the main qualitative conclusions change, but, obviously, there are changes in the quantitative conclusions. A further problem is reliance in the early years on quarterly data constructed by interpolation, using "related" series, long after the event. These qualifications should be kept in mind when judging the results.

The variability of many economic time series is lower after World War II. Comparison of the two postwar regimes shows similar levels of risk and uncertainty in each regime. Risk and uncertainty are higher for real GNP under fluctuating exchange rates. The increase in uncertainty about real GNP, though large relative to the increase in monetary uncertainty, is relatively small in absolute value. It seems likely that the increase is as much a consequence of the oil shocks of the 1970s as of the change in monetary regime. Uncertainty about the future price level declined marginally under fluctuating exchange rates.

The data suggest that the observed fluctuations in exchange rates from 1971 to 1980 have not had a large effect on the variance of forecast errors for GNP, prices, and money. Contrary to McKinnon (1984), fluctuating rates have not imposed a large excess burden, at least not for the United States. The rate of inflation is higher, but uncertainty about the future price level is lower than in the prewar regimes and not much changed from the Bretton Woods years.

The data suggest, more strongly, that the shift to fluctuating exchange rates did not trade greater internal for lesser external price stability. Further, a potential gain from fluctuating rates—improved monetary control—has not been achieved. The Federal Reserve has not increased monetary controls; uncertainty about money growth and future levels of the money stock is higher under fluctuating rates than under the Bretton Woods regime.[13]

These findings suggest that improvements in monetary arrangements can increase welfare by reducing uncertainty below current levels. A firm commitment to price stability, expressed in a monetary rule, would reduce inflation and uncertainty about future rates of price change. Further, a rule adopted by leading countries—the United States, Japan, Germany, and the United Kingdom—under which each nation agrees to maintain that rate of growth of its monetary base consistent with its own internal price stability would increase exchange rate stability for major currencies.

A rule of this kind has an additional benefit. Other countries can increase price stability by pegging to one of the major currencies or by pegging to a basket of the major currencies. Under the proposed regime, the stability of internal and external prices increases together for small countries.

A by-product of the empirical work presented in this chapter is the finding that the variance of forecast errors differs across regimes. At times, particularly in the 1930s, the variances are large relative to earlier or later periods. This suggests that a standard assumption in econometric work—that the variance of the error term is constant over time—may not hold across regimes. This finding is, of course, consistent with the presence of the so-called Lucas effect, under which parameters estimated from time series data depend on the policy regime during the period of observation.

REFERENCES

Barro, Robert J., and David B. Gordon. "A Positive Theory of Monetary Policy in a Natural Rate Model." *Journal of Political Economy* 91 (August 1983), 589–610.

13. Data end in 1980, so most of the period after 1979, in which the Federal Reserve attempted to control nonborrowed reserves, is omitted. Mascaro and Meltzer (1983) and Brunner (1983) suggest that uncertainty increased in this period.

Bomhoff, Eduard J. "Predicting the Price Level in a World That Changes All the Time." In *Economic Policy in a World of Change*, Karl Brunner and Allan H. Meltzer, eds. Carnegie-Rochester Conference Series on Public Policy, vol. 17. Amsterdam: North-Holland, 1982. Pp. 7–55.

———. *Monetary Uncertainty*. Amsterdam: North-Holland, 1983.

Bomhoff, Eduard J., and Clemens J. M. Kool. "Forecasts with Multi-State Kalman Filters." Appendix 1 to *Monetary Uncertainty*, Eduard J. Bomhoff. Amsterdam: North-Holland, 1983. Pp. 227–246.

Brennan, Geoffrey, and James M. Buchanan. *The Power to Tax: Analytical Foundations of a Fiscal Constitution*. Cambridge: Cambridge University Press, 1980.

Brunner, Karl. "Has Monetarism Failed?" *Cato Journal* 3 (Spring 1983), 23–62.

Brunner, Karl, and Allan H. Meltzer. "Money, Debt, and Economic Activity." *Journal of Political Economy* 80 (September/October 1972), 951–77.

———. "Strategies and Tactics for Monetary Control." In *Money, Monetary Policy, and Financial Institutions*, Karl Brunner and Allan H. Meltzer, eds. Carnegie-Rochester Conference Series on Public Policy, vol. 18. Amsterdam: North-Holland, 1983. Pp. 59–103.

Christ, Carl F. "On Fiscal and Monetary Policies and the Government Budget Restraint." *American Economic Review* 69 (September 1979), 526–38.

Cukierman, Alex, and Allan H. Meltzer. "A Theory of Ambiguity, Credibility and Inflation under Discretion and Asymmetric Information." *Econometrica*, 1986. Forthcoming.

Fellner, William. "Gold and the Uneasy Case for Responsibly Managed Fiat Money." In *Essays in Contemporary Economic Problems*. Washington, D.C.: American Enterprise Institute for Public Policy Research, 1981. Pp. 97–121.

Fischer, Stanley. "Stability and Exchange Rate Systems in a Monetarist Model of the Balance of Payments." In *The Political Economy of Monetary Reform*, Robert Z. Aliber, ed. New York: Allanheld, Osmun & Co., 1977. Pp. 59–73.

Flood, Robert P. "Capital Mobility and the Choice of Exchange Rate System." *International Economic Review* 20 (June 1979), 405–16.

Friedman, Milton. "A Monetary and Fiscal Framework for Economic Stability." *American Economic Review* 38 (June 1948), 245–64.

———. "Commodity-Reserve Currency." *Journal of Political Economy* 59 (June 1951), 203–32.

Friedman, Milton, and Anna J. Schwartz. *A Monetary History of the United States, 1867–1960*. Princeton: Princeton University Press, 1963.

Gordon, Robert J. "Price Inertia and Policy Ineffectiveness in the United States, 1890–1980." *Journal of Political Economy* 90 (December 1982), 1087–117.

Gould, John P., Merton H. Miller, Charles R. Nelson, and Charles W.

Upton. "The Stochastic Properties of Velocity and the Quantity Theory of Money." *Journal of Monetary Economics* 4 (April 1978), 229–48.

Hayek, Friedrich A. *Denationalization of Money*, 2nd ed. London: Institute of Economic Affairs, 1978.

Keynes, John Maynard. *A Treatise on Probability*. London: Macmillan, 1921.

―――. *The General Theory of Employment, Interest and Money*. New York: Harcourt, Brace and Co., 1936.

―――. "The General Theory of Employment." *Quarterly Journal of Economics* 51 (February 1937), 209–23.

Knight, Frank H. *Risk, Uncertainty and Profit*. Boston: Houghton Mifflin, 1921.

Kydland, Finn E., and Edward C. Prescott. "Rules Rather than Discretion: The Inconsistency of Optimal Plans." *Journal of Political Economy* 85 (June 1977), 473–91.

Mascaro, Angelo, and Allan H. Meltzer. "Long- and Short-Term Interest Rates in a Risky World." *Journal of Monetary Economics* 12 (November 1983), 485–518.

McCallum, Bennett T. "Are Bond-financed Deficits Inflationary? A Ricardian Analysis." *Journal of Political Economy* 92 (February 1984), 123–35.

McKinnon, Ronald I. *An International Standard for Monetary Stabilization*. Washington, D.C.: Institute for International Economics, 1984.

McNees, Stephen K. "The Recent Record of Thirteen Forecasters." *New England Economic Review* (September/October 1981), 5–21.

Meltzer, Allan H. "Rational Expectations, Risk, Uncertainty and Market Responses." In *Crises in the Economic and Financial Structure*, Paul Wachtel, ed. Lexington, Mass.: Lexington Books, 1982. Pp. 3–22.

―――. "Monetary Reform in an Uncertain Environment." *Cato Journal* 3 (Spring 1983), 93–112.

Mussa, Michael. "Empirical Regularities in the Behavior of Exchange Rates and Theories of the Foreign Exchange Market." In *Policies for Employment, Prices, and Exchange Rates*, Karl Brunner and Allan H. Meltzer, eds. Carnegie-Rochester Conference Series on Public Policy, vol. 11. Amsterdam: North-Holland, 1979. Pp. 9–57.

Report to the Congress of the Commission on the Role of Gold in the Domestic and International Monetary Systems, vols. 1 and 2. Washington, D.C.: The Secretary of the Treasury, March 1982.

Simons, Henry C. *Economic Policy for a Free Society*. Chicago: University of Chicago Press, 1948.

Vaubel, Roland. "The Government's Money Monopoly: Externalities or Natural Monopoly?" *Kyklos* 37 (1984, part 1), 27–58.

Webb, Roy H. "Forecasts 1983." Ferderal Reserve Bank of Richmond *Economic Review* 69 (January/February 1983), 3–6.

Accuracy of Forecasting as a Measure of Economic Uncertainty

CARL F. CHRIST

ALLAN MELTZER has given us new research results. They strongly suggest that the degree of uncertainty about real and nominal income, the price level, and the money stocks M1 and M2 in the U.S. economy decreased during the period from 1890 to 1980. Meltzer divides this period into six subperiods, according to the type of monetary regime that was in effect, and concludes that the last two regimes (fixed exchange rates under the Bretton Woods agreement and floating rates since 1971) were less uncertain than the two gold standard regimes, the mixed system of the 1930s, or the pegged interest rates of the 1940s.

His method is to measure the degree of variability of each of the five variables during each of the regimes and then to apportion it into the additive components that he calls *risk* and *uncertainty*. This is an ex post concept of risk and uncertainty, not an ex ante one.

There are many ways to define variability for this purpose. One definition would be the variance of the logarithm of the level of each variable during each period. This is equivalent to the mean square of the relative deviation of the variable from its geometric mean— that is, the mean square of $(X - Xg)/Xg$ if X is the level of the variable and Xg is its geometric mean. If this definition were used, it would imply that variability was high in any period when the variables in question were varying a great deal percentagewise in relation to their geometric means.

Meltzer uses a different definition of *variability*. He uses the variance of the error of the forecast of the logarithm of each variable during each period. This is equivalent to the mean square of the relative deviation of the variable from its forecast; that is, the mean square of $(X - Xf)/Xf$ if Xf is the forecast of X. When this definition is used, it implies that variability was high in any period when forecasts had large percentage errors.

The main question about this approach is, What is the forecasting

154

method? Meltzer uses the multistage Kalman filter technique (MSKF) to forecast each of the five variables, one quarter ahead, from 1890 to 1980, based solely on its own past values. It can yield genuine ex ante forecasts, for it uses no inputs except past data. However, Meltzer recognizes that his forecasts are not quite genuine ex ante forecasts, because the forecast for each quarter is based not on the preliminary estimates of past data actually available at the beginning of the quarter that is to be forecast but rather on past data that are now available, some years later.

Meltzer's model assumes that the logarithm x of each variable X in any quarter, $x = ln\ X$, is equal to the sum of five unobservable terms: (1) the expected value of x in the previous quarter, (2) the expected increase in x from last quarter to this quarter based on the expected growth rate of X, and three mutually and serially independent random disturbances having zero means and representing (3) a temporary shock to the level of X, (4) a permanent shock to the level of X, and (5) a permanent shock to the growth rate of X. The MSKF technique is a Bayesian way of using past observations of x to estimate, each quarter, the values of components 1 and 2 and obtain a forecast equal to their sum. Meltzer divides each of the three disturbances into normal values and outliers and assigns initial prior probabilities of 95 percent to each normal value and 5 percent to each outlier. Each forecast xf is a weighted average obtained by applying probability weights to the six forecasts based on the normal and outlier values of each of the three disturbances. The MSKF technique results in updated estimates each period of the probability weights and of the variances of the disturbances. It also allows the partition of the total variance of forecast error into three additive components, attributable to the three kinds of shocks.

Meltzer gives us in Table 4–2 the variance of the logarithm of the level of each variable for each regime. Similarly, in row 1 of Table 4–3 he shows 100 times the variance of error of the forecast of the logarithm of each variable for each regime. The first of these is a measure of the variability of actual values of the five variables. The second is a measure of the variability of the forecasting errors. In order to put them in comparable and familiar terms, I have computed the corresponding root mean squares of percentage deviations and of percentage errors. They are in Table 4–7.

The first row for each regime shows the root mean squares of the percentage deviations, $100(X - Xg)/Xg$ percent of the levels of the variables X from their geometric means Xg. The second row for each regime shows the root mean squares of the percentage errors of

Table 4–7. Root Mean Square Percentage Deviations of Variables from Geometric Means and Root Mean Square and Average Absolute Percentage Forecasting Errors One Quarter Ahead

Regime	Type of deviation or error	Nominal GNP	Price level	Real GNP	M2	M1
1	RMS percentage deviation from geometric mean	39.0	11.0	29.0	12.0	n.a.
	RMS percentage forecast error of MSKF	5.5	1.6	5.3	1.6	n.a.
2	RMS percentage deviation from geometric mean	26.0	16.0	16.0	29.0	20.0
	RMS percentage forecast error of MSKF	4.2	2.4	3.8	1.4	1.6
3	RMS percentage deviation from geometric mean	24.0	6.3	18.0	21.0	27.0
	RMS percentage forecast error of MSKF	7.5	1.6	6.3	4.0	2.1
4	RMS percentage deviation from geometric mean	18.0	18.0	8.4	25.0	24.0
	RMS percentage forecast error of MSKF	2.6	2.4	2.8	1.4	1.8
5	RMS percentage deviation from geometric mean	35.0	14.0	21.0	31.0	17.0
	RMS percentage forecast error of MSKF	1.1	0.4	1.0	0.6	0.7
6	RMS percentage deviation from geometric mean	27.0	19.0	8.4	21.0	17.0
	RMS percentage forecast error of MSKF	1.1	0.4	1.2	0.6	1.0
	RMS percentage forecast error from					
	ARIMA, 1970–73	1.0	0.5	1.1	n.a.	n.a.
	ASA–NBER survey, 1970–73	0.4	0.4	0.5	n.a.	n.a.
	Wharton model III, 1971–74	0.4	0.3	0.4	n.a.	n.a.
	Average absolute percentage forecast error from eight forecasters, 1976–80	1.1	0.2	0.7	n.a.	n.a.

NOTES: RMS percentage deviations from geometric means are computed from Meltzer's Table 4–2. RMS percentage forecast errors of the MSKF are computed from Meltzer's Table 4–3. RMS percentage forecast errors of the other three methods for periods approximating regime 6 are from Christ (1975), which compiled these results from references given there. The orders of the ARIMA forecasts for nominal GNP, price level, and real GNP were respectively (2, 2, 1), (1, 2, 1), and (1, 1, 1). Average absolute percentage forecast errors from eight forecasters for periods approximating regime 6 are computed from McNees' report (see reference in Meltzer) of eight forecasters who made forecasts early in each quarter for that same quarter's levels.

forecast, $100(X - Xf)/Xf$ percent, where Xf is the forecast. For comparison I also show, at the bottom of Table 4–7, the root mean square percentage errors of three other sets of ex ante one-quarter-ahead forecasts and average absolute percentage errors for eight other sets of forecasts, for periods approximating Meltzer's sixth regime (floating exchange rates).

In Table 4–5 Meltzer decomposes his measure of variability, 100 times the variance of the forecast error, into three additive components. The component attributed to temporary shocks in the level of the variable he calls *risk*. The other two components, attributed to permanent shocks in level and permanent shocks in growth rate, he calls *uncertainty*. This terminology is Knight's. The distinction is useful because it is easier to insure against risk than against uncertainty. Unfortunately, the uncertainty components are always much larger than the risk component. However, Meltzer notes that all three components of variability decline substantially from the early regimes to the latest two. He correctly observes that this result casts serious doubt, for this problem, on the frequently made assumption that econometric disturbances are homoskedastic.

Table 4–7 shows no great change in variability from the earlier regimes to the later ones if variability is defined in terms of the percentage deviations of a variable from its geometric mean for the period. As Table 4–7 also shows, this contrasts with the outcome when Meltzer's definition of variability is used, based on the MSKF's percentage forecast errors. That is, the variability of the levels of these five variables did not change much during the nineteenth century, but there was a substantial decrease in the errors of forecasting them by the MSKF method. Meltzer interprets this as an indication of reduced risk and uncertainty in the economy under the two most recent monetary regimes. Subject to some caveats noted next, this is a reasonable conclusion: it is not economic variability per se that creates risk and uncertainty; it is inability to forecast what will happen.

Table 4–7 shows that the largest changes in variability of levels among the five variables were the decline in the variability of real income over the entire period and the increase in the variability of the price level as the inflation rate rose in the 1970s. It is interesting that the accuracy of forecasts of the price level improved even while the price level itself was becoming more variable.

Is it possible that risk and uncertainty have not actually declined from 1890 to 1980—that Meltzer's results are an illusion or a statistical artifact? Three potential reasons suggest themselves. First, the data are presumably more accurate for the postwar period than earlier. If so, part of the higher forecasting errors noticed in the earlier regimes may be due to noise in the data. This is hard to test, but it seems possible.

Second, genuine quarterly data were used only since 1947; data for 1890–1946 were interpolated by Robert Gordon (see the reference in Meltzer's paper) from annual data by means of related series. Is it possible that errors in the interpolation process before 1947 contributed to Meltzer's result? This does not seem likely, for Gordon reports that his interpolation procedure, when applied to post-1946 annual data, yielded quarterly series very close to the actual quarterly data.

Third, when using the MSKF, it is customary to let the method make forecasts for several periods at the beginning of the data set, before starting to take the forecasts seriously, in order to allow the effects of any bad initial choice of prior probabilities to be washed out by the data. Meltzer did not do this; he presents all his forecasts right from the second quarter of 1890. I feared that this might have led to unusually large forecast errors at the beginning of his series. But he kindly made available a printout of the squares of forecast errors for each variable for each quarter, and this does not appear to have been a problem: the errors in the first twenty quarters from 1890(2) to 1895(1) are not particularly large, and are not even as large as those in the next twenty quarters.

If Meltzer's results are correct, is it possible that the reduction in uncertainty is coming from some source other than changes in monetary regimes? In principle, it is. The world may have become a more certain place for any number of other reasons, some of which he mentions: improved fiscal policy, lessened dependence on agriculture, and so on. He does not here tackle the problem of assessing this possibility.

How accurate are the MSKF forecasts? Table 4–7 shows that in the 1970s they were about as accurate as ARIMA forecasts (which are similar but less sophisticated), and less accurate than forecasts made by the ASA-NBER survey respondents, the Wharton model III, and other forecasters. Notice that the percentage forecast errors from the MSKF are typically much smaller than the percentage deviations of the variables from their geometric means. This is particularly true in the last two regimes. It means in effect that the correlation between the MSKF forecast and the actual values is rather high.

Readers may be interested in knowing what the MSKF's largest absolute percentage forecast error was for the entire 91 years for each of the five variables. Here they are, with the quarter in which each occurred:

Nominal GNP	Price level	Real GNP	M2	M1
22%	9.6%	20%	18%	6%
1933(3)	1946(4)	1933(2)	1934(3)	1943(4)

The MSKF usually recovered rapidly after making a large error. Only once in the 91 years was there a run of four consecutive quarters containing three or four errors over 10 percent (that happened for both nominal and real GNP in 1933), and only three other times were there runs of three consecutive quarters containing two or three errors over 10 percent (all were for nominal and real GNP, in 1895, 1897, and 1898).

A striking feature of the MSKF method is that it requires no knowledge of the phenomena being predicted. No economic theory is used in making the forecasts presented by Meltzer. Each variable is forecast in complete isolation from the others. No recognition is given to the fact that the five variables being predicted are connected to each other (for example, nominal GNP is the product of real GNP and the price level, and there is much evidence that the money supply affects real income in the short run and the price level in the long run). Is this the kind of forecasting method that is being used by economic agents? The fact that the ASA-NBER survey participants, the Wharton model III, and other forecasters made smaller percentage forecast errors than the MSKF in the 1970s suggests that it is not.

If other econometric models can fit data for the nineteenth century better than the MSKF does, it would be interesting to see whether their forecasts too have become more accurate since World War II.

Meltzer concludes with the recommendation that we not return to a gold standard but that instead we continue with a paper standard, governed by a monetary rule to maintain the growth of the money supply at a slow and steady rate. He bases his view partly on the belief that a stable price level is desirable, partly on the empirical results in his work, and partly on two other considerations: any country that adopts a gold standard (especially if it does so unilaterally) thereby imposes on itself large real adjustment costs in response to real or monetary disturbances that originate abroad, and there is a substantial resource cost in providing the monetary gold stock that a gold standard entails. Thus his view is that a properly managed paper standard (by which he means one subject to a monetary rule) is both higher in benefits and lower in costs than a gold standard. I am in general agreement with Meltzer's view. However, a monetary rule does need some limited flexibility so that it can take account of the likelihood of changes in the future (as in the past) of real output, of the velocity of each of the money stocks, and of the ratios of M1 and M2 to the monetary base and to each other. Meltzer is clearly aware of this need.

REFERENCE

Christ, Carl F. "Judging the Performance of Econometric Models of the U.S. Economy." *International Economic Review* 16 (February 1975), 54–74. Reprinted in *Econometric Model Performance: Comparative Simulation Studies of the U.S. Economy*, Lawrence R. Klein and Edwin Burmeister, eds. Philadelphia: University of Pennsylvania Press, 1976. Pp. 322–342.

Meltzer on Uncertainty under Different Monetary Regimes

STANLEY FISCHER

MELTZER addresses an important issue—that of short- and long-term uncertainty under alternative monetary regimes—with a welcome emphasis on empirical rather than theoretical reasoning. The structure of my comments follows that of Meltzer's paper: the first section engages in preliminary brush-clearing with pauses for rest and reflection; the second section examines the statistical procedures and results; and the final section asks what it all means.

Preliminaries

Monetary experience under the Bretton Woods and dirty floating systems has persuaded many people—for instance, Milton Friedman—that it must be possible to do better. Meltzer distinguishes three types of reform: a commodity standard, a monetary rule in a fiat money system, and deregulation.

He rightly emphasizes three points. First, a genuine commodity standard would be expensive to operate. Second, all monetary policies follow rules: the real questions are how to describe, prescribe, and proscribe the behavior of the central bank. Third, a priori reasoning will not indicate the optimal monetary rule, although it probably will reduce the range of possibilities. Accordingly, Meltzer does not pursue theory, preferring to let the facts of United States experience since 1890—interpreted through Kalman filters—speak to the issues, including the issue of how bad monetary policy has been since 1955.

In discussing commodity standards, Meltzer does not consider systems in which the medium of exchange function of money is separated from its standard of value function. Under Irving Fisher's proposal, the dollar would be exchangeable into a certain amount of gold, which amount would vary so as to maintain the real value of the monetary unit measured in terms of a commodity basket. The Fisher proposal sees the need to provide a mechanism that enforces the valuation announced by the monetary authority. In some of Robert Hall's proposals, there seems to be a view that the monetary authority can produce price stability merely by announcing that a dollar is worth a given amount in real goods. One way to understand such systems is to regard them as equivalent to compulsory indexation of all contracts. Even so, it is entirely unclear how they would work without a self-enforcing mechanism of the gold exchange type. Thus Meltzer is right to argue that the use of a commodity system would needlessly tie up real resources, even if reserves of gold or other commodities would not have to amount to a full 100 percent of the outstanding money stock.

I agree too with Meltzer's skepticism about the working of a fully competitive money system on Hayekian lines. Although there is as yet no full analysis of how such systems would work, there is certainly reason to think that a well-behaved single fiat money would be preferable to a multitude of competitive private monies.

A few comments about the first part of Meltzer's paper are in order before I proceed to its substance. First, Meltzer is careful not to claim that experience shows we could have done better than we have. There "may be room for a reduction in the variability of prices and output," monetary management "has not eliminated recessions," forecast errors are large, fiscal actions are less stabilizing than many "once believed." As a result of the Lucas critique, there are virtually no recent serious studies that examine behavior under alternative monetary rules.

Taylor (1979) suggests that the economy has been quite close to its efficiency frontier (in terms of the tradeoff between inflation and output variability) since World War II. Any analysis that blames monetary policy for short-run as opposed to long-run instability of prices will have to deal with the impressive stability—on a comparative historical and cross-sectional basis—of U.S. monetary growth. In the absence of careful studies, we are driven back to the sort of witch-hunting that deduces from the existence of economic maladies the presence of a devil in the shape of the Federal Reserve or the ghost of Keynes. A very urgent priority in this area is the resumption of serious empirical modeling of alternative monetary policies along the lines pursued a decade ago, before the rational expectations revolution made a priori reasoning about policy dominant. Meltzer's work is to be welcomed on these grounds.

Second, Meltzer is not in favor of a constant-growth-rate rule for money. He argues that monetary policy should be changed in response to permanent shifts in the growth rate of money demand. The criterion that justifies such activist policy is predictability of the price level path. Meltzer also argues that money growth should not be changed in response to transitory shifts in money demand. This argument is less persuasive, for if the Federal Reserve could identify such shifts, it could increase price-level stability by reacting to them.

Third, Meltzer's analysis of fixed exchange rate systems generally overlooks the $(n - 1)$ problem. The fixing of exchange rates provides no guidance as to the likely course of prices without knowing how the system is anchored—for instance, by one country pegging to gold or all major countries agreeing to fix their combined money growth rates. Given the size of the U.S. economy and the financial dominance of the dollar, the United States would likely be part of the anchoring system, and thus the discussion of the gold standard, money growth rules, etc., is needed in considering the behavior of a fixed-rate system as well as a closed economy.

Statistical Procedures and Results

The development and presentation of the empirical results depend on a complex distinction between risk and uncertainty. Intuitively appealing as the risk-uncertainty distinction is, it is rarely used successfully. Meltzer wants to distinguish routine events from major ones that are difficult to describe or even imagine, such as wars, the end of the world, or the invention of print. There appears to be no need for the distinction, however, for what is basically at issue is the difference between short- and long-run uncertainty about the inflation rate, output, and money.

The statistical model is given in equation (1d). Taking logarithms in that equation, we obtain, for any variable X:

$$ln\ X(t) = ln\ A(t) + b(t)t + ln\ u(t). \tag{1'}$$

In the statistical model used, $A(t)$ is regarded as a random walk, generating permanent changes in the level of X; $b(t)$, which is the growth rate of X, is described as a random walk, implying that there are permanent changes in the growth rate of X;[1] $ln\ u(t)$ is white noise.

Equation (1') is fitted to the major macroeconomic variables by means of Kalman filters. This is an interesting procedure, but it must be emphasized that the statistical model used to describe each $X(t)$

---

1. Some difficulties with this interpretation were pointed out in the discussion of Meltzer's paper at the conference; the model might instead simply have a random growth rate with constant mean to which it tends to return.

is simply a particular—and particularly simple—hypothesis about the behavior of the variables. Remarkably, there is no simultaneity in the determination of the variables. Nor do the dynamic processes assumed give much room for feedback effects. For instance, as pointed out by Meir Kohn at the conference, the gold standard was supposed to have a strong self-correcting element such that if the price level moved very far from equilibrium, it was likely to return. This would imply, for example,

$$P(t) = a + b(P^* - P(t-1)) + u(t), \qquad (1'')$$

where b is positive, and P^* is some equilibrium price level. Permitting dynamics like equation $(1'')$ makes a potentially large difference to the long-run uncertainty properties of the system.

The fundamental difficulty of the Meltzer presentation is that the risk-uncertainty distinction is being used to distinguish short-run from long-run uncertainty. We should be interested in measures of uncertainty about levels of variables at a variety of future dates. For instance, we would like to know the standard error of forecast for the price level 1 quarter ahead (short-run uncertainty), 12 quarters ahead (medium-run uncertainty), and perhaps 120 quarters ahead (long-run uncertainty). Given an underlying statistical model, we can construct such standard errors. The model may be simultaneous—for instance, a vector autoregressive system—and it may have other bells and whistles of the types that Meltzer uses (Bayesian estimation, permanent and transitory shocks, etc.), but fundamentally we want measures of uncertainty about levels of future variables. For instance, in the case of prices, we should focus on the price level.

Why focus on the price level and not the inflation rate? We do so because the price level determines the real value of nominal obligations entered into over the relevant horizon. Twelve-quarter uncertainty gives a measure of uncertainty about the real terms of nominal labor contracts; 120-quarter uncertainty gives a measure of uncertainty about the real terms of very long nominal bonds.

Let me illustrate with a particularly simple example, close to equation $(1'')$. Suppose

$$X(t) = a + b X(t-1) + u(t), \qquad (2)$$

where $u(t)$ is white noise with variance σ^2_u. Then the 1-period-ahead variance about the forecast, conditional on knowing $X(t-1)$, is σ^2_u. The 120-period-ahead variance is approximately $\sigma^2_u/(1-b^2)$ (see Pindyck and Rubinfeld 1981, pp. 561–62). As mentioned in connection with equation $(1'')$, the value of b significantly affects the relative variances of short- and long-run forecasts. With b close to unity in absolute value, the variance of forecast for the long run is very large; with *b* close to zero, the variance of the long-term forecast is much smaller than for *b* close to one. Despite the attraction and sophistication of Meltzer's forecasting methods, he should give systems with alternative dynamics a chance to generate the types of difference in dynamic uncertainty produced by variations in *b* in equation (2). Parameter uncertainty and learning, adjusted for in the Kalman filter, can also be included.[2]

Now we turn to Meltzer's results. With learning, uncertainty changes over time. Meltzer shows us in his tables the average levels of uncertainty in each of the regimes he distinguishes. In Table 4–2, column 2, we have measures of short-run uncertainty. In terms of uncertainty about real income and prices, the entire post–World War II period is a model of predictability. Perhaps things would be a little worse if the tables were updated to 1984, but it is clear that we are doing much better than in the bad old days before managed money. That overall conclusion is right, but the data problems pointed out by Meltzer must be taken with the utmost seriousness. The quarterly data used for the early regimes are interpolated from annual data, themselves of less reliability than modern data. It is entirely possible that much of the apparently increased certainty in the postwar period is a result of data improvements.[3]

Table 4–3 shows that even long-term uncertainty about both prices and real income is lower than it used to be. Here the caveats about data and the interpretation of the statistical results cast their shadow. It does appear, though, that the gold standard did poorly in creating long-run price stability. The recent period does well—and despite his past criticisms of the Federal Reserve, Meltzer gives credit to the new monetary regime as a source of stability.

There is one difficult but vital problem in the statistical work in this section. Meltzer divides 1890–1980 into six regimes and studies behavior in each, but a key uncertainty about such regimes is how long they can last. A full analysis of forecast errors would have to embody the probabilities that a given monetary regime will end up as another type. Although there are not enough data to construct

2. It is not comforting to realize that the uncertainty measures calculated by Meltzer, which are intended to represent the uncertainty experienced by economic agents under different regimes, rely on data that were not available during those regimes.

3. Romer (1984) presents results suggesting that data construction methods for the unemployment rate in the pre-1930 period are responsible for a large part of the apparently greater stability of the unemployment rate in the postwar period than in the pre-Depression economy. It is not yet known to what extent these results will generalize to other data.

these probabilities, we should recognize that some regimes—e.g., the gold standard—are more likely to end than others.

What Does It All Mean?

Meltzer's arguments and evidence against commodity systems are persuasive. The era of managed money is an unprecedented success—but the current system is not necessarily the best of all possible worlds.

Discussion of monetary rules would be much improved by recognizing that at issue are the location and frequency of decisions on changes in monetary policy. At the moment, the United States and most other countries have a maximum of flexibility. The United States could move to a constitutional amendment prescribing monetary policy, which would be a mistake in the current state of knowledge. Monetary policy could be moved into Congress, as is the case with fiscal policy. That would provide a monetary policy that probably changed relatively infrequently but would provide no assurances that the changes would make sense. Monetary policy could be moved into the Treasury, so that the Secretary of the Treasury could make the decisions. There are no obvious advantages to such a procedure except that the Treasury could no longer blame the Federal Reserve for its difficulties. As risk averters, we should prefer to see monetary and fiscal policy operated by different agencies, reducing the probability that both are poorly chosen at the same time.

There is much to be said for an independent central bank. The alternatives to moving monetary policy decisionmaking away from the Federal Reserve are to strengthen supervision of the Federal Reserve and to give it clearer guidelines for its objectives and decisions. Here the role of congressional committees in demanding accountability is crucial.

One source of evidence that Meltzer surprisingly overlooks is foreign experience. A number of European central banks have done well, even better than the Federal Reserve, in the post–World War II period. Since 1975, Japan has done likewise. Others have done badly. What distinguishes those countries? It is certainly not that some have more firm monetary rules than others. It may well be that the procedures for choosing monetary policymakers differ, as does the degree of independence of the central bank. A plausible hypothesis worth investigating is that the more independent the central bank, the better its performance. It may also be that different societies have different views about the relative costs of inflation and unemployment.

The final issue is that of the assumed desirability of price-level stability. Giving the Federal Reserve a goal of price-level stability—not a zero inflation rate, which permits forgiveness of past price-level changes—gives policy primacy to the goal of long-run price-level predictability. It is quite likely that increasing the long-run predictability of the price level will reduce its short-run predictability as the lags and uncertainties of policymaking become important.

There is no good reason to give monetary policy such a goal. There are few long-term (ten or more years) nominal contracts in any case. If we want to make the real terms of long-term contracts safe, we can instead have the government issue indexed bonds. These will permit private-sector issuers to follow suit. It is far better to have monetary policy focus on producing price-level predictability over the period relevant to most nominal contracts—three months to three years—than to set it the quixotic task of producing long-run price-level stability. There is no need to force the United States economy through the disaster that Britain went through in the 1920s in pursuit of a price level with only mystical significance.

REFERENCES

Hall, Robert E. "Optimal Fiduciary Monetary Systems." *Journal of Monetary Economics* 12 (July 1983), 33–50.

Pindyck, Robert S., and Daniel L. Rubinfeld. *Econometric Models and Economic Forecasts*, 2nd ed. New York: McGraw-Hill, 1981.

Romer, Christina. "Is the Stabilization of the Postwar Economy a Figment of the Data: Evidence from the Unemployment Rate Series." Cambridge: Massachusetts Institute of Technology, 1984.

Taylor, John B. "Estimation and Control of a Macroeconomic Model with Rational Expectations." *Econometrica* 47 (September 1979), 1267–286.

FIVE

The Monetary Regime of the Federal Reserve System

DAVID E. LINDSEY

A USEFUL definition of *monetary regime* is not easy to formulate. The standard concept seems useful only when important features of the overall context of policymaking are assumed away, a practice that subtly constrains economists' thinking about such issues as policy rules versus discretion. Thus, in the next section, I analyze and reject several meanings of the term before settling on the definition I prefer.

What Is a "Monetary Regime"?

The Federal Reserve System, as the central bank of the United States, is responsible for conducting domestic monetary policy. According to my Webster's and American college dictionaries, a regime is "a political system" or "a social system; social order," "a mode or system of rule or government," or "a ruling or prevailing system." The Federal Reserve System qualifies as a governmental system, as its designation makes clear, and its responsibility for monetary policy at first glance seems to justify considering the Federal Reserve as the prevailing monetary regime in the United States.

But this concept of monetary regime is too narrow to encompass the legal and regulatory framework in which monetary policy operates. This is no mere terminological quibble. Congress, the Executive Branch, and the courts are important elements of the overall monetary system. Congress created the Federal Reserve by the Federal Reserve Act, enacted in 1913. Subsequently, it has altered the Fed-

THE VIEWS in the paper are those of the author and not necessarily reflective of those of the Board of Governors or other members of its staff. For incisive comments on an earlier draft, I am grateful to Mendelle T. Berenson, Normand R.V. Bernard, Peter B. Clark, Jared J. Enzler, Edward C. Ettin, Donald L. Kohn, Kenneth J. Kopecky, William Lee, Joan H. Lindsey, David H. Small, Nancy Steele, P.A. Tinsley, and John R. Williams. In addition, Anil K. Kashyap and Michael R. Maryn provided excellent research assistance and Laurel A. Stende and Audrey L. McVean provided superb typing. The remaining errors are my responsibility alone.

eral Reserve's authority and has reshaped the financial system generally through amendments to this act set forth in the Banking Act of 1935, the 1970 amendments to the Bank Holding Company Act, the International Banking Act of 1978, the Full Employment and Balanced Growth Act of 1978, the Depository Institutions Deregulation and Monetary Control Act of 1980, and the Garn–St Germain Depository Institutions Act of 1982. In addition, Congress has specified macroeconomic objectives in the Employment Act of 1946 and later the Full Employment and Balanced Growth Act of 1978.

In making policy in the areas of international finance and debt management, the Treasury has affected key aspects of the U.S. monetary system, as have the other federal financial regulatory agencies, particularly in the areas of deposit insurance, bank supervision, and the specification of permissible deposit rates and types of accounts. Court decisions also have played a role in guiding monetary arrangements.

On the other hand, to identify the Federal Reserve System as the prevailing monetary regime (in the sense of monetary policy regime) would convey a broader meaning of *policy regime* than the definition of the term as used by economists. Robert Lucas (1976) originally identified a *policy* (he did not use the word *regime*) as the particular coefficients of the system of policy reaction functions. These coefficients specify how policy instruments are adjusted systematically to movements in other economic variables. (Lucas allowed the setting of policy instruments to have a purely random component as well.) Following Lucas, economists typically define a *change in policy regime* as a change in the coefficients of the policy reaction functions. Lucas argued that such a discretionary change would alter the way policy instruments affect other economic variables through the role played by expectations.

The observed monetary policy regime in this very narrow sense has undeniably undergone successive changes. Obvious examples are the switch in October 1979 from the federal funds rate to nonborrowed reserves as the operating target for open-market operations, the shift in emphasis in the fall of 1982 from M1 to the broader monetary aggregates as intermediate targets, and the accompanying transition from nonborrowed to borrowed reserves as the operating target.

These changes, however, are best viewed as discretionary procedural adjustments within an overall monetary policy structure that displayed a basic continuity over these years. By contrast, the history of the Federal Reserve System indicates it has experimented with a range of fundamentally different policies, so that we may usefully think of the Federal Reserve as comprising several regimes histori-cally. In Chapter 4, for example, Allan Meltzer identifies four periods during which Federal Reserve policy differed sufficiently to be con-sidered four different regimes.

To refer to the Federal Reserve System as a monetary regime, then, is really to refer to the general structure of policymaking that was followed over a particular period or is likely to be followed. In contrast to a pure gold standard, for example, one salient feature of the present Federal Reserve System is the greater potential for dis-cretionary monetary management. Of course, the authorities them-selves can exercise their potential discretion to varying degrees. Thus, in evaluating the modern Federal Reserve as a more broadly defined regime, one must in practice evaluate both the dominance of author-ities over rules and the actual ways in which the discretion granted the monetary authorities has been used. My primary focus is on the latter aspect of the issue, although my evaluation of different policy procedures has important implications for the fundamental issue of the optimal degree of discretion in monetary policy.

To conduct a systematic analysis of alternative structures for con-ducting monetary policy, therefore, I classify together those specific policies (in Lucas's original sense) that are broadly similar. Each general classification groups together systems of reaction functions with qualitatively similar structures, despite differences among them in the particular values of the reaction coefficients or in the particular functional forms. With a nondiscretionary policy mode, the policy-maker would always stick to a particular system of reaction functions. This particular system would fall within one of the general structural classifications and would constitute a nondiscretionary policy within that general regime.

If the policy mode were discretionary, each classification could be thought of as identifying a separate discretionary policy regime, since each contains only a limited set of discretionary options for choosing among systems of reaction functions of the same structural type. The discretionary switch to a system of reaction functions outside the scope of the prevailing general policy structure would constitute a policy regime change.[1]

1. An alternative way to broaden the concept of policy regime is to identify the behavioral patterns of policymakers that lie behind specific policy changes, that is, to specify the reaction coefficients themselves as functions of their determinants and of the influences that cause those determinants to change over time. The determinants are the underlying preferences of the policymakers, as well as the preferences and behavioral patterns of private economic agents together with the factor endowments, institutional arrangements, and technology that represent the underlying structure

By adopting this concept of policy regime, I do not mean to deny that discretionary actions within the same regime can have Lucas effects on relationships connecting objective variables to policy instruments. Nor do I mean to ignore the practical difficulties the public could face in interpreting discretionary policy changes within the same regime. Nonetheless, looking at policymaking this way suggests that the public's interpretation, as well as economists' research, will be less problematic to the extent that both understand the basic character of the prevailing policy regime and of any significant discretionary moves taken within it.[2]

---

of the economy. This approach would try to describe the metaregime that subsumes specific policies.

Such an approach is, however, flawed, as it simply pushes the problem back one step. The particular coefficients in the expanded system of reaction functions would then represent a particular metaregime, but even these coefficients—and hence the metaregime—would vary over time. Instabilities in parameters certainly would arise in the application of this approach because in practice no empirical specification of the metaregime, even for past periods, could adequately specify those determinants or incorporate all the important influences on them other than random noise.

The flaws of such an approach extend beyond the practical shortcomings of any specific research effort. Policy decisions are made by bodies comprising separate individuals that make decisions by majority rule. Describing a consistent set of preferences for policy bodies is ruled out by the Arrow impossibility theorem. Also, the makeup of the groups changes over time, as do the political and economic ideologies that underlie the views of the members. Further, advances in scientific knowledge may even improve an understanding of how macroeconomic policies affect the economy and induce policymakers to alter their basic behavior patterns. To make matters worse, the underlying structure of the economy is frequently changed by shifting preferences, regulatory reforms to financial and other arrangements, technological innovations, and global shocks. Most fundamentally, some of the major influences on the determinants of Lucas's reaction coefficients in the future are sure to be truly novel and thus (by definition) unforeseeable.

This is another way of saying that even this approach, let alone Lucas's original overall analytic framework, cannot come to grips with the actual context of discretion in policymaking. In Lucas's original framework, a discretionary policy change represents an exogenous jolt to an otherwise constant economic structure—apart from random noise with known properties—which is overlaid by public expectations that the earlier policy regime would be maintained indefinitely. The public then expects the new policy to be permanent. In that context, discretionary actions take on a somewhat artificial or unnatural character. However, this framework ignores the essentials of economic life discussed above. In the more "realistic" context of the previous paragraph, in which Lucas's framework is less appropriate, discretionary policy changes assume a more natural, if not inevitable, character; instead, what seems artificial are assumptions that the economy's underlying structure is fixed and that the public expects the policy regime to remain invariant.

2. Theoretical and econometric policy analysis is not an easy task in this context, as evidenced by the current turmoil in academic macroeconomic thought. If discretionary policy changes for some extended period can be characterized by coefficient

Alternative Monetary Regimes

Table 5-1 shows five types of policy structures that, along with discretionary versus nondiscretionary policy modes, form ten general categories of monetary policy regimes. Because these demarcations reflect a high level of generality, subcategories of each regime would have to be considered for some purposes. Still, the alternative regimes shown seem adequate for present purposes, since the main debates on the desirability of alternative monetary regimes have concerned the pros and cons of moving from one cell to another in this table.

The upper-left cell denotes the class of nondiscretionary simple rules without feedback from other economic variables. This cell encompasses, for example, the classical gold standard and a constant-money-growth rule. The upper-right cell comprises simple rules without regular feedback that are subject to alteration on rare occasion through discretionary action, for example, a change of the specific growth rate or of the definition of money embodied in the constant money growth rule or a devaluation of the domestic currency against gold under a gold standard.

The next row describes simple feedback reaction functions, nondiscretionary versions of which have been proposed by Weintraub (1983), Hall (1984), Meltzer (1984), and McCallum (1984). McCallum, for example, would have the Federal Reserve adjust the growth rate of the monetary base each month or quarter in response to the divergence of the actual level of nominal GNP from a target level. (Presumably, the growth rate would be adjusted in the opposite

---

variations in reaction functions with the same functional form, perhaps these coefficients could be represented econometrically as autoregressive processes, similar to the time-varying coefficient format used by Swamy and Tinsley (1980). One might expect the policy response to measured inflation to be larger, for example, during episodes of high inflation owing to reinforcement by public opinion when the need for restrictive policy is more readily perceived. As a first step, Abrams, Waud, and Froyen (1983) have examined policy reaction rules with purely stochastic coefficients.

Since the Arrow impossibility theorem rules out reaction functions with fixed functional forms as well as fixed coefficients, more significant discretionary moves would have to be characterized as changes in functional forms, not simply variations in coefficient values. The problems created by such changes for econometric methods are obvious. As another approach, Tinsley and von zur Muehlen (1981) have advanced the notion that a consensus will be reached among policy strategies that yield a common distribution of probable outcomes acceptable to a majority of voting members.

Problems of public interpretation of policy changes have been examined by Taylor (1975), B. Friedman (1979), and Cooley, LeRoy, and Raymon (1984).

Table 5–1. Alternative Monetary Policy Regimes

Type of policy structure	Type of policy mode	
	Nondiscretionary	Discretionary
Simple rules without feedback		
Simple feedback rules		
Intermediate nonmonetary targeting with feedback		
Intermediate monetary targeting with feedback		Federal Reserve policy regime since early 1970s
Ultimate targeting with continuous feedback to instruments		

direction by a fixed fraction of the percentage divergence.) The target path for nominal GNP would specify a nominal GNP growth rate of 3 percent annually.

The discretionary version of this general regime is represented by the adjoining cell, in which the constant coefficients used in the simple feedback rules are subject to change, perhaps in response to occasional macroeconomic difficulties. Under McCallum's policy, for example, lags in the impact of policy actions would raise the potential problem of dynamic instability, since monetary base growth would continue to rise even during the early to middle phases of expansion in the business cycle, when nominal GNP rapidly approaches its target level from below.

The third row conveys the class of policy structures in which nonmonetary variables are used by the central bank as intermediate targets and in which feedback rules may be complex. The general targeting approach can be viewed as the successive determination of long-run goals for ultimate targets (such as real GNP, prices, and unemployment); of long-run objectives for the intermediate targets (such as nominal GNP, a nominal interest rate, or a real interest rate); and of short-run settings for the operating instruments (such as the nominal federal funds rate, the discount rate, or some form of reserve aggregate). Gordon (1985), Tobin (1983), and Stein (1982), among others, have advocated nominal GNP as an intermediate target.

Under this policy structure, feedback involves resetting the instruments in response to emerging divergences of the intermediate variables from their long-run objectives, as revealed by direct or inferential evidence from a variety of incoming data. In addition, the intermediate targets are reset, presumably less frequently, as incoming data suggest emerging divergences of the ultimate variables from their goals.

The fourth row represents the use of monetary aggregates as intermediate targets. Again, the feedback rules may be complex.

Any reliance on intermediate targets, whether monetary or nonmonetary, has been criticized as inefficient from the perspective of optimal control by Tinsley (1974), Benjamin Friedman (1975), and Bryant (1980, 1983), among others. These authors argue for dispensing with the intermediate step of the last two structures in favor of continual adjustments to the operating instruments in response to information about movements of the ultimate variables. While data on intermediate variables would provide some of the inferential evidence, no intermediate variable would be interpreted as a surrogate target. The fifth row in Table 5–1 represents this general policy structure. In the last three rows, discretionary variations over time in the coefficients of the feedback rules or their functional forms are incorporated in the cells of the right-hand column.

At the level of generality in the table, the Federal Reserve's policy regime since the early 1970s falls in the cell labeled "discretionary intermediate monetary targeting with feedback." The three-step schema for intermediate targeting described for nonmonetary variables needs to be refined with a further step to represent the Federal Reserve's use of monetary aggregates over this period. Between the determination of long-run (annual) objectives for the intermediate monetary targets and the determination of short-run (weekly to monthly) settings for the operating targets, the Federal Reserve has interposed the determination of shorter-run objectives (originally two-month, then quarterly) for the intermediate monetary aggregate variables.

Following the broad classifications in the table, the two major discretionary shifts by the Federal Reserve in operating procedures in 1979 and 1982, as mentioned, represent switches among subcategories of this general policy regime, involving changes in the functional forms of a certain subset of monetary policy reaction functions as well as changes in the coefficients of at least part of the remaining subset. At the lower level of generality associated with finer structural classifications, these shifts could, of course, be viewed as changes in the monetary policy regime.

Structure of Monetary Policy Implementation

This section discusses in less abstract terms the prevailing structure of Federal Reserve monetary policy implementation and its recent evolution. Three subperiods are delineated.

1970 through October 1979. Over the 1970s, the Federal Reserve gradually strengthened its reliance on monetary aggregates.[3] Step by step, the monetary aggregates—mainly M1 and M2—supplanted interest rates as the primary intermediate targets for monetary policy. In the early 1970s, the Federal Reserve began focusing internally on the growth rates of monetary aggregates as indicators of monetary stimulus or restraint. The Federal Reserve started announcing publicly its desired ranges for annual growth rates for selected monetary aggregates in response to a joint resolution of Congress passed in 1975. Later, Congress legislatively mandated this practice.

The current provisions of the Federal Reserve Act, as amended by the Full Employment and Balanced Growth Act of 1978, require the Board of Governors of the Federal Reserve System to report to the Congress twice each year on the "objectives and plans of the Board of Governors and the Federal Open Market Committee with respect to the ranges of growth or diminution of the monetary and credit aggregates." This section of the act also states that "nothing in this Act shall be interpreted to require that the objectives and plans [for the monetary and credit aggregates] . . . be achieved if the Board of Governors and the Federal Open Market Committee determine that they cannot or should not be achieved because of changing conditions . . . provided . . . the Board of Governors shall include an explanation of the reasons for any revisions to or deviations from such objectives and plans."

The reports to Congress are made in February and July. In July of each year, tentative ranges for money and credit aggregates are announced for the subsequent year. These ranges are reaffirmed or revised in the following February and July reports, in light of a review of the behavior of the monetary and credit aggregates in the period just past in relation to previously announced objectives and to the

3. Space constraints prevent a thorough analysis here of the interplay of economic developments, emerging schools of competing macroeconomic thought, and the evolution of monetary policy regimes even over this relatively short period, let alone a longer one. Some of these interactions are discussed in Lindsey (1983a). A different perspective is offered by Brunner (1983).

evolving economic and financial conditions that influenced attainment of these objectives and their appropriateness.

The reports also show associated ranges of projections by members of the Federal Open Market Committee of growth rates in nominal GNP, real GNP, and prices and of the unemployment rate one to two years ahead that they believe are consistent with the announced ranges for money and credit and with the prospective stance of fiscal policy. The plans for the monetary and credit aggregates are also related, as required by law, to the administration's short-term economic goals.

Table 5–2 shows the initial ranges from March 1975 through March 1976 and subsequent ranges from the fourth quarter to the fourth quarter for money and credit through 1985, together with the observed outcomes.[4] The Federal Reserve's record in attaining the announced annual ranges for M1 and M2 from 1976 to 1979 was somewhat mixed. The ranges for the calendar year also are shown by the lines in Figure 5–1 and the actual growth rates of M1 and M2 are shown by X's, using the definitions of these aggregates in force during these years. Over each of these calendar years, only one of the aggregates grew within its range, while the other exceeded its upper bound. In addition, M1 exceeded its upper limit during the first three quarters of 1979.

For most of the decade, the Federal Reserve relied on the federal funds rate—the interest rate that banks charge one another on overnight loans of reserves—as its operating target in attempting to attain its monetary objectives. When money growth was faster than desired, the Federal Open Market Committee raised its operating range for the funds rate, shown by the solid bands in the bottom panel of Figure 5–1. The committee lowered the range when money growth was undesirably weak. The trading desk at the Federal Reserve Bank of New York altered the supply of nonborrowed reserves relative to demand to keep the actual funds rate, shown by the crosses, generally within the operating range.

Through these procedures, the Federal Reserve sought to influence directly the quantity of money demanded by the public. It tried to select a level of the funds rate that would make the public want to hold an amount of money equal to the targeted value. When the trading desk raised the funds rate, other short-term interest rates tended to rise in sympathy. The public then found market instruments more attractive relative to money balances, which were subject

4. Before the establishment of the annual growth rate ranges for 1978:4 to 1979:4, the ranges were reset each quarter for the subsequent four-quarter period.

Figure 5–1

Adopted Ranges and Actual Growth Rates for M1 (currency and demand deposits), 1976-1979

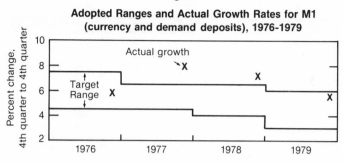

Adopted Ranges and Actual Growth Rates for M2 (M1 plus savings and small time deposits at commercial banks), 1976-1979

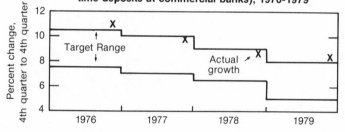

Short-run Tolerance Ranges and Actual Levels of Federal Funds Rate

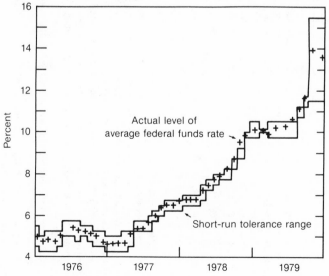

Table 5–2. Longer-run Growth Rate Ranges Adopted for the Monetary and Credit Aggregates; annual rates and percentages

Period	M1		M2		M3		Bank credit or domestic nonfinancial debt[a]	
	Range adopted	Actual	Range adopted	Actual	Range adopted	Actual	Range adopted	Actual
March 1975–March 1976	5 –7½	5.3	8½–10½	9.7	10 –12	12.3	6½– 9½	3.2
1975:4–1976:4	4½–7½	5.8	7½–10½	10.9	9 –12	12.7	6½– 9½	4.3
1976:4–1977:4	4½–6½	7.9	7 –10	9.8	8½–11½	11.7	7 –10	11.1
1977:4–1978:4	4 –6½	7.2	6½– 9	8.7	7½–10½	9.5	7 –10	13.5
1978:4–1979:4[b]	3 –6	5.5	5 – 8	8.3	6 – 9	8.1	7½–10½	12.3
1979:4–1980:4[c]	4 –6½	7.3[d,e]	6 – 9	9.6	6½– 9½	10.2	6 – 9	8.0
1980:4–1981:4	3½–6	2.3[d,f]	6 – 9	9.5	6½– 9½	11.4	6 – 9	8.8[g]
1981:4–1982:4	2½–5½	8.5[d]	6 – 9	9.2	6½– 9½	10.1	6 – 9[h]	7.1[g]
1982:4–1983:4	5 –9[i]	7.2	7 –10[j]	8.3	6½– 9½	9.7	8½–11½	10.5
1983:4–1984:4[k]	4 –8		6 – 9		6 – 9		8 –11	
1984:4–1985:4[l]	4 –7		6 – 8½		6 – 9		8 –11	

[a]Until 1983, ranges are for bank credit; afterward ranges are for domestic nonfinancial sector debt. Before 1977, the bank credit proxy was used as the measure for bank credit.

[b]At the February 1979 meeting, the FOMC adopted a range for M1 for 1978:4 to 1979:4 of 1½ to 4½ percent. This range anticipated that shifting to ATS and NOW accounts in New York State would slow M1 growth by 3 percentage points. At the October meeting, it was noted that such shifts would reduce M1 growth by no more than 1½ percentage points. Thus the longer-run range for M1 was modified to 3–6 percent.

[c]Adopted at the February 1980 meeting, when the monetary aggregates on which these targets were based were redefined and new target ranges adopted.

[d]The figures shown reflect target and actual growth of M1-B in 1980 and of shift-adjusted M1-B in 1981. M1-B was relabeled M1 in January 1982. The targeted growth for M1-A was 3½ to 6 percent in 1980 (actual growth was 5.0 percent); in 1981 targeted growth for shift-adjusted M1-A was 3 to 5½ percent (actual growth was 1.3 percent).

ᵉWhen these ranges were set, shifts into other checkable deposits in 1980 were expected to have only a limited effect on growth of M1-A and M1-B. As the year progressed, however, banks offered other checkable deposits more actively, and more funds than expected were directed to these accounts. Such shifts are estimated to have decreased M1-A growth and increased M1-B growth each by at least ½ percentage point more than had been anticipated.

ᶠAdjusted for the effects of shifts out of demand deposits and savings deposits into other checkable deposits. At the February FOMC meeting, the target ranges for observed M1-A and M1-B in 1981 on an unadjusted basis, expected to be consistent with the adjusted ranges, were −4½ to −2 and 6 to 8½ percent, respectively. Actual M1-B growth (not shift adjusted) was 5.0 percent.

ᵍAdjusted for shifts of assets from domestic banking offices to international banking facilities.

ʰRange for bank credit is annual growth from the December 1981–January 1982 average level through the fourth quarter of 1982.

ⁱBase period, adopted at the July 1983 FOMC meeting, is 1983:2. At the February 1983 meeting, the FOMC had adopted a target range for 1982:4 to 1983:4 for M1 of 4 to 8 percent.

ʲBase period is the February–March 1983 average.

ᵏAdopted at the February 1984 meeting.

ˡTentatively adopted at the July 1984 meeting.

179

to interest-rate ceilings or outright prohibitions on the payment of interest. The resulting transfer of funds from monetary to other financial assets was reflected in a reduced stock of money. Over time, as well, the higher interest rates and accompanying tighter credit conditions tended to damp spending and hence transaction demands for money. In practice, when money demand strengthened, the committee did not always alter the funds rate promptly enough or sufficiently to keep monetary aggregates consistently within their ranges, even over the longer run.

October 1979 through the Fall of 1982. On October 6, 1979, facing above-target monetary expansion, worsening inflation, and their consequences in domestic and international financial markets, and dissatisfied with the old procedures, the Federal Reserve switched its operating target from the federal funds rate to nonborrowed reserves as a sign of its commitment to longer-run restraint on money growth.[5] The Board of Governors of the Federal Reserve System (1979) announced that it had switched procedures "to support the objective of containing growth in the monetary aggregates [by] . . . placing greater emphasis on the supply of bank reserves and less emphasis on confining short-term fluctuations in the Federal funds rate."

Holding to a nonborrowed reserves target path essentially gives the short-run money supply curve a positive slope (when the stock of money is on the horizontal axis and the interest rate is on the vertical axis). The curve is positively sloped mainly because an increase in short-term interest rates relative to the discount rate induces depository institutions to increase their borrowing at the discount window. With nonborrowed reserves fixed, total reserves will be higher, and hence the stock of reservable deposits that can be supported by the outstanding nonborrowed reserves will be larger.

The increase in borrowing induced by a given rise in short-term interest rates has a limit though, because depository institutions are expected not to make repeated or continuous use of the discount facility for adjustment credit under normal circumstances. Thus banks experience some rising implicit cost to added use of the discount window as they anticipate more administrative pressure to adjust reserve positions in some other way. Banks will increase their borrowing until the implicit cost on the last dollar of discount borrowings has risen by an amount equal to the initial change in market interest

5. For a more detailed discussion of the issues in this subsection, see Lindsey (1982b, 1983b).

rates. In equilibrium, the marginal cost to a bank on each of its managed liabilities is equalized, including the sum of the explicit discount rate and the implicit marginal cost of discount window borrowing.

A nonborrowed reserves operating target, therefore, provides an automatic self-correcting mechanism acting partially to resist divergences of the money stock from its targeted value that could be mimicked only through judgmental adjustments under a federal funds rate guide. Under the nonborrowed reserves procedure, a rightward shift of the nominal money demand curve—owing to an increase in real income, a rise in the price level, or a positive random disturbance—will be partially checked by the induced rise in short-term interest rates.

Figure 5–2 shows how this automatic mechanism worked during the three years after October 1979. The top two panels indicate monthly levels of M2 and M1 relative to the upper and lower bounds of their annual ranges. A strengthening of money relative to target raised required reserves. Since nonborrowed reserves were held to a fixed path by the trading desk, reserve positions of depository institutions were automatically tightened as institutions in the aggregate were forced to borrow the extra reserves at the discount window. These adjustment plus seasonal borrowings are shown in the third panel.

Institutions were induced to borrow additional reserves at the window only after they had first attempted to acquire the needed reserves from other institutions. In doing so, they bid up the federal funds rate relative to the discount rate. This response of the funds rate may be seen in the bottom panel. Higher short-term interest rates in turn encouraged depository institutions and the public to make secondary adjustments to balance sheets that curtailed deposit expansion and helped to bring money back to path. This process occurred automatically in the absence of additional deliberate actions by the Federal Reserve. However, the Federal Reserve also frequently opted to amplify these automatic effects. For example, in the case of a monetary overshoot, it might have lowered the nonborrowed reserves target or raised the discount rate.

From October 1979 to the fall of 1982, divergences of money, especially M1, from long-run targets were closely associated with changes in borrowed reserves and the federal funds rate in the same direction. Such variations in short-term interest rates were part and parcel of the process that returned money to longer-run objectives over time in the face of divergences. Figure 5–3 indicates that for

Figure 5—2

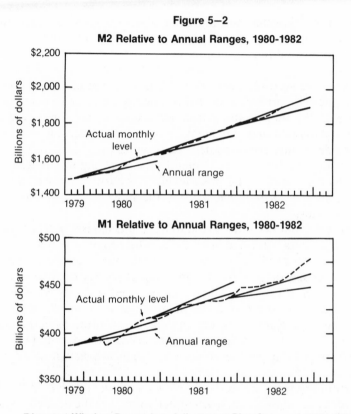

M2 Relative to Annual Ranges, 1980-1982

Actual monthly level

Annual range

M1 Relative to Annual Ranges, 1980-1982

Actual monthly level

Annual range

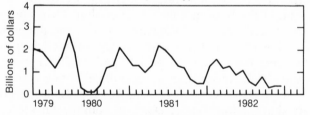

Discount Window Borrowing, Adjustment Plus Seasonal, 1979-1982
(monthly)

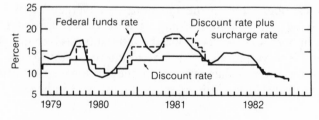

Federal Funds Rate and Discount Rate, 1979-1982
(monthly)

Federal funds rate

Discount rate plus surcharge rate

Discount rate

182

those three years the nonborrowed reserves operating procedures permitted short-term interest rates to move over a much wider range in the intermediate run than under the previous procedures.

Over those three years the Federal Reserve slowed the trend rate of money growth, and while real economic activity stagnated and unemployment rose to a postwar record, the rate of inflation essentially was halved. But as monetarist critics noted, money growth as well as interest rates showed more intermediate-term variability. What explains this behavior? That money and interest rates moved in the same direction establishes a prima facie case that the demand curve varied over a wider range than the supply curve did. Moreover, there is evidence that the Federal Reserve in fact confronted a more unpredictable demand for money after the inception of the new procedures.

Consider the forecasting performance of the equation for M1 demand then used in the Board's quarterly econometric model, shown in Figure 5–4. This standard equation, fit from the early 1950s through 1974:2, treats M1 demand as determined by real income, the price level, and interest rates. The figure shows this equation's dynamic simulation errors in predicting the quarterly growth, at an annual rate, of actual M1—the solid line—and an M1 measure that abstracts from the estimated impact of the authorization of new types of deposits—the dotted line. In the three years after 1979:3, these errors jumped noticeably in absolute value relative to earlier experience. This as well as other money demand functions had shown a deterioration in the mid-1970s, but the absolute errors in the later period generally were larger still.

The greater instability in the demand for M1 seemed to have causes other than the switch in operating procedures itself.[6] The errors in the second and third quarters of 1980, and the movements in the income scale variable over those quarters, accompanied the imposition in March 1980 of the credit control program (part of a broader antiinflationary program of the Carter administration) and its subsequent removal in July of that year. At the start of 1981, negotiable order of withdrawal accounts (NOWs) were authorized nationwide, boosting actual M1 demand. Working in the other direction, cash

---

6. Walsh (1984) presents a theoretical argument suggesting that the policy change itself induced a reduction in the interest elasticity of money demand (and hence the appearance of larger intercept errors in postsample simulations of money demand equations fit to previous data). The problem with this explanation is that, as discussed later, a larger, not smaller, interest elasticity of money demand than in standard equations is needed to reduce the observed residual errors over this period, especially in 1982.

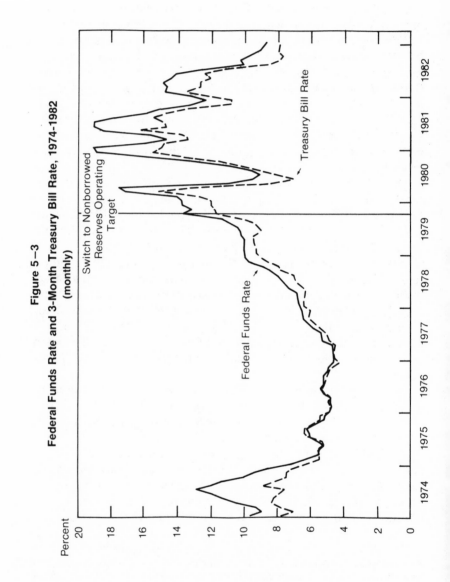

Figure 5–3

Federal Funds Rate and 3-Month Treasury Bill Rate, 1974-1982 (monthly)

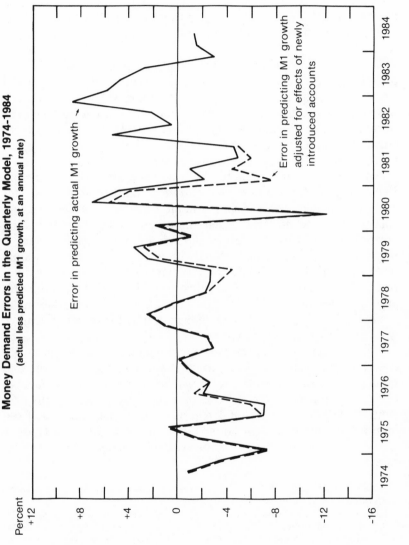

Figure 5–4

Money Demand Errors in the Quarterly Model, 1974-1984
(actual less predicted M1 growth, at an annual rate)

Error in predicting actual M1 growth

Error in predicting M1 growth adjusted for effects of newly introduced accounts

Note: Based on dynamic simulation of the old standard M1 equation in the Federal Reserve Board's quarterly econometric model.

management techniques evidently spread to medium-sized corporations, and some demand depositors also shifted into money market mutual funds. As in the mid-1970s, the high market interest rates that accompanied high rates of inflation prompted money holders to economize on conventional checking account balances subject to interest-rate ceilings, and prompted Congress and the financial regulatory agencies to allow the creation of new accounts paying higher returns.

In 1982, the recession heightened public uncertainties about income prospects, and precautionary motives apparently swelled the demand for M1.[7] In addition, the growth of fixed-ceiling NOWs had evidently raised the interest elasticity of M1 demand, as discussed later; the sizeable declines in rates in the second half of the year began to engender a larger increase in desired money holdings than suggested by conventional money demand functions.

Given the greater instability of M1 demand over the period from 1979:3 to 1982:3, the observed variations in short-term interest rates cannot be blamed on loose short-run monetary control. Interest rate variations would not have been smoothed merely by eliminating erratic growth in total reserves and money, that is, introducing a vertical money supply curve along with the well-known institutional reforms needed to stabilize the position of the curve given total reserves.[8] In that case, interest rates would have become more volatile because the partial short-run accommodation to variations in demands for reserves and money permitted by the discount window would no longer have been available.

Under a nonborrowed reserves operating target, the discount window provided some elasticity to the supply of total reserves and money. This supply elasticity softened the interest rate consequences of shifting demands for reserves and money. By contrast, with rigid control of the supply of total reserves and money on, say, fixed month-to-month paths, variation in demands for reserves and money would have been reflected in more sizeable changes in the interest rate.[9]

7. This partial explanation for the behavior of money demand in 1982 also has been offered by M. Friedman (1983).

8. Lindsey (1982a) discusses a variety of such regulatory changes.

9. The implications for short-term interest rate volatility of attempts to restore M1 more rapidly to the long-run target following divergences from target under nonborrowed reserves versus total reserves operating targets, under the institutional structure prevailing at the time, are explored by Tinsley, von zur Muehlen, and Fries (1982). For the consequences for interest rate volatility of either operating target under alternative institutional arrangements that provide for tighter monetary control, see Tinsley et al. (1982).

The Federal Reserve dealt with disturbances to money demand by adjusting the announced ranges or by permitting the disturbances, in varying degrees, to show through in actual money growth relative to the ranges. In February 1981, for example, the Federal Reserve took account of nationwide NOWs by introducing a range for a "shift-adjusted" M1 (M1 was called M1-B at the time) that was 2.5 percentage points below the range for actual M1. Staff estimates from surveys and cross-sectional regression analysis indicated that M1 growth for the year was boosted 2.7 percentage points by shifts of funds from non-M1 sources into regular NOWs. However, not all the downward movement in underlying M1 demand, shown by the dashed lines in Figure 5–4, was foreseen when the ranges were constructed. The unexpected portion of this demand shift, which approximately neutralized the impact of NOW accounts, also was accommodated, and the 5 percent growth in actual M1 for the year was about at the midpoint of the 3.5 to 6 percent shift-adjusted range.

In the first quarter of 1982, the error reversed dramatically, as M1 growth surged while short-term interest rates moved up and nominal GNP declined. Again in the fourth quarter, this model substantially underpredicted M1 growth, the first of a string of such underpredictions that carried into 1983. For 1982 as a whole, M1 growth substantially exceeded its upper bound, while the measured velocity of M1 posted a nearly 6 percent decline, unprecedented in the postwar period.

The Fall of 1982 to the Present. During October 1982, interpretation of M1 movements was complicated further by the nearly $35 billion of all savers' certificates scheduled to mature, a portion of which was likely to be placed, at least temporarily, in M1.[10] In addition, Congress had just authorized, effective in mid-December, the money market deposit account (MMDA). This ceiling-free account had limited transaction features and could be expected to attract M1 deposits into M2, though in uncertain amounts. In light of these circumstances, Chairman Volcker announced on October 9 that for the time being the committee was placing reduced emphasis on M1 as a guide to policy relative to broader monetary aggregates.

Under these alternative institutional arrangements that help to stabilize the money supply function, using total reserves as the operating target produces closer short-run control over M1 than does using the monetary base, owing to the effects of shocks to currency demand, in simulations of the board monthly model with historical errors reported in Lindsey et al. (1981).

10. This period is discussed in more detail in Simpson (1984).

Subsequently, the Depository Institutions Deregulation Committee authorized the super NOW account, effective in early 1983. These were NOW accounts with balances larger than $2,500 not subject to a rate ceiling. These accounts could be expected to pull funds into M1 from sources outside M1, although again in an unpredictable magnitude. Within a month of their introduction, super NOWs totaled $20 billion.

The initial shift of funds into MMDAs was even more phenomenal: those accounts had attracted more than $250 billion by early February 1983. As Figure 5–5 shows, in February 1983 the committee chose a February and March 1983 average as the base for the M2 range that year to get past the initial bulge in that aggregate. Minimal impacts were expected on M3 growth for the year, as depository institutions were thought likely to reduce their reliance on large CDs in response to the influx of core deposits.

Estimates by the board's staff based on survey and econometric evidence of the impact on M1 of flows of funds into MMDAs from M1 accounts and into super NOWs from outside M1 suggested sizeable gross effects—on the order of $11 billion in each case over the year. But the two effects were approximately offsetting, so there was apparently little net impact. Nonetheless, the demand for M1 remained strong through the first half of 1983. The conventional demand equation depicted in Figure 5–4 again yielded sizeable underpredictions, and M1 velocity did not rebound in typical cyclical fashion during the recovery. In July, the committee rebased the monitoring range for M1 to 1983:2 and raised the growth bands 1 percentage point.

The strength in M1 growth in the first half of 1983 continued to be concentrated in checkable accounts other than demand deposits and can be attributed mainly to lagged effects of earlier declines in short-term interest rates interacting with an altered demand for M1 function. As noted, the growth of fixed-ceiling NOW accounts made the other checkable deposit component, and M1 as a whole, more elastic with respect to market interest rates than was true of demand deposits or currency. After all, using hypothetical figures, a fall in short-term market rates from 15 percent to 10 percent represents a decline of one-third in the marginal opportunity cost of holding a demand deposit (even one paying a positive average implicit return via services independent of account size).

By contrast, the marginal opportunity cost of holding a NOW account paying a 5 percent explicit rate of return is reduced by one-half. A new equation for the demand for M1 developed by Brayton, Farr, and Porter (1983) incorporates these and other features, including interest rate spread elasticities that rise with higher spreads and

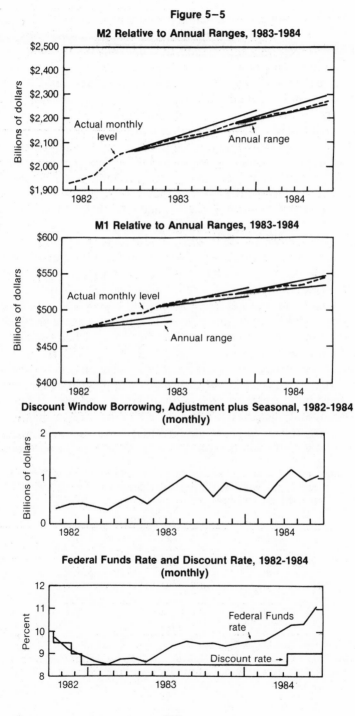

Figure 5-5

M2 Relative to Annual Ranges, 1983-1984

M1 Relative to Annual Ranges, 1983-1984

Discount Window Borrowing, Adjustment plus Seasonal, 1982-1984 (monthly)

Federal Funds Rate and Discount Rate, 1982-1984 (monthly)

189

a term that captures the availability of certain accounts. This equation does not go so far astray as the conventional equation in postsample simulation over the entire 1982 through mid-1983 period, though sizeable errors for individual quarters remain.[11]

During the second half of 1983 and so far in 1984, the predictability of M1 demand has improved, especially as judged by the Brayton, Farr, and Porter equation. At the same time, the velocity of M1 has returned to patterns more consistent with historical experience. In February 1984, the committee announced a 1984 target range for M1, with qualifications, as opposed to the monitoring range in 1983, and in July, the committee indicated that roughly equal weight would be placed on each of the three monetary aggregates.

The July 1984 report to Congress and Chairman Volcker's accompanying testimony regarding plans for the monetary aggregates emphasized, however, that "appraisals of their movements, and relationships among them, will continue to be judged in the light of developments in economic activity, inflationary pressures, financial market conditions, and the rate of credit growth" (Volcker 1984, p. 634). Chairman Volcker had made clear a year and a half earlier that policy reactions to movements in monetary aggregates relative to their ranges were to be more flexible than they had been over the previous three years, with the context of overall economic and financial developments allotted a larger role. As he put it in his testimony of February 16, 1983: "I neither bewail nor applaud the circumstances that have put a greater premium on judgment and less 'automaticity' in our operations; they are simply a fact of life. In making such judgments, the basic point remains that, over time, the growth of money and credit will need to be reduced to encourage a return to

11. Recent refinements of the equation are described in Brayton (1984). With the refined equation, the equation's errors for quarterly growth rates for M1 are as follows (expressed at an annual rate, in percentages):

	Quarter			
Year	1	2	3	4
1979	n.a.	n.a.	n.a.	−1.6
1980	3.8	−9.0	5.7	−1.6
1981	−5.8	2.3	−1.8	−5.3
1982	1.5	−3.8	−0.1	7.0
1983	1.5	1.4	2.5	−1.7
1984	−0.1	−0.7	n.a.	n.a.

Note, however, that for 1983 the equation has a term that adjusts for the availability of super NOWs but not for the introduction of MMDAs, which biases the M1 growth errors downward, especially in the first two quarters of the year.

reasonable price stability. The targets set out are consistent with that intent" (p. 174).

The deemphasis of M1 in the fall of 1982, together with the more flexible strategy that followed regarding the monetary aggregates more generally, was mirrored by a shift in operating procedures. A nonborrowed reserves operating target is not well suited for controlling M2 and M3 because the vast bulk of their nontransaction components are not subject to reserve requirements. Beyond transaction deposits, which are subject to a 12 percent reserve requirement, the only other reservable component of the broader aggregates under the new reserve requirement structure of the Monetary Control Act of 1980 comprises certain nonpersonal time deposits subject to a 3 percent requirement.[12] Thus, the nonborrowed reserves operating procedure, with its automaticity deriving mainly from variations in required reserves on transaction deposits, has to be modified if M1 is dethroned as the primary intermediate monetary target (or if a more judgmental approach is taken in reacting to M1 movements).

Governor Wallich has explained that the Federal Reserve did not return to a federal funds rate operating target: "Since the fall of 1982, the nonborrowed reserve strategy and its automaticity have given way to a technique that allows the funds rate to be determined by the market, through the targeting of discount window borrowing from one reserve maintenance period to the next, implemented by allowing a flexible nonborrowed reserves path."[13] Over longer periods, "the degree of restraint on reserve positions," as reflected in the level of adjustment plus seasonal borrowings at the discount window, has been altered more judgmentally in response to movements in monetary aggregates relative to short-term objectives against the background of other economic and financial developments.

As Figure 5–5 indicates, this shift in operating procedures has weakened the earlier monthly correspondence between movements in monetary aggregates relative to their ranges, on the one hand, and in discount borrowings and the federal funds rate, on the other (although the correlation between borrowings and the spread of the funds rate over the discount rate in the relatively low-frequency

12. After a transitional period of nearly four years, the old structure of reserve requirements on member bank savings and time deposits was fully phased out, and the new structure for members fully phased in, on February 2, 1984. At the same time essentially contemporaneous reserve requirements were introduced, but only on transaction deposits.

13. See Wallich (1984, p. 26). This article provides a detailed description of the operating procedures used since the fall of 1982, as well as their relation to contemporaneous reserve requirements.

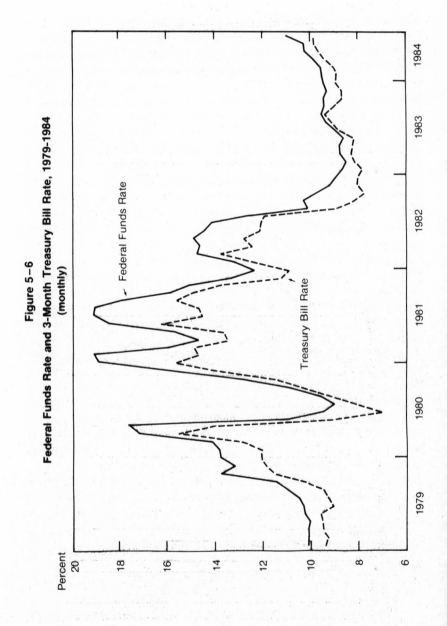

Figure 5-6

Federal Funds Rate and 3-Month Treasury Bill Rate, 1979-1984

(monthly)

Federal Funds Rate

Treasury Bill Rate

Percent

observations in the chart is apparent). More basic to the lessening in intermediate-term fluctuations in borrowings and the funds rate since mid-1983 is the fact that, with the demand for money more stable and the economy at large performing well, M1 and M2 generally have remained within their long-run ranges. (In contrast, M3 has run above its upper limits, reflecting the financing of strong credit growth at depository institutions, which was buoyed at commercial banks this year in part by a spate of large oil-related mergers and leveraged-buyout activity.)

For these reasons, as Figure 5–6 shows, short-term interest rates since the fall of 1982 have displayed a much smoother pattern than they did during the previous three-year period. Rounding out the economic picture since the fall of 1982, real economic activity and employment have rebounded strongly, while inflation has been subdued. However, problems have emerged regarding one large bank, along with heightened market sensitivity about loans to developing countries by other large domestic and foreign banks. Fiscal policy has remained very stimulative, and accompanying the federal government's Brobdingnagian appetite for credit, real interest rates have been historically high. At the same time, a strengthening international value of the dollar has contributed to the emergence of a record current account deficit.

Analytic Underpinnings and Evaluation of the Prevailing Monetary Regime

The analytic underpinnings of the monetary regime of the Federal Reserve System since the early 1970s can be brought out through a comparison with a simple money growth rule, and in my view the prevailing regime compares favorably.

A Fixed Money Growth Rule. Evaluation of any alternative monetary regime rests on two basic questions: Does it provide a reliable long-run anchor for nominal macroeconomic magnitudes? Does it provide reasonable shorter-run stability for nominal and real macroeconomic variables? A nondiscretionary rule for domestic money growth gets high marks on both counts, according to its advocates. In fact, old-line monetarists such as Milton Friedman have argued that the two criteria are inextricably linked, in that satisfying the first will contribute to satisfying the second. Newer-vintage monetarists of the rational expectations school could argue that because the public would catch on to any nondiscretionary policy regime that is permanently maintained, satisfaction of the first criterion through a simple money growth rule is a sufficient, though not a necessary, condition for satisfaction of the second. In fact, some have asserted that precommitment to a simple rule, by helping to anchor not only actual prices but also expectations about policy as well as prices, will mitigate short-run departures in real variables from their "natural" levels.

Clearly, the argument that a reasonably predictable trend for the average price level, ideally near zero, will by itself contribute to improving real economic performance is unexceptional. Even so, I see a distinct tension between the two criteria since I am not persuaded that a regime designed to satisfy one of the criteria will necessarily meet the other. The money growth rule is a good case in point.

A money growth rule of, say, 3 percent annual growth of M1 would satisfy fairly well the criterion of anchoring nominal economic magnitudes over the long run. To put perhaps too fine a point on it, I will quantify my subjective judgment. If this policy were maintained for two decades, starting from initial conditions in the U.S. economy of 1 percent per year inflation and real GNP at its potential level, the rate of change in the GNP deflator over the twenty years could be expected to average between -1 and $+3$ percent per year with, say, a 70 percent probability, and between -3 and $+5$ percent with a 95 percent probability.

These ranges allow for some uncertainty about future trends of potential real GNP growth, fiscal policy and the "natural" real rate of interest, elasticities of M1 demand with respect to real income and nominal interest rates, and financial innovations affecting M1 demand. (The ranges assume that any new financial instrument with a measured turnover rate above some prespecified cutoff is simply added to the definition of M1.) The ranges also incorporate some likelihood that essentially one-time effects on the equilibrium price level associated with any external "supply shocks" will not approximately cancel out over the entire period.[14]

Despite minor quibbles about my figures, many economists would not consider my assessment of the odds on the twenty-year outcome for average inflation under this rule to be especially controversial (although some might find the tails of the ranges troubling to the case for the rule). Such a consensus would testify to the widespread

14. Even monetarists have conceded that the oil-price shocks raised the equilibrium level of prices given the stock of money, since U.S. wealth in effect was transferred to OPEC states and thus potential real GNP fell (e.g., Mayer 1975).

acceptance of the quantity theory of money as a long-run proposition. In this regard, the monetarist counterrevolution has prevailed.

The consensus would break down, however, with respect to the shorter-run behavior of nominal and real variables under a strict monetary rule. The view that macroeconomic cycles could well be troublesome, even given the initial conditions of my twenty-year thought experiment, is not uncommon. This concern, which I share, represents one holdover from the original Keynesian revolution.

The problem of short- and intermediate-run macroeconomic instability under a simple monetary rule is the decisive consideration justifying feedback and discretion in policymaking. At the same time, the long-run anchor to nominal values could be perceived as being less assured under more flexible policy regimes, exemplifying the tension noted between the two criteria.

I have several reasons for my concern about shorter-run macroeconomic instability under a monetary rule. First of all, the historical correlation between current and lagged growth in the money stock and current growth in nominal GNP is not all that close in the short run. Even before 1982, only about half of the quarterly variance in nominal GNP growth since 1960 could be accounted for by St. Louis-type reduced-form equation estimates, which also included a fiscal policy variable (Simpson 1979). In 1982 and 1983, such equations performed quite poorly (Axilrod 1984; Simpson 1984).

I consider even these statistical relationships to be a weak reed on which to assess likely relationships under a monetary rule, only in part because the Lucas effect of a regime change might result. (A simple example of this effect, in the context of a Barro-type model with unanticipated money shocks disturbing real variables, is given by Sachs 1982.)[15] A more important problem is that the money stock has had an endogenous component in the short run, even with intermediate monetary targeting. As a consequence, an element of spurious correlation between money and GNP that masquerades as a causal relationship has been introduced into historical data. Various aspects of this phenomenon have been analyzed by Tobin (1970), Cagan (1965), Temin (1976), Blinder and Goldfeld (1972), Lindsey (1982b), Litterman and Weiss (1983), Sims (1980, 1982, 1983), and McCallum (1983).

One of these aspects is that to the extent Federal Reserve operations historically have had the effect of smoothing interest rate movements in the short run, positive shocks to spending would have

---

15. Sachs appears to have real rather than nominal income in mind.

shown up in the data not only as an increase in GNP but also as a contemporaneous accommodating increase in the observed quantity of money. If money had been held fixed, by contrast, GNP would have risen less since interest rates would have gone up more, but money would not have changed at all, eliminating this source of correlation. (With a positive shock to money demand, GNP would remain unchanged if the increased demand were fully matched by an accommodating increase in the money supply, leaving interest rates unchanged, while GNP would fall if money were held fixed. No contemporaneous correlation is induced in either of these extreme cases.)

Moreover, the lag in the historical data going from movements in money to movements in GNP is also partly a statistical artifact of historical money endogeneity. The observed lagged relation evidently reflects in part the influence of movements in interest rates on both GNP and money, with the mean lag for the quantity of money demanded historically shorter than that for spending. This is the conclusion of the second generation of causality tests conducted by Litterman and Weiss (1983) and by Sims (1980, 1982, 1983). Including lagged interest rates in estimated vector autoregressions for GNP usurps explanatory power from lagged values of the money stock (cf. McCallum 1983).

Apart from the spurious causation reflected in historical data, certain known causal patterns bring into question the short-run stability of nominal and real GNP under a monetary rule. Empirical evidence strongly suggests that the quantity of money demanded is responsive to nominal interest rates. When money growth is fixed, shocks to spending or to inflation expectations that alter nominal interest rates will show up in part as variations in the velocity of money and hence nominal GNP, even if the money demand function is perfectly stable.

Moreover, lags in the responsiveness of spending or money demand to interest rates and income will produce cycles in nominal and real GNP that would not occur if money demand were totally insensitive to interest rate movements (although interest rate cycles could be severe). As a thought experiment confined to the interaction of the IS (spending) and LM (monetary) sectors of the economy, assume that potential real GNP is fixed, and for the time being, assume also that both actual and expected inflation are always equal to their steady-state values and to the fixed rate of money growth. Then short-run changes in nominal interest rates will equal changes in real interest rates, which, in standard IS equations, affect real aggregate demand with a distributed lag.

Consider a permanent downward shock to real spending. With real income initially lower, the quantity of money demanded can be maintained on the fixed-growth path only by a sharp fall in interest rates; because short-run interest elasticities are smaller than long-run elasticities, interest rates will fall well below their new, lower steady-state level. Even though interest rates subsequently will rise as output gradually recovers in response to the initial drop in interest rates, the cumulative effects on real spending of initial interest rates that are below steady-state values could cause output next to over-shoot its steady-state level. Interest rates must then rise above their steady-state value to keep the quantity of money demanded in line with the money supply track, owing to the stimulation of the quantity of money demanded coming from the lagged impact of the initially low interest rates and, increasingly over time, to the higher than steady-state level of real GNP. Afterward, real output could be pushed below its steady-state level and the process could begin again.

Enzler and Johnson (1981) examined this case by simulating a simple IS–LM model. Given a range of plausible spending and money demand elasticities and lag structures, a permanent shock to real aggregate demand gives rise to oscillating cycles of real GNP, damped or undamped depending on particular coefficient values, of some three to five years in duration.

Now append to this conventional IS–LM structure a Lucas-type aggregate supply function (or inflation-adjusted Phillips curve) in which the gap between actual and potential real GNP (or the gap between the natural and the actual rate of unemployment) is positively related to the deviation between the actual and the expected rates of inflation. Further assume a simple adaptive-expectations mechanism in which the expected rate of inflation in the current year equals the observed rate last year. The change in the rate of inflation from one year to the next is then a negative function of the size of the output gap (and of the deviation between the natural and the actual unemployment rate).

This mechanism is consistent with a renormalization of the familiar Milton Friedman (1968)–Edmund Phelps (1972) accelerationist theory of the determination of price (and wage) behavior, in which a slower rise in prices (and wages) each year is associated with output below potential GNP (or unemployment above the natural rate). When account is also taken of identifiable special factors, such as wage and price controls and oil-price shocks, such a process fits the data on postwar U.S. aggregate prices and wages very well (see, e.g., Ando and Kennickell 1983; Eckstein 1983; Perry 1983; Blanchard 1984; and Gordon 1984).

Anderson and Enzler (n.d.) explain why this inflation process, in conjunction with fixed money growth, would impart a pronounced cyclical tendency to real GNP and inflation over time:

> It is now fairly easy to show why holding the money growth rate constant might not result in a stable simulation path for a macromodel containing this mechanism. Such a policy starts with a given money stock and holds money to a fixed growth rate. Thus, both the steady-state rate of inflation and the steady-state price level at each point of time are predetermined. Now consider what happens if the price level is disturbed upward. The demand for money will be increased and interest rates will rise. This depresses output and increases unemployment. The increased unemployment, in turn, depresses the rate of change of prices. As long as the price *level* is too high unemployment will be above its natural level and the *rate of inflation* will fall. The declining rate of inflation eventually returns the price level to its steady-state value, but when the *level* of prices is at its steady-state value, allowing the unemployment rate to return to the natural rate, *inflation* will be too low to be consistent with the fixed money growth path and the price level will pass through the steady-state level.* This reduces the demand for money causing interest rates to fall until unemployment is below the natural rate. Inflation will now accelerate until at some point it reaches its steady-state value. But now the *level* of prices is too low, and overshooting occurs again.
>
> This same argument applies to another often suggested monetary policy-making procedure—targeting nominal GNP. The specification of a steady growth path for nominal GNP also determines both the steady-state price level and the rate of inflation. Once again, since deviations in the price level are corrected through changes in the rate of inflation, overshooting occurs. (Pps. 12–13)

In Enzler and Johnson's simulations of a simple but standard IS-LM macro model with adaptive expectations and with a range of plausible coefficients and lag structures, this process imparts a regular cycle to real GNP and inflation of about fifteen years in duration, damped or undamped depending on particular coefficient values. The interplay of the two cyclical processes causes irregular cycles that can be damped or explosive. The large-scale MIT–Penn–SSRC (MPS) quarterly econometric model also exhibits a pronounced cyclical tendency in similar simulations for similar reasons.

Some macroeconomists would respond that such a scenario is unrealistic because sooner or later the public will recognize the processes giving rise to such inflation and output cycles and form more

---

*An asymptotic approach to the steady state would require inflation to gradually approach the target rate as the price level approached its steady-state path, but that is possible only if inflation accelerates while unemployment is above its natural rate, and the model contains no mechanism to make this happen.

sophisticated inflation expectations based on the interaction of the monetary regime with the economy. They would point out that in the simple model of our example, rational inflation expectations combined with public knowledge of the economic structure will eliminate the cycle in real output (though not the cycle in prices and interest rates). These economists are not persuaded that problems of cyclical instability undermine the case for a fixed money growth rule, even considering that production-adjustment lags, or inertia in wage and price contracting, captured in more complicated theoretical models with rational expectations, can induce a residual, if damped and moderate, cyclical tendency in response to shocks.

Perhaps their view is correct. But as Anderson and Enzler note, it is based on a speculative theory of inflation expectations, without strong empirical support in the postwar behavior of U.S. prices and wages. Even in the context of Enzler and Johnson's deterministic simulations of a simple four-equation model with fixed coefficients, the mechanisms at work are not easy to understand. With these processes further obscured in the real world by random disturbances to functions for prices, labor markets, spending, and money demand, not to mention permanent structural changes in the economy, I do not trust the public's expectations to serve well enough as an automatic stabilizing device to support the legislative or constitutional enshrinement of a permanent rule fixing money growth.

Policy Feedback. Skepticism about the stabilizing effect of the public's expectations in a realistic economic setting under a money growth rule leads to consideration of policies involving feedback. Besides simple, nondiscretionary feedback rules, two other basic approaches can be envisioned. The first, the optimal control approach, relies on formally solving large-scale econometric models, coupled with a specified loss function, for instrument resettings in light of recent errors. In resetting the instruments, formal account can be taken of uncertainty about the economic structure.

The second feedback approach is more informal and judgmental and can be carried out—given the general goals of policymakers—without reliance on particular econometric models or on an explicit loss function. To expand on an analogy occasionally used by macroeconomists, this approach is like turning the steering wheel when the car starts to veer off the road and easing up on the accelerator and stepping on the brake when the road turns sharply, while watching where the car is going and making new adjustments accordingly.

By contrast, the first approach is like solving the engineering equations that describe the car's steering and propulsion systems and how the car's momentum and direction are affected by gravity, wind resistance, and the friction and position of the wheels, taking due account of traffic and highway conditions. The driver's preferences regarding time of arrival, gas mileage, and so on also would have to be specified. Though in principle it yields settings of the steering wheel, accelerator, and brake at each point in time that would guide the car safely and efficiently to its destination, this approach is obviously impractical and also unnecessary. The driver does not really need to comprehend quantitatively all the physical mechanisms at work to get from Minneapolis to Dayton, even though admittedly the driver will not keep the car at the exact center of the lane at all times.

To be sure, macroeconomic policymaking does not involve manipulating a mechanical system such as a car. But it seems that the inherent uncertainties about the mechanisms at work, especially expectational ones, as well as structural changes and short-run noise, make the second approach even more appropriate, despite the availability of formal procedures to account for uncertainty. I do not understand why the possibility that the mechanisms themselves may respond to policy actions would imply in practice that policymakers should not in turn react to the observed effects of such responses on macroeconomic outcomes. Nor do I see why flexible feedback adjustments necessarily would run into problems of credibility if the overall macroeconomic outcomes are reasonably satisfactory over time. Indeed, policy flexibility—that is, the capacity to respond to a variety of unforeseen contingencies—seems to be a prerequisite for attaining those reasonably satisfactory outcomes.

The type of practical feedback I have in mind should not be confused with fine tuning, the possibility of which is, of course, ruled out by random disturbances and by long and variable policy lags. But judgmental feedback can still moderate, even if it cannot eliminate, departures of macroeconomic variables from desired paths. Random disturbances and long and variable lags are factors in driving a car as well, but they normally cause fatal mistakes only when a driver operates at overly high speeds. Judgmental feedback correction with sequential trial-and-error instrument adjustments still suffices for most drivers.

To investigate aspects of this second approach, several authors have experimented with a variety of responsive but relatively ad hoc policy reaction rules. These reaction functions range from relatively simple feedback reactions to a sequential set of conditional rules of thumb. In deterministic simulations over very long periods, some serve fairly well in stabilizing simple models and the large-scale MPS econometric model (Enzler and Johnson 1981; Anderson and Enzler, n.d.). These also do a reasonable job in stochastic simulations of the MPS model over shorter periods (Tinsley and von zur Muehlen 1983a, b).

Simulations of the MPS model with historic errors suggest, however, that the 1970s constituted a difficult period under any monetary policy reaction function examined because oil-price shocks necessitated a sustained increase in unemployment above the natural rate to contain the acceleration in inflation. Monetary policy can do little to improve this tradeoff in the face of supply shocks, and no reaction function studied showed much improvement over actual policy (Anderson and Enzler, n.d.; Clark 1984).[16]

Monetary Aggregates as Intermediate Targets. The car analogy, though imperfect, nonetheless yields another useful insight about the prevailing structure of monetary policymaking. The use of monetary aggregates as intermediate targets, like reference to the speedometer and the highway's centerline, provides presumptive indications that satisfactory progress is being made toward the ultimate objective. Maintenance of a particular speed and a particular distance from the centerline for given highway conditions is not an end in itself but rather a rule of thumb allowing for frequent checks on performance and the appropriateness of the current settings of the operating instruments. Of course, not all speeds or all routes will prove consistent with a trip's satisfactory progress. Similarly, intermediate monetary targets must be selected with care and adjusted as the need arises.

A transition from automotive to economic reasoning is no doubt overdue. Reliance on monetary aggregates as intermediate targets has intuitive appeal in light of their properties in the well-known Poole (1970) framework, in which the ultimate target variable, nominal GNP, is unobservable in the short run because the data lag behind. The central bank chooses between maintaining the money stock or an interest rate, both observable, at a value determined at the start of the current period to be consistent with attainment of the nominal GNP target in the absence of random disturbances to the IS or LM functions. Still a third alternative is generally optimal:

---

16. As reported by Kalchbrenner and Tinsley (1976), a full-blown optimal control reaction function with quarterly feedback performed worse in model simulation than actual policy during the period after the first oil-price shock. Another study of the period after the first oil-price shock (Craine, Havenner, and Berry 1978) provides support for feedback strategies versus fixed rules. Of course, by no means all of the observed inflation of the 1970s or early 1980s can be attributed to oil-price shocks. Clark (1984) makes this point quantitatively with MPS model simulation results.

the central bank maintains these two observable variables in the predetermined combination that would minimize the expected deviation of nominal GNP from target in the face of shocks. The slope of the combination policy line (in a diagram with the interest rate and the money supply on the axes) depends on the interest elasticities and historical variances of the IS and LM functions.

Several special cases in this framework are instructive. If the IS and LM functions have equal variances, then for all permissible values of interest elasticities a money-stock intermediate target is always preferable to an interest-rate target, although a combination policy is generally even better. However, if the IS and LM functions also have equal interest elasticities (in absolute value), then the optimum combination policy corresponds exactly to a pure money-stock policy (LeRoy and Lindsey 1978). The intuition behind this result is that when the money stock is held at its predetermined target value, an unexpected upward or downward movement in the interest rate is just as likely to arise predominantly from an IS shock as from an LM shock. In this special case, movements in interest rates give no information about the nature of the shocks, before direct observations on income and hence on the primary type of shock, that would suggest altering the original expectation of the GNP outcome, given the target money stock.

This special case may crudely approximate the real world when interest rate ceilings on regular NOWs are further liberalized in early 1985 and then eliminated in early 1986—moves that will reduce the responsiveness of M1 demand to movements in market interest rates. Without information about upcoming special factors affecting the IS or LM function, it is not obvious which function would be subject to greater variance and interest sensitivity at the start of any given control period. This situation seems to imply that the Federal Reserve should keep aiming at preset monetary aggregate targets, at least until incoming data begin to indicate the sources of disturbances and the extent to which they are transitory. As such evidence accumulates, it will make sense to adjust the intermediate monetary targets to maintain consistency with ultimate goals over time.

In the Poole framework, the intermediate target in any event must be reset at the beginning of each new control period in response to movements in exogenous variables, evolving lag effects, autocorrelated error terms, and so on. Even the special case being considered—in which a pure money stock intermediate target is optimal within a given control period—provides in this sense analytic support for policy activism rather than a fixed monetary rule.

However, the Poole framework assumes that the policymaker knows the economic structure and the stochastic processes governing the additive error terms, an assumption that lessens its applicability in the actual context of macroeconomic stabilization. In addition, Poole's framework does not really address the main concern of monetary policy in cyclical macroeconomic stabilization, which involves influencing trends in ultimate variables over the intermediate run, not minimizing undesired variations in them over such short control periods that data on these variables are unavailable. After all, data for prices and output lag by a quarter at most, with indicative pieces of data coming in sooner. Resisting quarter-to-quarter random wiggles in prices and output is not nearly as important as affecting developments covering a year or more.

In this more relevant context, monetary aggregates lose some of the intuitive appeal as intermediate targets that they possess in the Poole framework. One issue that immediately arises is how flexible the Federal Reserve should be in attempting to hold monetary aggregates along preset paths in the short run in the face of purely random and self-reversing shocks to real aggregate demand and money demand, as well as to real aggregate supply. An inflexible control procedure that kept money on track in the short run would transmit those shocks fully into variations in interest rates and credit market conditions more generally, with adverse side effects for the efficient functioning of those markets but without much, if any, lasting gain in macroeconomic performance.

Sustained episodes of systematic strengthening or weakening of aggregate demand relative to capacity (as opposed to temporary random shocks) seem to call more clearly for the resistance associated with attainment of intermediate monetary targets. However, over such longer time periods, a second issue arises. How flexible should the Federal Reserve be in adjusting its monetary targets in response to documented financial innovations, shifts in money demand functions, and marked changes in inflationary expectations and in nominal interest rates, as well as swings in aggregate demand? Without flexibility in making such intermediate target adjustments, these developments would, other things being equal, induce sustained movements of ultimate variables away from their goals.[17]

Through the judgmental feedback embodied in the informal reaction functions actually used to set intermediate and operating targets,

---

17. The role for policy flexibility is analyzed in formal models incorporating rational expectations by Rogoff (1983) and Canzoneri (1983).

and through discretionary changes in these feedback rules over time, the Federal Reserve has exercised flexibility in both regards. As discussed in the previous section, the extent of flexibility has depended on particular economic circumstances, but discretionary policy flexibility has remained within the general structure of intermediate monetary targeting with feedback.

This structure is desirable for reasons that relate to the first criterion of policy discussed earlier: tying down nominal economic values in the long run. Monetary aggregates as intermediate targets, even if used flexibly in the short and intermediate run, focus the attention of both the Federal Reserve and the public on the basic long-run determinant of inflation. The kernel of truth in the familiar aphorism that inflation results from too much money chasing too few goods emerges over the long run, and there is widespread public agreement that the central bank ought to prevent the growth of money from getting out of control.

The presumption that, over long periods, money growth should average in the low single digits serves as a perpetual reminder to the central bank that the trend of money growth needs to be reduced from the pace observed since the mid-1960s if reasonable price stability is to be achieved and maintained. Use of monetary, as opposed to nonmonetary, intermediate targets forces the central bank to keep the ultimate destination in mind, even during the detours taken to avoid immediate dangers along the way.

Conclusion

As I sd to my
friend, because I am
always talking,—John, I

sd, which was not his
name, the darkness sur-
rounds us, what

can we do against
it, or else, shall we &
why not, buy a goddamn big car,

drive, he sd, for
christ's sake, look
out where yr going.

Robert Creeley (1962)

REFERENCES

Abrams, Richard K., Roger Waud, and Richard Froyen. "The State of the Federal Budget and the State of the Economy." *Economic Inquiry* 21 (October 1983), 485–503.

American College Dictionary, 1961 ed., s.v. "regime."

Anderson, Robert, and Jared J. Enzler. "Toward Realistic Policy Design: Simulating the Use of Policy Reaction Functions Involving Economic Forecasts." Washington, D.C.: Board of Governors of the Federal Reserve System, n.d.

Ando, Albert, and Arthur Kennickell. "'Failure' of Keynesian Economics and 'Direct' Effects of Money Supply: A Fact or a Fiction?" Washington, D.C.: Board of Governors of the Federal Reserve System, March 1983.

Axilrod, Stephen H. "Issues in Monetary Targeting and Velocity." In *Monetary Targeting and Velocity*. Conference proceedings. December 4–6, 1983. San Francisco: Federal Reserve Bank of San Francisco. Pp. 4–13.

Blanchard, Olivier J. "The Lucas Critique and the Volcker Deflation." *American Economic Review* 74 (May 1984), 211–15.

Blinder, Alan S., and Stephen M. Goldfeld. "Some Implications of Endogenous Stabilization Policy." *Brookings Papers on Economic Activity* 3 (1972), 585–644.

Board of Governors of the Federal Reserve System. "Monetary Policy Actions." *Federal Reserve Bulletin* 65 (October 1979), 830–32.

Brayton, Flint. "The Demand for M1 in the Quarterly Model." Washington, D.C.: Board of Governors of the Federal Reserve System, July 12, 1984.

Brayton, Flint, Helen T. Farr, and Richard D. Porter. "Alternative Money Demand Specifications and Recent Growth in M1." Washington, D.C.: Board of Governors of the Federal Reserve System, May 23, 1983.

Brunner, Karl. "Has Monetarism Failed?" *Cato Journal* 3 (Spring 1983), 23–82.

Bryant, Ralph C. *Money and Monetary Policy in Interdependent Nations.* Washington, D.C.: Brookings Institution, 1980.

———. *Controlling Money: The Federal Reserve and Its Critics.* Washington, D.C.: Brookings Institution, 1983.

Cagan, Phillip. *Determinants and Effects of Changes in the Stock of Money: 1875 to 1960.* Washington, D.C.: National Bureau of Economic Research, 1965.

Canzoneri, Matthew B. "Monetary Policy Games and the Role of Private Information." Washington, D.C.: Board of Governors of the Federal Reserve System, November 1983.

Clark, Peter B. "Inflation and Unemployment in the United States: Recent Experience and Policies," Working Paper Series 33. Washington, D.C.: Board of Governors of the Federal Reserve System, January 1984.

Cooley, Thomas F., Stephen F. LeRoy, and Neil Raymon. "Econometric Policy Evaluation: Note." *American Economic Review* 74 (June 1984), 467–70.

Craine, Roger, Arthur Havenner, and James Berry. "Fixed Rules versus

Activism in the Conduct of Monetary Policy." *American Economic Review* 68 (December 1978), 769–83.

Creeley, Robert. "I Know a Man." In *For Love: Poems, 1950–1960*. New York: Scribners, 1962. P. 38.

Eckstein, Otto. "Disinflation." In *Inflation: Prospects and Remedies, Alternatives for the 1980s*, no. 10, William D. Nordhaus, ed. Washington, D.C.: Center for National Policy, 1983.

Enzler, Jared, and Lewis Johnson. "Cycles Resulting from Money Stock Targeting." In *New Monetary Control Procedures*, Federal Reserve Staff Study, vol. 1. Washington, D.C.: Board of Governors of the Federal Reserve System, February 1981. Pp. 11–18.

Friedman, Benjamin M. "Targets, Instruments, and Indicators of Monetary Policy." *Journal of Monetary Economics* 1 (October 1975), 443–73.

———. "Optimal Expectations and the Extreme Information Assumptions of 'Rational Expectations' Macromodels." *Journal of Monetary Economics* 5 (January 1979), 23–42.

Friedman, Milton. "Why a Surge in Inflation Is Likely Next Year." *Wall Street Journal*, September 1, 1983.

———. "The Role of Monetary Policy." *American Economic Review* 58 (May 1968), 1–17.

Gordon, Robert J. "Discussion" of Ray C. Fair, "Estimated Trade-offs between Unemployment and Inflation." In *Price Stability and Public Policy*. Kansas City: Federal Reserve Bank of Kansas City, August 2–3, 1984. Pp. 83–94.

———. "The Conduct of Domestic Monetary Policy." In *Monetary Policy in Our Times*, Albert Ando, Hidekazu Eguchi, Roger Farmer, and Yoshio Suzuki, eds. Cambridge: MIT Press, 1985. Pp. 45–81.

Hall, Robert E. "Monetary Strategy with an Elastic Price Standard." In *Price Stability and Public Policy*. Kansas City: Federal Reserve Bank of Kansas City, August 2–3, 1984. Pp. 137–59.

Kalchbrenner, John, and P. A. Tinsley. "On the Use of Feedback Control in the Design of Aggregate Monetary Policy." *American Economic Review* 66 (May 1976), 349–55.

LeRoy, Stephen F., and David E. Lindsey. "Determining the Money Instrument: A Diagrammatic Exposition." *American Economic Review* 68 (December 1978), 929–34.

Lindsey, David E. "Comment on 'How Regulations Affect Monetary Control.' " *Journal of Money, Credit and Banking* 14 (November 1982a, part 2), 788–95.

———. "Recent Monetary Developments and Controversies." *Brookings Papers on Economic Activity* 1 (1982b), 245–68.

———. "Repercussions of the Great Depression on Stabilization Policy." Lecture to American History class, Earlham College. Washington, D.C.: Board of Governors of the Federal Reserve System, February 23, 1983a.

———. "Nonborrowed Reserve Targeting and Monetary Control." In *Improving Money Stock Control: Problems, Solutions and Consequences*, Laurence H. Meyer, ed. Economic Policy Conference Series, cosponsored by the Center for the Study of American Business at Washington University and the Federal Reserve Bank of St. Louis. Boston/The Hague/London: Kluwer-Nijhoff, 1983b. Pp. 3–41.

Lindsey, David E., et al. "Monetary Control Experience under the New Operating Procedures." In *New Monetary Control Procedures*, Federal Reserve Staff Study, vol. 2. Washington, D.C.: Board of Governors of the Federal Reserve System, February 1981. Pp. 1–102.

Litterman, Robert, and Laurence Weiss. "Money, Real Interest Rates and Output: A Reinterpretation of U.S. Post-War Data." Staff report. Minneapolis: Federal Reserve Bank of Minneapolis, 1983.

Lucas, Robert E., Jr. "Econometric Policy Evaluation: A Critique." In *The Phillips Curve and Labor Markets*, Karl Brunner and Allan H. Meltzer, eds. Carnegie-Rochester Conference Series on Public Policy, vol. 1. Amsterdam: North-Holland, 1976.

Mayer, Thomas. "The Structure of Monetarism." *Kredit und Kapital* 8 (Jahrgang 1975), Heft 2, 3, 191–218, 293–316.

McCallum, Bennett T. "A Reconsideration of Sims' Evidence Concerning Monetarism." *Economic Letters* 13 (1983), 167–71.

———. "Monetarist Rules in the Light of Recent Experience." *American Economic Review* 74 (May 1984), 388–91.

Meltzer, Allan H. "Overview." In *Price Stability and Public Policy*. Kansas City: Federal Reserve Bank of Kansas City, August 2–3, 1984. Pp. 209–22.

Perry, George. "What Have We Learned about Disinflation?" *Brookings Papers on Economic Activity* 2 (1983), 587–608.

Phelps, Edmund S. *Inflation Policy and Unemployment Theory: The Cost-Benefit Approach to Monetary Planning*. New York: W.W. Norton & Co., 1972.

Poole, William. "Optimal Choice of Monetary Policy Instruments in a Simple Stochastic Macro Model." *Quarterly Journal of Economics* 84 (May 1970), 197–216.

Rogoff, Kenneth. "The Optimal Degree of Commitment to an Intermediate Monetary Target: Inflation Gains versus Stabilization Costs." International Finance Discussion Papers, no. 230. Washington, D.C.: Board of Governors of the Federal Reserve System, September 1983.

Sachs, Jeffrey D. "Comments and Discussion." *Brookings Papers on Economic Activity* 1 (1982), 157–62.

Simpson, Thomas D. "A Proposal for Redefining the Monetary Aggregates." *Federal Reserve Bulletin* 65 (January 1979), 13–42.

———. "Changes in the Financial System: Implications for Monetary Policy." *Brookings Papers on Economic Activity* 1 (1984), 249–65.

Sims, Christopher A. "Comparison of Interwar and Postwar Business Cycles: Monetarism Reconsidered." *American Economic Review* 70 (May 1980), 250–57.

———. "Policy Analysis and Econometric Models." *Brookings Papers on Economic Activity* 1 (1982), 107–52.

———. "Is There a Monetary Business Cycle?" *American Economic Review* 73 (May 1983), 228–33.

Stein, Herbert. "Problems in the Conduct of Monetary Policy." *AEI Economist* (July 1982), 1–8.

Swamy, P.A.V.B., and Peter A. Tinsley. "Linear Prediction and Estimation Methods for Regression Models with Stationary Stochastic Coefficients." *Journal of Econometrics* 12 (February 1980), 103–42.

Taylor, John. "Monetary Policy during a Transition to Rational Expectations." *Journal of Political Economy* 83 (October 1975), 1009–21.

Temin, Peter. *Did Monetary Forces Cause the Great Depression?* New York: W.W. Norton & Co., 1976.

Tinsley, Peter A. "On Proximate Exploitation of Intermediate Information in Macroeconomic Forecasting." Special Studies Paper 59. Washington, D.C.: Board of Governors of the Federal Reserve System, 1974.

Tinsley, Peter A., and Peter von zur Muehlen. "A Maximum Probability Approach to Short-Run Policy." *Journal of Econometrics* 15 (January 1981), 31–48.

———. "Conditional Intermediate Targeting." Washington, D.C.: Board of Governors of the Federal Reserve System, October 1983a.

———. "The Reliability of Alternative Intermediate Targets." Washington, D.C.: Board of Governors of the Federal Reserve System, November 1983b.

Tinsley, Peter A., Peter von zur Muehlen, and Gerhard Fries. "The Short-Run Volatility of Money Stock Targeting." *Journal of Monetary Economics* 10 (September 1982), 215–237.

Tinsley, Peter A., Helen T. Farr, Gerhard Fries, Bonnie Garrett, and Peter von zur Muehlen. "Policy Robustness: Specification and Simulation of a Monthly Money Market Model." *Journal of Money, Credit and Banking* 14 (November 1982, part 2), 829–56.

Tobin, James. "Money and Income: Post Hoc Ergo Propter Hoc?" *Quarterly Journal of Economics* 84 (May 1970), 301–17.

———. "Monetary Policy: Rules, Targets and Shocks." *Journal of Money, Credit and Banking* 15 (November 1983), 506–18.

"Statement by Paul A. Volcker, Chairman, Board of Governors of the Federal Reserve System, before the Committee on Banking, Housing and Urban Affairs of the U.S. Senate, Febuary 16, 1983." *Federal Reserve Bulletin* 69 (March 1983), 167–74.

"Statement by Paul A. Volcker, Chairman, Board of Governors of the Federal Reserve System, before the Committee on Banking, Housing and Urban Affairs of the U.S. Senate, July 25, 1984." *Federal Reserve Bulletin* 70 (August 1984), 626–32.

Wallich, Henry C. "Recent Techniques of Monetary Policy." Federal Reserve Bank of Kansas City, *Economic Review* (May 1984), 21–30.

Walsh, Carl E. "Interest Rate Volatility and Monetary Policy." *Journal of Money, Credit and Banking* 16 (May 1984), 133–50.

Webster's New World Dictionary of the American Language, College Edition, s.v. "regime."

Weintraub, Robert. "What Type of Monetary Rule?" *Cato Journal* 3 (Spring 1983), 171–83.

A Monetarist View of the Federal
Reserve System

DAVID I. FAND

ONE MAY evaluate Lindsey's analysis of the monetary regime of the Federal Reserve System on either of two criteria. As an exposition of what the Federal Reserve does, and especially how it rationalizes its actions, it is a very good piece. As a defense of Federal Reserve policy, however, especially against the criticisms of those who analyze monetary policy from a monetarist perspective, his presentation fails. My criticisms of Lindsey concern five general points.

The Federal Reserve's Performance in the 1970s

Lindsey passes rather lightly over the performance of the Federal Reserve System during the 1970s. While this is perhaps understandable, it is not entirely proper. For example, he states, "The Federal Reserve's record in attaining the announced annual ranges for M1 and M2 from 1976 to 1979 was somewhat mixed." That is more than a slight understatement. In fact, the Federal Reserve missed its monetary targets, changed its monetary targets, used multiple monetary targets, and allowed base drift in those targets. The monetary authorities acted as if the enunciation of the targets were a routine that they were required to go through but were not required to adhere to. For this reason, it is difficult to know what to make of Lindsey's claim that, during the 1970s, "the Federal Reserve gradually strengthened its reliance on monetary aggregates." The Federal Reserve does not appear to have been relying on those aggregates to help it attain the low and stable money growth rates advocated by those who also advocate the use of monetary aggregates as policy targets. Moreover, much of the monetary growth in the 1970s was procyclical.

David I. Fand

The Instability of Money Demand

Essential to Lindsey's overall argument is his claim that the marked instability in both money growth rates and interest rates after October 1979 was due to money demand fluctuations. In October 1979, the Federal Reserve shifted from a federal-funds-rate operating target to a nonborrowed-reserves target in which changes in money demand are not completely acccommodated. Thus, he writes:

Under the nonborrowed reserves procedure, a rightward shift of the nominal money demand curve—owing to an increase in real income, a rise in the price level, or a positive random disturbance—will be partially checked by the induced rise in short-term interest rates.

Figure 5–2 shows how this automatic mechanism worked during the three years after October 1979. The top two panels indicate monthly levels of M2 and M1 relative to the upper and lower bounds of their annual ranges. A strengthening of money relative to target raised required reserves. Since nonborrowed reserves were held to a fixed path by the trading desk, reserve positions of depository institutions were automatically tightened as institutions in the aggregate were forced to borrow the extra reserves at the discount window.

These statements would lead the reader to believe that most of the variations in money growth in 1980 were due to movements in borrowed reserves, but this is not the complete story. The movements in the money stock also reflect the movements in nonborrowed reserves. The results would have been different if Lindsey had plotted the behavior of nonborrowed reserves, since most of the increase in required reserves due to the growth in money was supplied by non-borrowed reserves. Acccordingly, the sharp drop in money growth in the first half of 1980 and its sharp acceleration in the second half of 1980 can be attributed to nonborrowed reserves—and Federal Reserve policy—rather than shifts in money demand.

In discussing the fact that money growth as well as interest rates evidenced more intermediate-run variability following the October 1979 change in targets, Lindsey writes, "That money and interest rates moved in the same direction establishes a prima facie case that the demand curve varied over a wider range than the supply curve did." Actually some research suggests that interest rates tend to move in response to the weekly release of the money-supply figures every Friday afternoon because those announcements may affect the expectations of bond traders. Accordingly, the correlation between money-supply and interest-rate changes noted by Lindsey may be due to temporary shifts in money demand caused by the Federal Reserve's missing its money-supply target in the first place.

The Operating Procedures of the Federal Reserve

The history of monetary policy in the United States since 1951 illustrates the importance of the operating procedures followed by the Federal Reserve in contributing to actual rather than stated policy outcomes. The change in operating targets in October 1979 seemed to be a harbinger of a policy of lower and steadier money growth. The result was quite different. Although Lindsey states that the Federal Reserve slowed the trend of money growth during the three years following October 1979, the difference between the average money growth rate over the twelve quarters before that date and the average money growth rate over the twelve subsequent quarters is not statistically significant. This is due in part to the high variance of the quarterly growth rates after October 1979. A total-reserves target would have resulted in less variability in the money supply and so, plausibly, less uncertainty about the actual stance of the Federal Reserve. This, in turn, might have reduced the extreme sensitivity of bond traders to the weekly announcements of money-supply figures, thereby reducing the fluctuations in short-term interest rates.

At present, however, a comparison of nonborrowed reserves and total reserves as targets for monetary policy is beside the point: the Federal Reserve has shifted to yet another procedure. Lindsey quotes Governor Wallich as follows: "Since the fall of 1982, the nonborrowed reserve strategy and its automaticity have given way to a technique that allows the funds rate to be determined by the market, through the targeting of discount window borrowing from one reserve maintenance period to the next, implemented by allowing a flexible nonborrowed reserves path."

It appears that the monetary authorities are returning to a borrowing or free reserves target, the predominant target from 1951 to the early 1970s. Studies by Meigs (1962) and by Brunner and Meltzer (1964) have dealt thoroughly and critically with this operating procedure (See Fand 1963). Meigs's study shows that what is significant is the difference between the actual level of free reserves and the level of free reserves desired by banks. He concludes that the use of the absolute level of free reserves as an indicator of tightness or ease was hazardous.

The Federal Reserve's View of the Economy

If the discretionary monetary policy based on feedback that Lindsey favors is to succeed, the monetary authorities must understand the behavior of the economy fairly well. In view of the Federal Reserve's past statements and Lindsey's summary of the analytical models used by the staff of the Board of Governors, there is little reason for optimism on this score. It is worth recalling that, in testimony before Congress in early 1983, officials of the Federal Reserve predicted that the recovery in that year was going to be very weak due to high interest rates. They expected those high interest rates to deter investment substantially, leaving an anemic, consumer-led recovery. The fact that the United States experienced a vigorous recovery with strong increases in capital spending suggests that the Federal Reserve's model failed to capture some important features of the U.S. economy.

It is also sobering to note the degree to which the Federal Reserve rejects analytical developments in economics that call into question the wisdom of its dedication to discretion in the formulation of monetary policy. In particular, the rational expectations hypothesis, which has been applied successfully to the analysis of domestic financial markets, foreign exchange markets, and commodity markets, is dismissed as merely a "speculative theory of inflation expectations, without strong empirical support in the postwar behavior of U.S. prices and wages."

Lindsey and others at the Federal Reserve apparently prefer the hypothesis that expectations are formed adaptively: instead of forming their expectations by looking forward, people are assumed to form them by looking backward. Although it is easy to understand why the Federal Reserve might prefer the implications of the hypothesis of adaptive expectations as described by Lucas (1972), the claim that it is a more realistic depiction of the U.S. economy than one derived from the hypothesis of rational expectations is difficult to support. Lindsey informs us that "when account also is taken of identifiable special factors, such as wage and price controls and oil-price shocks, such a process fits the data on postwar U.S. aggregate prices and wages very well."

While it may be possible to obtain a respectable R^2 in fitting a model such as the one Lindsey describes to postwar U.S. data, this is no indication of its usefulness in answering the question Lindsey is posing, which is, How would the U.S. economy perform under a stable-money-growth rule? As Lucas (1976) has pointed out, the properties of an econometric model may be specific to the type of policy regime that is in effect during the period of observation. Simulations based on a model fitted to a period of variable money growth are unreliable indicators of the way in which the economy would perform under a different monetary rule.

The Shortcomings of Discretion

Lindsey concludes his analysis of the monetary regime of the Federal Reserve with an endorsement of discretionary, flexible response by the monetary authorities to changes in economic conditions. He does not propose anything so mechanical as fine tuning but believes it is important to allow good sense to override any adherence to intermediate targets when it becomes apparent that hitting those targets will cause an avoidable deterioration in aggregate economic performance. While it is certainly difficult to oppose in principle the exercise of good sense, the results likely under Lindsey's approach cause me to wonder whether we can expect to find that his proposal makes good sense in practice.

The essence of Lindsey's position is that he favors "tying down nominal economic values in the long run" while allowing policymakers discretionary flexibility in the short run. The problem with this prescription for the formulation of monetary policy is that it is impossible to achieve. If the exercise of policymakers' good judgment results in periods of relatively high money growth, then there must also be periods of relatively low money growth if the goal of long-term stability of nominal magnitudes is to be met. Lindsey does not explain how we can both allow the monetary authorities flexibility in the short run and be assured that in the long run we will achieve the desired average rate of money growth.

Throughout his analysis, Lindsey is essentially conducting the following thought experiment: in one room we have disinterested, objective scientists formulating a rule-based monetary policy, while in another room we have equally adept and hard-working scientists formulating a discretionary monetary policy. Lindsey concludes that the resulting discretionary policy will be superior to the resulting nondiscretionary policy. Even if that were a correct conclusion under the circumstances, it does not solve the real world problems of monetary policy.

Those who argue for rules do so in part because they believe that under a discretionary regime policies become hopelessly mired in politics. A rule is necessary to free the policymaker from the inevitable pressures of politics; one cannot abstract from the political problem. The Federal Reserve does not operate in a political vacuum. Indeed, it is quite sensitive to political pressure. As Robert Weintraub put it, if one wants to know what the Federal Reserve is doing, look not at who the chairman of the Federal Reserve Board is, but rather look at who the president of the United States is. That will continue to be true until we abandon our current discretionary monetary regime in favor of a rule-based regime.

REFERENCES

Brunner, Karl, and Allan H. Meltzer. *The Federal Reserve's Attachment to the Free Reserve Concept.* Subcommittee Print. U.S. Congress, House, Committee on Banking and Currency, Subcommittee on Domestic Finance, 88th Cong., 2d sess., 1964.

Fand, David I. "Review of A. James Meigs, Free Reserves and the Money Supply." *Journal of Business* 36 (July 1963), 372–75.

Lucas, Robert E., Jr. "Econometric Testing of the Natural Rate Hypothesis." In *The Econometrics of Price Determination*, Otto Eckstein, ed. Washington, D.C.: Board of Governors of the Federal Reserve System, 1972. Pp. 50–59. Reprinted in Robert E. Lucas, Jr. *Studies in Business-Cycle Theory.* Cambridge: MIT Press, 1981. Pp. 90–103.

———."Econometric Policy Evaluation: A Critique." In *The Phillips Curve and Labor Markets*, Karl Brunner and Allan H. Meltzer, eds. Carnegie-Rochester Conference Series on Public Policy, vol. 1. Amsterdam: North-Holland, 1976. Pp. 19–46. Reprinted in Robert E. Lucas, Jr., *Studies in Business-Cycle Theory.* Cambridge: MIT Press, 1981. Pp. 104–30.

Meigs, A. James. *Free Reserves and the Money Supply.* Chicago: University of Chicago Press, 1962.

Monetary Procedures and Monetary Policy

KENT P. KIMBROUGH

DAVID LINDSEY essentially deals with two issues. First, he examines the conduct of monetary policy since 1970, focusing on its implementation and its results in terms of the behavior of the money supply, interest rates, and inflation. Second, Lindsey speculates on the prospective behavior of the economy if policies in line with those currently adopted by the Federal Reserve were continued versus what might arise if some version of the constant-money-growth rule were adopted. The picture Lindsey paints is one of a beleaguered Federal Reserve System trying desperately to control money-supply growth but forever being challenged by unpredictable shifts in money demand and financial innovations that make this task virtually impossible. Yet despite (or perhaps because of) this, we are told that the Federal Reserve's power and wisdom are such that the goals of economic prosperity and stability will be best served by discretionary monetary policy of the current variety rather than by a rule.

The picture Lindsey paints does not seem to be an accurate one, and the comments that follow attempt to explain where it goes astray. Four main issues are addressed. First, several well-known problems with the Federal Reserve's operating procedures that have heightened monetary instability since 1970 are outlined. Second, the impact of Federal Reserve procedures on monetary instability are quantified by comparing actual money supply variability with levels that could be achieved by adopting procedures aimed at directly controlling the monetary base. Judged on this basis, Federal Reserve policies hardly seem to be as succcessful as Lindsey seems to believe they have been. Third, a case for rules (or commitments) as opposed to Federal Reserve–like discretion is outlined. Fourth, some arguments in favor of coupling a flexible exchange rate with a constant money growth rate, perhaps tied to the trend rate of real output growth, are put forward.

These four points parallel Lindsey's organization. To start, the three periods from 1970 to the present that Lindsey examines are used as a backdrop against which to discuss issues relating to mon-

215

etary procedures and money supply variability. Then, having argued that the Federal Reserve can in fact control the money supply fairly precisely, I take up the issue of whether rules or discretion will best promote prosperity and economic stability.

Monetary Procedures and Money Supply Behavior in the 1970s

In the first part of his paper Lindsey divides the period from 1970 to the present into three periods and looks at the implementation of monetary policy during each of these periods. The periods are 1970–October 1979, October 1979–fall 1982, and fall 1982–the present. The breaks correspond to the October 6, 1979, shift in Federal Reserve operating procedures from using the federal funds rate as its instrument for controlling the money stock to using nonborrowed reserves, and to the passage of the Garn-St Germain Depository Institutions Act of 1982, which allowed commercial banks and thrift institutions to offer accounts competitive with money market funds.

As noted, until October 6, 1979, the Federal Reserve openly used the federal funds rate (the rate at which banks borrow and lend funds deposited with the Federal Reserve to one another) as its instrument for controlling the money supply. To understand the workings of this procedure, suppose that the Federal Reserve thought the federal funds rate was too high to assure desired money supply growth. In such a case, the Federal Reserve would purchase Treasury securities and credit the reserve accounts of the selling banks the appropriate amount. As a result, these banks would experience an increase in their excess reserves and would offer to lend them on the federal funds market. This would reduce the federal funds rate, while, simultaneously, the increase in reserves would lead to the desired increase in the money supply.

The problem with this procedure is that the Federal Reserve must rely on liquidity effects to control short-run interest rate movements, while in the long run their main impact on interest rates is via inflationary expectations. Since the liquidity effects and inflationary expectations effects of changes in the money supply typically run in opposite directions, rather than policy errors being reversed they are actually sustained and magnified by the policy of using the federal funds rate as an instrument. In the example, the downward pressure on interest rates would ultimately be reversed as the increase in the money supply raised inflationary expectations. As interest rates began to rise toward, or perhaps even above, their initial levels, Federal

Reserve operating procedures would call for another round of Treasury security purchases and monetary expansion to reduce interest rates. This in turn would only heighten inflationary expectations and call forth another round of monetary expansion, and so on. Since using the federal funds rate as an instrument magnifies policy errors rather than reversing them, such a procedure cannot help but result in unnecessarily high money supply variability.

In light of such criticisms, on October 6, 1979, the Federal Reserve announced it would replace the federal funds rate with nonborrowed reserves as its instrument for controlling the money supply. However, despite this change in operating procedures, money supply growth has been even more volatile, as has been well documented. The major problem seems to have been the targeting of nonborrowed reserves coupled with the use of lagged reserve requirements.[1] Operationally, lagged reserve requirements mean that banks' required reserves were determined by deposits held two weeks earlier. However, economically, their main impact was to eliminate the responsiveness of required reserves to interest rate movements. With required reserves predetermined at any point in time, any discrepancy between required reserves and total reserves had to be eliminated entirely by changes in excess reserves.

Therefore, under lagged reserve requirements, equilibrating movements in the federal funds rate tended to be much larger than they would have been under contemporaneous reserve requirements. In order to ease the federal funds rate movements that would result from lagged reserve requirements and monetary base targeting, the Federal Reserve chose to control nonborrowed reserves and to allow member bank borrowing at the discount window to act as a shock absorber and clear the market for reserves. However, since it is total reserves that govern the behavior of the monetary base and ultimately the money supply, the Federal Reserve's policy of controlling only a portion of total reserves, the nonborrowed portion, essentially took control of the money supply out of their hands, thus exacerbating the problem of monetary instability.

Since February 1984, the Federal Reserve has operated under a system of contemporaneous reserve requirements. However, problems still remain. To begin with, contemporaneous reserve requirements apply only to what the Federal Reserve classifies as *transactions balances* (roughly, this means checkable deposits); all other deposits are still subject to lagged reserve requirements. As a result, the goal

---

1. The issues discussed in this paragraph are examined in detail by Goodfriend (1984).

of interest rate smoothing that was a key source of the problem with Federal Reserve procedures discussed in the previous paragraph is still likely to be present. In addition, the problem of targeting non-borrowed reserves, rather than total reserves or the monetary base, is also still present.

So far, a number of reasons—using the federal funds rate as an instrument, lagged reserve requirements, and targeting nonborrowed reserves—have been given as to why monetary instability under actual Federal Reserve procedures has been excessive, but no benchmark against which to judge their performance has been offered. As a benchmark against which to judge Federal Reserve operating procedures, consider the often-proposed alternative of using open market operations to control the monetary base. Results of research for the Shadow Open Market Committee discussed by Brunner and Meltzer (1983), and reported initially by Johannes and Rasche (1979), indicate that by controlling the monetary base, money supply growth can be reliably held to within plus or minus 1 percent (i.e., 1 percentage point) of the midpoint of the target range over periods as short as a quarter. More precisely, by controlling the monetary base, the Federal Reserve could keep actual money supply growth within plus or minus 1 percent of some prespecified target 95 percent of the time.

A similar calculation from the M1 data presented in Lindsey's Table 5–2 suggests that actual Federal Reserve procedures over the period 1975–79 resulted in a 95 percent probability of money growth being within 1.5 percent of the midpoint of the target range, and over the longer period 1975–83 resulted in a 95 percent probability of money growth being within plus or minus 2.2 percent of the target. The upshot is that actual Federal Reserve policies increased monetary instability some 50 percent to 120 percent above what could be achieved with a policy of controlling the monetary base. As a consequence, price level uncertainty has been higher than necessary and overall economic performance poorer than it could have been. That is the history of Federal Reserve monetary procedures from 1975 to 1983.

Rules versus Discretion

Given that the Federal Reserve can in fact control the money supply with a high degree of precision, the question of what that power should be used for naturally arises. The Federal Reserve System began operation in 1914 in the wake of two decades characterized by bank panics and sluggish economic performance. The idea was that a central bank like the Federal Reserve would help to promote prosperity and economic stability. Today, these continue to be the objectives that most economists and policymakers would like to see the Federal Reserve pursue. There are two basic monetary regimes the Federal Reserve can adopt to achieve these objectives: a rule—say 3 percent constant money growth or a fixed exchange rate—or discretion. The Federal Reserve has, of course, always opted for discretion.

In comparing the two regimes the Federal Reserve could adopt, Lindsey makes the standard claim that "evaluation of any alternative monetary regime rests on two basic questions: Does it provide a reliable long-run anchor for nominal macroeconomic magnitudes? Does it provide reasonable shorter-run stability for nominal and real variables?" The first criterion rests on the widely accepted view that in the long run monetary policy cannot influence real variables such as output and employment.[2] Therefore, in the long run, monetary policy should concern itself with managing the price level or the inflation rate.

The second criterion is based on the notion that in the short run systematic monetary policy, such as leaning against the wind, can influence real activity. This is a more controversial view. Without going into the details here, let it suffice to say that there is a substantial body of empirical evidence that suggests this is not the case (see Barro 1981a and 1981b for a discussion of this literature). This evidence suggests that only unanticipated changes in the money supply have real effects, and this rules out any potential for systematic efforts to stabilize real activity, like leaning against the wind, to be successful. If this view is accepted, the only role for monetary policy, short run or long run, is to control nominal magnitudes such as the price level. In light of the tight long-run relationship between money growth and inflation, this view cries out for adopting some sort of rule. However, even if this view is not accepted, a strong case can be made against discretion and in favor of rules.

Lindsey states that "the problem of short- and intermediate-run macroeconomic instability under a simple monetary rule is the decisive consideration justifying feedback and discretion in policymaking." However, for considerations of short-run economic stability to come down decisively in favor of discretion, discretion as actually exercised by the Federal Reserve must have reduced instability below levels that might reasonably be attained under a rule. Brunner and

---

2. However, see the recent work on Friedman's (1977) upward sloping long-run Phillips curve by, for instance, Stockman (1981).

Meltzer (1983) present evidence to indicate that Federal Reserve policies have actually been destabilizing. They find that over the period 1969–80, which corresponds roughly to the period considered by Lindsey, the standard deviation of nominal GNP growth, a measure of instability, was 2.43 percent, while a constant-money-growth rule would have resulted in a standard deviation of 1.98 percent.[3] That is, compared with what could have been achieved with a rule, the actual exercise of discretion by the Federal Reserve increased macroeconomic instability by about 25 percent. This hardly seems to be evidence in favor of discretion.

Why have discretionary policies been so damaging? Recall that Federal Reserve policies increased money growth instability relative to what could have been attained by controlling the monetary base by 50 percent to 120 percent over part of this period. Increased monetary uncertainty makes it harder for the price system to allocate resources efficiently. This reduction in efficiency occurs because producers and consumers find it more difficult to use market prices to distinguish relative price shifts, which call for a reallocation of resources, from shifts in the general level of prices, which do not call for a reallocation of resources.[4] This means that periods of increased monetary uncertainty are typically accompanied by yo-yo-like movements of resources in and out of various activities as individuals more frequently find, ex-post, they have misinterpreted market price signals. The result is increased macroeconomic instability.

Additionally, it is a feature of discretionary policy, and one that increases uncertainty, that it is time inconsistent. The policy that policymakers adopt today and say they plan to continue tomorrow may not look to be the best policy when tomorrow arrives. Hence, under discretion policymakers have an incentive to renege on their commitments. As Barro discusses in Chapter 1 of this volume, this results in suboptimal economic performance.

Finally, the criteria that Lindsey and others use to justify discretionary policy are inherently inconsistent and thus assure that individuals are confronted with an uncertain monetary environment. Recall that Lindsey argues that short-run monetary policies should

---

3. I would prefer to have figures on real GNP growth, but I could not come up with them. The reason I would prefer them is that if P is the rate of growth of the price level, y the rate of growth of real GNP, and Y the rate of growth of nominal GNP, it follows that $\text{Var}(Y) = \text{Var}(P) + \text{Var}(y) + 2\text{Cov}(P,y)$. Hence Federal Reserve policies could have destabilized nominal GNP growth while stabilizing real GNP growth. This seems to be an unlikely outcome, however.

4. For a discussion of the price system as a mechanism for providing information, see Hayek (1945).

be aimed at stabilizing real and nominal magnitudes, while long-run policy should be focused on stabilizing nominal magnitudes. The problem with this is that the long run is not independent of the short run—the long-run money supply path is simply the sum of its short-run paths. To see this, suppose that the Federal Reserve adopts Lindsey's two criteria by announcing on January 1 that its long-run price-level goals can be achieved if the money supply grows 3 percent over the year (roughly speaking, this would require money growth to average ¼ percent per month). In addition, it is also announced that, should a recession develop, the Federal Reserve will increase the money growth rate to stabilize the economy. Suppose that all goes smoothly for the first ten months of the year—no recession materializes, and the Federal Reserve increases the money supply ¼ percent each month as its long-run price level goals dictate.

However, suppose that early in November a recession develops. In accord with its short-run stabilization objectives, the Federal Reserve responds by pumping money supply growth up to ½ percent in November. However, December arrives and the recession has deepened. The Federal Reserve now has a dilemma. The money supply has already grown 3 percent over the first eleven months of the year $(10 \times \frac{1}{4}\% + \frac{1}{2}\% = 3\%)$. Therefore, the Federal Reserve cannot both meet its long-run money growth target and expand the money supply in order to combat the recession as its short-run objectives require. A choice must be made, and the private sector is likely to be left to guess which objective will win out when the Federal Open Market Committee meets. The two criteria that Lindsey proposes, and that history indicates the Federal Reserve has adopted, thus lead to a chronic conflict between short-run and long-run money growth goals, and this contributes to a high degree of monetary uncertainty.

One rule with much to recommend it was proposed by Friedman (1948, 1953). It calls for coupling a flexible exchange rate with a constant-money-growth rule. The money growth rate could easily be tied to the average growth rate of real output over a certain preannounced period so as to prevent the inflation rate from drifting off course if the trend rate of growth of real output changed. This proposal has several advantages. First, it allows a country to pick the inflation rate it deems optimal. In light of the fact that the refusal of other countries to accept inflation rates imposed on them by U.S. policies was a cause for the collapse of the Bretton Woods system, this has a strong practical appeal. It also has a sound economic appeal in light of the optimal inflation literature (see, for instance, Aschauer and Greenwood 1983). Second, when left free to respond to market forces, the exchange rate, like other prices, provides information to economic actors. As discussed by Kimbrough (1984a), this information helps producers and consumers to allocate resources efficiently and to stabilize the economy.[5] Third, many economists argue that national price levels are slow to adjust to changes in underlying economic conditions. Therefore, exchange rate movements have an important role to play in facilitating short-run relative price adjustments. Fourth, there is the well-known argument that flexible exchange rates help to promote free trade by eliminating balance of payments objectives as a source of protectionist measures. (I am skeptical of this argument.) Finally, despite much lip service in the popular press and in academic circles, there is no evidence to indicate that the U.S. economy has experienced more instability since the demise of Bretton Woods and the move to floating rates. Preliminary work in Kimbrough (1984b) indicates that during the Bretton Woods era (1948–72) the standard deviation of U.S. real output about its natural level (calculated as a simple autoregressive process plus trend) was 3.8 percent and, since the adoption of floating rates (1973–82), has been 4.3 percent. This difference is statistically insignificant, which is noteworthy, since no attempt has been made to control for destabilizing factors emerging during the floating rate period, such as increased monetary instability and the major oil price shocks. Were these factors controlled for, it would be reasonable to expect that the evidence would come down in favor of floating rates.

REFERENCES

Aschauer, David, and Jeremy Greenwood. "A Further Exploration in the Theory of Exchange Rate Regimes." *Journal of Political Economy* 91 (October 1983), 868–75.
Barro, Robert J. "The Equilibrium Approach to Business Cycles." In *Money, Expectations, and Business Cycles*. New York: Academic Press, 1981a. Pp. 41–78.
———."Unanticipated Money Growth and Economic Activity in the United States." In *Money, Expectations, and Business Cycles*. New York: Academic Press, 1981b. pp. 137–69.
Brunner, Karl, and Allan H. Meltzer. "Strategies and Tactics For Monetary Control." In *Money, Monetary Policy, and Financial Institutions*, Karl Brunner and Allan H. Meltzer, eds. Carnegie-Rochester Conference Series on Public Policy, vol. 18. Amsterdam: North-Holland, 1983. Pp. 59–103.

5. Under fixed exchange rates money supply or balance of payments figures can, in principle, provide essentially the same information. However, because of reporting errors in early estimates and the infrequent reporting intervals, this information will be inferior in quality to that provided directly by the exchange rate.

Friedman, Milton. "A Monetary and Fiscal Framework for Economic Stability." *American Economic Review* 38 (June 1948), 245–64.

———."The Case for Flexible Exchange Rates." In *Essays in Positive Economics*. Chicago: University of Chicago Press, 1953. Pp. 157–203.

———."Nobel Lecture: Inflation and Unemployment." *Journal of Political Economy* 85 (June 1977), 451–72.

Goodfriend, Marvin. "The Promises and Pitfalls of Contemporaneous Reserve Requirements for the Implementation of Monetary Policy." Federal Reserve Bank of Richmond, *Economic Review* 70 (May/June 1984), 3–12.

Hayek, Friedrich A. "The Use of Knowledge in Society." *American Economic Review* 35 (September 1945), 519–30.

Johannes, James M., and Robert H. Rasche. "Predicting the Money Multiplier." *Journal of Monetary Economics* 5 (July 1979), 301–25.

Kimbrough, Kent P. "Aggregate Information and the Role of Monetary Policy in an Open Economy." *Journal of Political Economy* 92 (April 1984a), 268–85.

———."Exchange Rate Regimes and Output Fluctuations: U.S. Evidence." Duke University, Durham, North Carolina, 1984b.

Stockman, Alan C. "Anticipated Inflation and the Capital Stock in a Cash-in-Advance Economy." *Journal of Monetary Economics* 8 (November 1981), 387–93.

SIX

Optimal Monetary Institutions and Policy

ROBERT E. HALL

IN THE BEST of all possible worlds, the dollar would be a unit of purchasing power with the same stability as the inch and the gallon. Markets would clear instantly, so there would be no adverse consequences for real economic activity when monetary policy single-mindedly kept the price level on target. In the modern U.S. economy, however, there is a strong suspicion that purely nominal changes in monetary policy have real consequences in the short run. Moreover, the same suspicion exists for every other economy, both contemporary and historical. Though economics has not been notably successful in proving that monetary policy affects employment and output as well as the price level, and though economists differ acrimoniously about the strength of the real effects, almost nobody would assert that there are no real effects at all.

This chapter proposes a design of monetary policy for an economy where there is a suspicion of sluggish price movement and consequent real effects of monetary change. Its purpose is to recommend a practical policy that is as close as possible to the theoretical optimum. Though the recommendation is pratical in the sense that it considers all the issues that would arise if the policy were put in place in the modern U.S. economy, it does not consider the question of the political acceptability of the policy.

Three major objectives enter into the design of the policy:

1. *Microeconomic efficiency.* A monetary policy should avoid deadweight loss. Two major sources of loss in the current system are requirements that banks hold non-interest-bearing reserves and the prohibition of bearer securities in small denominations that would compete with Federal Reserve currency.

2. *Stability.* Every monetary system involves a unique asset—gold, silver, currency, or reserves—that unambiguously discharges a debt. In times of financial crisis, the demand for this asset rises sharply. A good monetary system will insulate the price level and real activity from these shifts in demand.

3. *Macroeconomic efficiency and robustness.* If markets do not clear instantly and monetary actions have real effects, policy faces a

224

tradeoff between price stability and real stability. An aggressive policy for price stabilization may bring sharp fluctuations in output and employment. Fundamentally, the choice between price and output stability involves subtle issues about the benefits of each. However, a very basic requirement is that policy minimize real fluctuations for whatever amount of price variability is chosen. Such a policy is efficient. Moreover, because of our ignorance about the structure of the economy, a policy should be robust; it should bring an acceptable result, both in an economy with perfectly flexible prices and in an economy with quite sticky prices.

All three of these objectives can be met—there is no tradeoff among them. Deadweight loss can be made inconsequential by basing the monetary system on interest-bearing reserves. Because the reserves are attractive financially, there is no need for reserve requirements or for the prohibition of private competitors. Further, by letting a substantial fraction of the federal debt serve as reserves, the problem of instability is solved. Sudden increases in demand during crises have much smaller consequences within a large market for hundreds of billions of dollars of federal debt than within a market for tens of billions of dollars of reserves.

A policy that is efficient from the macroeconomic point of view takes into account departures of the price level from its target and departures of real activity from its potential level. A remarkably simple characterization of efficient policies is this: all efficient policies make the price-level departures proportional to the unemployment departures. Another way to think of efficiency is by considering what I call an *elastic price target*. The price-level target is a constant plus an elasticity times the unemployment rate. The elasticity might be 8. Hawks (those who put heavy weight on price stability or believe that prices are highly flexible) would choose an elasticity below eight; doves might choose an elasticity even higher than eight. The simple consideration of efficiency, however, quite apart from the welfare value of price stability or the flexibility of prices, tells us to pursue a policy within the family of elastic price targets. All other policies, including especially the type of policy followed by the United States for the past few decades, are nonstarters. An elastic target policy can deliver better performance in terms of both price and employment stability.

Monetary Saturation

Milton Friedman (1969) has made the basic case for monetary saturation. Basically, if monetary instruments cost no more to issue and service than do nonmonetary instruments, then simple minimization of deadweight loss requires that the yields of the two types of instruments be equal. In an economy where no interest is paid on monetary instruments, saturation can occur only when the nominal interest rate on nonmonetary instruments is zero. As Friedman pointed out, policy can achieve zero nominal rates by deflating at the negative of the real interest rate. But in a modern economy without legal or technological restrictions on paying interest on monetary instruments, saturation can be achieved with stable prices (or any other policy for the price level) by paying market interest rates on monetary instruments.

To make this discussion specific, I will consider the possibility that the Federal Reserve pays the three-month Treasury bill rate on reserves, minus a small differential. The actual magnitude of the differential is what much of the rest of this chapter is about; for now, I only stress that the diffferential is small. Because reserves pay a yield close to other short-term instruments, the demand for reserves would be substantial even though reserve requirements would no longer exist. Much of the wealth currently held by banks in the form of federal debt would be held as reserves instead. In 1983, commercial banks alone held $188 billion in Treasury securities, as against only $40 billion in reserves.

The portfolio of the Federal Reserve would swell to meet the added demand for reserves. Around half the $380 billion in short-term (less than one-year maturity) federal debt should be monetized to get close to saturation.

To achieve saturation in currency, a technological solution to the problem of paying interest is needed. Mere restoration of banks' rights to issue non-interest-bearing notes is probably a step backward because it trades tax revenue for the wasteful techniques that banks would use to keep their notes in circulation. The best step would be to grant all financial institutions the right to issue interest-bearing notes in small denominations. A note with a constant face value of $100 could earn interest for the holder, which would be credited to that person's Visa account. Each time a bank paid a depositor with a note, it would record the fact electronically with Visa so that interest could be credited to the current holder.

Deregulation of bearer notes would eliminate part of the deadweight loss associated with currency today, but I suspect that considerable demand for Federal Reserve notes would remain. The Federal Reserve would continue to earn substantial seigniorage on its currency issue.

Stability. Saturation of the economy in reserves should help to stabilize the economy by reducing the frequency of financial crises and by limiting their consequences when they do occur. In a crisis, debtors struggle to obtain the asset that underlies the monetary system—the asset that has the power to discharge a debt unambiguously. Under the gold standard, a crisis takes the form of a move out of paper assets and into gold. In a fiduciary monetary system, debtors move into the reserves at the central bank. Although the founding principle of the Federal Reserve System was that discretionary policy could accommodate such a move by issuing added reserves, monetary history suggests that the Federal Reserve can always think of a good reason not to follow through in any given crisis. In any case, it is difficult for the Federal Reserve to determine how much to expand reserves, especially when a crisis occurs during inflation.

When the economy is saturated in reserves, as it would be if those reserves paid virtually the market rate, it stands to reason that the demand for them will be more stable. In the existing system, there is outstanding at any time several trillion dollars' worth of promises to pay reserves, either on demand or at a specified term. In 1983, there was only $40 billion in reserves, and essentially all of it was tied up as required reserves. A little nervousness on the part of debtors adds tremendously to demand for reserves. As it stands, the economy can accommodate this demand only by sharply increasing interest rates. Were the economy saturated in several hundred billion dollars of reserves, a modest rearrangement of reserves would satisfy the new demand from nervous debtors.

The Interest-Rate Differential as the Instrument of Monetary Policy

Once the Federal Reserve has established the policy of paying interest on reserves so as to saturate the economy in reserves, it opens up the possibility of using, as a policy instrument, the differential between the reserve interest rate and other interest rates. Raising the differential—that is, lowering the reserve rate relative to other rates—stimulates the economy. It is equivalent to increasing the quantity of reserves because a larger differential decreases the demand for reserves. Similarly, reducing the differential constitutes monetary contraction.

Manipulation of the interest-rate differential offers an advantage over open-market operations as a technique for carrying out mon-

etary policy, by avoiding the brokerage costs of open-market operations. Under present policy, the Federal Reserve churns its portfolio
of government securities in the process of trying to stay within its
target ranges for the levels of monetary aggregates and interest rates.
The process of crediting reserve accounts with interest, on the other
hand, is purely a matter of making accounting entries and involves
no brokerage.

Efficient and Robust Monetary Policy

Even though monetary saturation would improve macroeconomic
performance by reducing the frequency and severity of financial crises,
stabilization policy would retain many of its current problems. From
time to time, unexpected shocks to aggregate demand would push
unemployment above or below its normal level. These shocks would
affect the price level as well, perhaps with a lag. A greater challenge
to policy occurs when the price level jumps suddenly. In an economy
with sticky prices, a sharp increase in the price of one factor such as
oil has the initial impact of raising the general price level, though
ultimately a price stabilization policy can effect a lowering of the
prices of other factors of production as needed to keep the overall
price level on target.

The success of monetary policies can be judged in terms of two
basic outcomes in the economy: the variability of the price level and
the variability of unemployment. The basic goal of monetary policy
in the longer run is price stability. Every departure of the price level
from a constant target is a shortcoming. Long-range financial planning by individuals and businesses is most effective if the future value
of the dollar can be relied on, even many decades hence, to be close
to its current value.

With respect to unemployment, there are many reasons to believe
that the average level of unemployment is inefficiently high. In such
a case, a reduction in unemployment below the rate at which the
economy will tend toward unaided would be socially beneficial. It
might seem that the level of unemployment, not just its variability,
could be considered in judging monetary policies. However, as Milton Friedman (1968) argued persuasively, monetary policy is powerless to influence the average level of unemployment. It is reasonable
to suppose that the marginal social cost of unemployment rises with
the level of unemployment. The best that monetary policy can do is
to limit fluctuations in unemployment, since each fluctuation has a
net social cost when the upside outweighs the downside.

As a general matter, then, we can judge monetary policies by use of a diagram pioneered by John Taylor (1980), where the horizontal axis is unemployment variability (measured by the standard deviation of the departure of unemployment from its normal or natural level) and the vertical axis is price variability (measured as the standard deviation of the percent deviation from a constant target). Figure 6–1 is such a diagram. Any point in the diagram is a combination of unemployment and price variability that might be brought by a particular monetary policy rule. In general, points close to the origin represent the best combinations. But structural characteristics of the economy limit the points that are attainable by even the best policy. There is a curve in Figure 6–1, labeled the *policy frontier*, made up of the points closest to the origin that can actually be achieved with a practical policy, given the degree of price stickiness in the economy.

Each point on the policy frontier corresponds to a policy that is efficient in the sense that no other policy gives better performance in terms of both unemployment variability and price variability. The policy frontier has a critical role in deriving optimal policy. Without knowing anything about social preferences for unemployment versus price stability, we can make the strong statement that any policy not on the frontier is irrational. Preferences turn out to have a sharply

Figure 6–1

The Policy Frontier for Unemployment and Price Variability

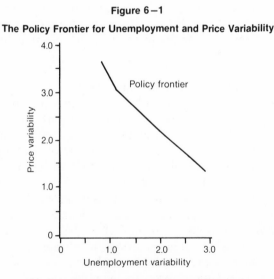

Note: Each point on the frontier is as close as any policy can get to small values of both unemployment and price variability. The axes are the standard deviation of the unemployment rate around its normal level of 6 percent and the standard deviation of the percent departure of the price level from a constant target level.

limited role in policy choice—the class of efficient monetary policies is quite small. The most important thing for policymakers to do is to get to the frontier. As I will show, actual policy since the mid-1960s put the U.S. economy at a point far above the frontier. Great improvements of the Pareto-superior type—reductions in both unemployment and price variability—could have been achieved without taking any position on the relative importance of unemployment and price stability.

Robustness. As I have stressed, economists don't really know how much influence monetary policy has on unemployment. The prevailing Keynesian model says that monetary policy moves affect unemployment during a transition period; during the same period, the price level is less sensitive to monetay policy than in the long run. The policy frontier in Figure 6–1 describes this case. But there are alternative models, not totally refuted by the data, where monetary policy cannot influence unemployment at all. Then the policy frontier is a vertical line.

A robust monetary policy gives reasonable performance under a wide variety of conditions. It gives a determinate price level, without too much variability, in the case where unemployment is unaffected by monetary policy. It gives a reasonable point on the policy frontier for the type of economy that the majority of practical macroeconomists believe we inhabit. Finally, it does not bring outrageous unemployment variability if prices prove less flexible than is generally thought.

Efficiency. Generally, the efficient monetary policy in a given macroeconomic model can be derived by minimizing the variance of the price level, given the objective of attaining a particular variance of unemployment. The structural equation of the model that matters for this calculation is the price adjustment equation, or Phillips curve. If that equation has a complicated form, the efficient policy may be correspondingly complicated. However, I avoid a detailed analysis of this type for two reasons. First, there is no professional consensus on the details of price adjustment. The only consensus is that prices move somewhat slowly to clear markets and that unemployment is one of the variables that might reasonably indicate the direction and magnitude of price adjustments. Second, as pointed out by Robert Lucas (1976) in his famous paper on econometric policy evaluation, the Phillips curve may change when a new policy comes into use. To estimate the shift requires a theory of price adjustment. Since the whole point of this chapter is to avoid commitment to a particular theory, that avenue would be self-defeating.

What I will do instead is to examine the very simplest case, where the rate of inflation is governed, negatively, by the unemployment rate, without any expectational shifts or other modern complications. The absence of an expectational term is appropriate in considering alternative policies, all of which stabilize the price level. The shifting Phillips curve is a phenomenon of an economy with chronic upward drift in its price level. No policy considered here permits chronic drift.

In addition to a negative relation between the rates of unemployment and inflation, the Phillips curve in my analysis shifts randomly. Inflationary shocks from all sources other than aggregate demand— world oil and food markets, episodes of aggressive wage demands, and so forth—are wrapped into the shift. As it turns out, almost nothing is lost by treating these as a single composite rather than looking at them individually.

The problem, then, is to describe policies that bring efficient combinations of unemployment and price variability in an economy with a simple Phillips curve. I will assume that monetary policy has a single dimension that influences unemployment and prices. Specifically, when the interest-rate differential on reserves is raised, unemployment falls and prices rise in some combination; when it is lowered, unemployment rises and prices fall.

As a final step in setting the stage, let me assume that the inflationary shocks that perturb the Phillips curve are unpredictable from one year to the next. In dealing with this year's stabilization problems, monetary policy cannot anticipate what new shock will occur next year.

In this setup, efficient stabilization policies can be characterized in a particularly simple way:

> The efficient policy can be expressed as a requirement that the deviation of the price level from target be a fixed multiple, A, of the deviation of unemployment from normal.

> Any policy that keeps the price deviation in proportion to the unemployment deviation is efficient.

To carry out an efficient policy, the Federal Reserve simply pegs the price level at a multiple of the unemployment rate (when they are expressed as deviations from a constant long-run price target and the normal unemployment rate, respectively). Suppose the elasticity of the policy (the multiple, A) is chosen to be 8, which I consider a reasonable choice. If the Federal Reserve finds that prices are on target but that unemployment is a percentage point too high, it will launch an expansion, which will bring down unemployment by one point, raise the price level by eight points, or have a combination of effects such that the new price level is 8 times the new unemployment rate.

An important feature of this type of policy is that it does not rest on any particular belief about the immediate impact of monetary policy. The opinion of a majority of economists is that the earliest effects are mostly real. In that case, policy will make adjustments that shift unemployment relative to an unresponsive price level in order to achieve the elastic target. Should the price level respond rapidly, the policy will work just as well. The elastic price target is a robust policy as a result.

The elastic price target achieves price stability in the long run without fail. No matter what happens to the economy, the average unemployment rate in the long run will equal the normal rate. Consequently, under this policy, the average price level must be equal to the target. Price-level drift, a major failing of actual U.S. policy since 1965, will not occur under the elastic target. If policymakers are unable to adjust the target formula to offset permanent changes in equilibrium unemployment, the level of prices may differ permanently from the target, but the average rate of change of prices will be zero.

The elasticity of the target provides the only necessary control over the choice between unemployment and price stability. A low elasticity keeps prices close to target at all times, at the cost of wide swings in unemployment. An elasticity of zero, which is an efficient policy, is strict price stabilization, as proposed by Knut Wicksell (1962). Under such a policy, the Federal Reserve is oblivious to unemployment and adjusts the reserve differential aggressively enough to keep prices right on target. If the majority of economists are right about the Phillips curve, then this policy involves hideous jumps in unemployment when inflationary shocks strike (e.g., the two oil price shocks of the 1970s).

An elasticity of 2.5 or 3 is a close approximation to nominal GNP targeting, a policy recommended by many economists in its own right. Under this policy, shocks are partially acccommodated in the short run. Prices are to rise and output is to fall by the same percentage, so that the product, nominal GNP, remains at a predetermined level. By Okun's law, the corresponding change in unemployment is ⅓ or 1/2.5 percentage points for each percentage of output, so the elasticity of the target should be 2.5 or 3. Stating the policy in terms of an elastic price target with respect to unemployment avoids the inconvenience of having to prescribe a target path for nominal GNP.

Nominal GNP targeting, or its equivalent—an elastic price target with an elasticity around 3—turns out to be a fairly harsh policy because it calls for aggressive contraction when adverse price shocks occur. A more forgiving policy, with smaller unemployment fluctuations and correspondingly larger and longer departures of the price level from target, is obtained with an elasticity of 8.

Simulation of three variants of the elastic price target for the period 1952–83 for the U.S. economy, with a Phillips-curve tradeoff of 0.5 percent lower inflation for each extra percentage point of unemployment, gave the following three points on the policy frontier (for details, see Hall 1984):

Elasticity	Standard deviation of price	Standard deviation of unemployment
0	0	2.79
3	2.64	0.88
8	3.50	0.44

Pure price stabilization—an elasticity of zero—requires powerful expansion and contraction of real activity to offset price shocks. The standard deviation of unemployment of almost 3 percentage points means that unemployment rates of 9 percent are common and that rates of 12 percent occur about one time in twenty.

The next line shows that nominal GNP targeting—an elasticity of 3—gives much better real performance at the cost of some deviations of the price level from target. Unemployment is between 5 and 7 percent for more than two-thirds of the time. Rates above 8 percent are rare. The price level spends more than two-thirds of its time in a band between 97 percent and 103 percent of the target level.

The third line, corresponding to an elasticity of 8, gives even better real stability. The standard deviation of 0.44 percentage points for unemployment means that the rate is almost never above 7 percent or below 5 percent. The cost is a standard deviation of the price level of 3.5 percent.

What is most instructive is to contrast these three points on the policy frontier with the actual behavior of the price level and the unemployment rate over the same period, 1952–83. The actual standard deviation of unemployment was 1.74 percentage points, about double what it would have been under nominal GNP targeting. The high variability of unemployment should have given us an extremely stable price level, with a standard deviation of about 1 percent around a constant level. Instead, the price level had an extraordinary degree of variability because it rose so much. Obviously, there was no constant target for the price level. One way of describing the failure of the policy is in terms of the standard deviation of the price level around its average for the period; this standard deviation was a staggering 38.4 percent. Actual policy was outside the policy frontier by miles. This illustrates my most basic point: it is much more important to have any efficient policy than to have an inefficient one. The actual choice of a point on the frontier is a subsidiary matter.

Properties of a Robust Policy. A monetary policy based on an elastic price target is robust. It is always efficient, regardless of the characteristics of the economy. It delivers a degree of unemployment stability that can be improved only by accepting more price instability. It has two other robustness properties.

Although an arbitrary choice of the elasticity always gives an efficient policy, the best policy is the one on the frontier that touches the highest social indifference curve between price and unemployment variability. Generally, the position of the policy frontier depends on the slope of the Phillips curve, so the tangency occurs at different points in the diagram for different slopes. The choice of the optimal policy rests on knowledge of the slope of the Phillips curve and on preferences about inflation and unemployment variability.

The interesting feature of the optimal choice, however, is that the optimal elasticity of the price target is very insensitive to the slope of the Phillips curve. It is true that an economy with a more responsive inflation rate—that is, a steeper Phillips curve—will have a more favorable policy frontier, closer to the origin. But the policy frontiers for different slopes are roughly concentric—one is more or less like another magnified. Mathematically, the policy frontier is approximately homothetic. The slopes of different frontiers corresponding to different Phillips curve parameters are the same along a ray from the origin. If the social indifference curves are roughly homothetic as well, then the expansion path showing the alternative optima for different Phillips curves' slopes is a ray from the origin. But all policies along a ray from the origin involve the same elasticity; the slope of the ray is the elasticity. A policy of making price deviations proportional to unemployment deviations makes the standard deviations of the two variables stand in the prescribed proportion as well.

The conclusion that emerges is the following: for a given set of social preferences, the choice of the elasticity of the elastic price target is roughly independent of the slope of the Phillips curve. If the best elasticity is 8 for an economy with a Phillips curve slope of

0.5, 8 will be a good choice for slopes of 0.1 and 2.0 as well. Because we don't really know the slope of the Phillips curve, this type of robustness is an important feature of the policy. It will not go badly astray even if the existing econometric evidence about price adjustment is severely biased, as some critics have charged.

The final robustness property of the policy concerns its performance in an economy with perfectly flexible prices. Certainly it would be an embarrassment to propose a policy that left the price level indeterminate in such an economy. A robust policy should make the price level determinate and not too unstable in an economy with instant market clearing. By the criteria of this chapter, only one policy is optimal for that economy: exact price stability. An elastic price target is a little suboptimal because it makes the price level vary as unemployment varies, even though there is no social gain from the elasticity. If we were completely confident that prices were fully flexible, we would set the elasticity at zero. But the cost of making the elasticity positive is not very high. The price level is determinate because the policy is one of pegging the price level to the unemployment rate, which is exogenous to price determination in an economy with perfectly flexible prices.

Taken together, these considerations suggest that an elastic price target with an elasticity of 8 is a desirable one, given our limited knowledge of the operating characteristics of the economy. It seems to give a reasonable simulated performance over the post–World War II period under the assumption that the slope of the Phillips curve is 0.5. Its performance would be much better if the Phillips curve were significantly steeper, or much worse if it were flatter, but it is not clear that we would choose a different elasticity in either of those cases. Even if the professional consensus on the transitory real effects of monetary policy is wrong, and the optimal policy is complete price stability, the cost of using the elastic target policy is not too high.

Automatic Execution of the Efficient Policy

Proponents of nominal GNP targeting have generally offered the target as a guide to making monetary policy in its present form. Their hope is that the Federal Reserve would trade government securities as necessary to keep nominal GNP on its target path. The chairman of the Federal Reserve Board would report to Congress periodically on the success of policy; the principal criterion for judging this success would be how close nominal GNP came to its prescribed level. Some type of penalty would be imposed if nominal GNP went too far astray.

That type of policymaking would be a big improvement over the current policy. It could not help but move us closer to the policy frontier. But the two basic ideas of this chapter can be linked to give a completely automatic policy. We can make the reserve-interest differential the instrument of monetary policy and then change it by formula so as to achieve the elastic price target. The result is a policy that is close to ideal on both microeconomic and macroeconomic grounds.

The basic idea of the automatic policy is to raise the reserve differential whenever the economy drops below the elastic target and to lower it when the economy is above target. However, some subtleties need to be handled in order to make the policy work smoothly. If policy responds just to the current state of the economy, and there is some lag before a policy change has much effect on either unemployment or the price level, then there is a potential for unstable feedback. Even if the system were not unstable under such a policy rule, a response this month to economic data from last month could be seriously disruptive if it is not self-limiting.

Both the price level and the unemployment rate are measured with a certain amount of unavoidable error. If the price level were high and unemployment low in a particular month, an aggressive policy might call for a reserve differential that would be so low as to attract a large amount of wealth into reserves. The immediate impact of this monetary contraction would be high interest rates and financial disruption. If the reserve differential were kept low for the whole month, without responding to anything that happened during the month, there could be a month-long economic crisis. Even if unemployment and prices responded a bit during the month, the crisis could easily extend into the second month as well. The response in later months could be so strong as to call for a later expansionary move to a high reserve differential.

All of these problems can be avoided by linking the reserve differential not to the most recent data but to future data, say for the forthcoming year. In other words, the elastic target is to be achieved over the average of the forthcoming twelve months, not for the current month alone. The advantage of imposing the target on expectations rather than on historical data is that expectations are instantly responsive to policy. The month-long crisis I just described could not occur if the reserve differential were linked to the near future instead of the immediate past. If a situation threatened where a higher differential might raise the demand for reserves and contract the economy, the expectation of that contraction would show immediately in higher expected unemployment and lower expected prices. Quickly, a new equilibrium would be reached, where the amount of the differential was just enough to put the economy on the elastic price target in terms of expectations for the coming twelve months.

Many other economists have pointed out the virtue of guiding monetary policy by expectations or forecasts instead of the most recent actual behavior of the economy. Some economists have proposed that the Federal Reserve look at futures markets for commodities or for the cost of living index or, in the case of nominal GNP targeting, at nominal GNP forecasts from reliable outside forecasters. These all are good ideas. But when the reserve differential is used as the instrument of monetary policy, there is a particularly simple way to link policy to expectations. All that needs to be done is to pay interest later, once the actual performance of the economy becomes known.

The specific operating rule I have in mind is the following: the Federal Reserve keeps track of the average balance over the past twelve months for each reserve account. Each month, it credits each account for 1 percentage point of interest on its average balance for each point by which the price level exceeds the elastic target. The interest is credited toward the end of each month, when the price level and unemployment rate for the previous month are announced. In addition, interest is credited daily for each account on that day's balance at the three-month Treasury bill rate less 0.5 percent.

Under this system, it is impossible for the public consensus about the price level and the unemployment rate over the next twelve months to differ significantly from the elastic target. Suppose, for example, that the public believed that the price level would be 1 percent above the elastic target on average over the next twelve months. They would also believe that reserves were going to pay 0.5 percent more than Treasury bills. Such a situation would be highly contractionary. But this only shows that their original belief was incorrect—the price level could not be so far above target in the face of such a negative policy.

The policy of retrospective payment of interest based on departures from the target is close to the ideal implementation of the elastic target. It avoids the central problem of earlier proposals for nominal GNP targeting: What do we do when the Federal Reserve misses the target? Monetary policy would be in the hands of a perfectly reliable automaton. Unlike other proposals to put monetary policy on automatic pilot, such as the constant money growth rule, this one is guaranteed to stay out of trouble. Its sensitivity to unemployment as well as to the price level means that it cannot bring the sharp recession or uncontrolled boom that is the bugaboo of constant money growth.

The proposed policy has two parameters that might benefit from fine tuning. One is the twelve-month period over which expectations are relevant. It might work a little better to use twenty-four months or six months. I have chosen twelve months because it appears that a substantial fraction of the total impact of monetary policy on the real variables takes place within that span. The other parameter is the number of percentage points of interest per point of departure from the target. One for one seems reasonable, but the system might work more smoothly with a smaller or larger multiplier.

Conclusion

I have recommended a completely practical general approach to monetary policy with a number of important properties of optimality. The approach has no political appeal whatsoever; it seems complicated and arcane and would require that the Federal Reserve give up all of its revenue and all of its responsibility for monetary policy. Nevertheless, the basic ideas of monetary saturation and an elastic price standard should be investigated by economists.

Let me conclude by restating the policy I have in mind and by listing its virtues. The Federal Reserve would monetize about half of the short-term federal debt; the actual amount is relatively unimportant. To do this, it would pay interest on reserves at about 50 basis points below the Treasury bill rate. Deadweight loss in financial markets would be further reduced by eliminating reserve requirements and by lifting restrictions on interest-bearing competitors to currency.

In addition to paying daily interest linked to Treasury bills, the Federal Reserve would credit each account monthly in proportion to its average balance over the preceding twelve months. The extra interest would be 1 percent (at annual rates) for each point by which the price level exceeded 8 times the unemployment rate. The price level would be stated as a deviation from a fixed target, and the unemployment rate as a deviation from the normal rate of 6 percent.

The effect of this policy would be to saturate the economy in reserves. Saturation has chronic microeconomic benefits in the form of eliminated deadweight loss. In addition, saturation would help stabilize financial markets and the economy as a whole. Episodes of economic crisis when the public shifts portfolio demands toward reserves, are less disruptive in an economy in which large volumes of reserves are held for portfolio motives in the first place. Saturation provides the needed elasticity of reserves that the Federal Reserve was created to provide, but that it has failed to provide too many times.

By linking the reserve differential to the prospective behavior of the economy, the policy also achieves the efficient stabilization policy. It correctly balances price stability against unemployment stability. When an adverse inflationary shock hits the economy, the policy absorbs the shock first in the form of a higher price level and then gradually works the price level back to its fixed long-run target. Such a response is optimal.

The proposed policy is robust, in the sense that it functions well in economies with very different degrees of price flexibility and real responsiveness to monetary change. If prices are completely flexible, the policy simply pegs the price level to an exogenous variable, the unemployment rate. If prices and unemployment are related in the way suggested by mainstream macroeconomics, then the elastic price target is the efficient stabilization policy. That property holds for any degree of price stickiness. Moveover, the choice of the optimal policy from among the efficient ones—that is, the choice of the optimal elasticity of the target—is almost independent of the amount of price stickiness. An elasticity of 8 seem a good choice whether the slope of the Phillips curve is 0.1 points of inflation per point of unemployment or 1.0.

REFERENCES

Friedman, Milton. "The Role of Monetary Policy." *American Economic Review* 58 (March 1968), 1–17.
———. "The Optimum Quantity of Money." In *The Optimum Quantity of Money and Other Essays*. Chicago: Aldine Publishing Co., 1969. Pp. 1–50.
Hall, Robert E. "Monetary Strategy with an Elastic Price Standard." In *Price Stability and Public Policy*. Kansas City: Federal Reserve Bank of Kansas City, August 2–3, 1984. Pp. 137–59.
Lucas, Robert E. "Econometric Policy Evaluation: A Critique." In *The Phillips Curve and Labor Markets*, Karl Brunner and Allen H. Meltzer, eds. Carnegie-Rochester Conference Series on Public Policy, vol. 1. Amsterdam: North-Holland, 1976. Pp. 19–46.
Taylor, John B. "Output and Price Stability: An International Comparison." *Journal of Economic Dynamics and Control* 2 (1980), 109–32.
Wicksell, Knut. *Interest and Prices*, R.F. Kahn, trans. New York: Augustus M. Kelley, 1962.

Hall's Proposals for Monetary Reform

LELAND B. YEAGER

SO FAR, American monetary policy has been inefficient. The United States has suffered more unemployment than necessary to keep inflation down to a given rate and more inflation than necessary to keep unemployment down. For each condition, high levels and high variability have gone together. Robert Hall proposes to make policy efficient, with no more variability in either unemployment or inflation than necessary for holding down the variability of the other.

Let me see if I understand Hall's proposal. A hybrid rule would target on both prices and unemployment. Monetary policy would aim at keeping a price index at 100 plus or minus some multiple of the number of percentage points by which the unemployment rate exceeded or fell short of 6 percent. Monetary policy should be easier with unemployment at 10 percent, for example, than with unemployment lower. Policy would then aim at a price level higher by some multiple of 4 percentage points than the target of 100 that would be appropriate if unemployment were only 6 percent, the assumed natural level. The just-mentioned multiple is what Hall calls the *elasticity* of the price target.

The ideal elasticity depends on the degree of price stickiness. If stickiness were zero—if prices were perfectly flexible—then the elasticity should be zero, meaning that policy would always target a price index of 100. The stickier prices were, the more the policy would temporarily compromise with the goal of a steady price level for the sake of lower unemployment. Hall suggests an elasticity of 8 for illustrative purposes but says that the effectiveness of his policy is not sensitive to the particular elasticity adopted in the rule. That is what he means in calling his policy *robust*.

An example illustrates the logic of his proposal. Suppose some supply shock like an oil price increase mechanically, arithmetically, raises the general price level. Total real money balances shrink, and with them the volumes of transactions, production, and employment they can support. To restore real money balances partially, accommodate the shock, and fight unemployment, Hall's rule would call

240

for accepting an increased target price level and so for expanding the nominal money supply. In the longer run, price stickiness would be overcome, declines in other prices would average out the rises in oil and oil-linked prices, and these price declines would promote the clearing of the labor market and other markets. Real money balances would recover in this way without requiring full maintenance of the nominal monetary accommodation, which would turn out to have been necessary only temporarily. The decline in unemployment would, by Hall's rule, bring the target price level back down toward 100.

His rule, as I understand it, is designed to cope with price- and unemployment-boosting supply shocks. Barring supply shocks, success in always simply targeting on a price index of 100 would avoid demand shocks.

Now I turn from the targeting rule to Hall's innovative policy procedure. Reserve requirements would be dropped, but the central bank would pay interest on base money, the ultimate means of settlement. These interest payments would entice financial institutions and the public to hold more base money and fewer government securities than they do now. Having much more base money would greatly lessen the danger of a crisis caused by scrambles to convert other claims into it. The central bank would hold the securities no longer held outside it, collecting interest on them that would go toward covering its interest payments on base money. In effect, the government (counting the central bank as part of the government) would owe more of its debt in the form of base money and less in the form of bonds and bills.

I don't quite understand Hall's method of paying interest on hand-to-hand currency, but I'll mention a suggestion once made in conversation by J. Huston McCulloch. Currency could double as lottery tickets, with drawings periodically held to determine the winning serial numbers.

The interest rate on base money would be set slightly below the rate on Treasury bills or other open-market instruments. Hall speaks of the central bank's shrinking or expanding this differential from time to time, but it should be acceptable for simplicity to speak of raising or lowering the interest rate on base money.

Suppose that Hall's price and unemployment rule calls for tightening monetary policy. The central bank would raise the interest rate on base money, thereby inducing financial institutions to maintain larger reserve ratios and accordingly to curtail their other extensions of credit and their monetary and quasimonetary liabilities. (The total volume of base money and the central bank's asset portfolio would presumably remain almost steady all along or else grow only moderately.) In opposite conditions, when Hall's rule called for monetary ease, the central bank would cut the interest rate on base money, encouraging financial institutions to reduce their reserve ratios and to expand their money and credit activity.

If I recall correctly, James Tobin was urging manipulation of interest on reserve money as a policy weapon some years ago. Hall adds a new argument for this policy: it would avoid the brokerage and other costs of the central bank's constantly churning around in the securities market.

Hall reminds us of Milton Friedman's microefficiency argument for monetary saturation. Saturation could be practically achieved by allowing competition to press private issuers to pass most of the interest earned on their portfolios on to the holders of their deposits and small-denomination bearer securities.

Hall suggests an interesting twist. Ideally, policy should be shaped for the future, not the past, and it should enlist expectations on its side. Success in doing so would circumvent the problem of lags that is routinely urged against the ordinary proposal for targeting the management of fiat money on a price index. Therefore, the interest rate on reserves held last year (or whatever the specified period might be) should not be decided until the current year and in light of what Hall's rule would call for under current conditions. Last year, when institutions were making their reserve-holding decisions, they would not yet have known the interest rate they would receive. They would have been consulting their expectations of that rate and of future conditions affecting its determination. At each time, expected future conditions would be exerting their appropriate influence in advance.

Hall's rule does not require any specific quantity of money. It becomes unnecessary to try to define (and to keep redefining) money and to keep measuring its quantity. The central bank would not have to try to regulate its creation and factors affecting the demand for it (not directly, anyway—not apart from manipulating the interest rate paid on base money). Hall's proposal seems compatible with complete financial deregulation.

I'll close with some questions or suggestions. First, I wish Hall would explain more fully why he expects short-run deviations from the target of a steady price level to wash out in the long run. Second, I wish he would amplify his argument about enlisting expectations of the future through retroactive determination of the interest rate on base money. Third, should the degree of price stickiness simply be taken as given? Wouldn't a thoroughly credible policy reduce the degree of price stickiness and thereby reduce the appropriate extent of temporary departures from a steady-price-level target? Moreover, wouldn't a simple price-level rule itself be more credible than a complicated rule? Fourth, isn't it true that a simple rule could pretty much avoid demand shocks? Aren't the complexities of Hall's rule designed to cope with supply shocks instead? If this is true, and if major supply shocks are rare anyway, don't these facts add force to my third point and support the case for a relatively simple rule? Fifth, in the light of public-choice theory and of accumulated experience, can we really trust the government to behave itself and obey a monetary rule? Shouldn't we rather look for ways to get money entirely out of the government's control?

Finally, I congratulate Robert Hall on his fertility in coming up with ideas for monetary reform. His present proposal is one more in a varied series.

Comments on Hall's Proposals

MICHAEL R. DARBY

IN THE 1960s at Dartmouth College I learned that when investment shifts down, the government should increase spending to offset investment's effect on output. Yes, orthodox Keynesian doctrine from Gardner Ackley's old textbook was taught here too. It wasn't long before I learned that things were not so simple, that no lights went off telling us when and by how much investment shifted, and that there were all sorts of problems in implementing macroeconomic policy. That's why I always enjoy reading each of Robert Hall's successive proposals for optimal monetary institutions and policy.

Hall replaces the dismal science with a Humphreyesque economics of joy. How can we not be elated to learn that there are so many different monetary arrangements—ranging from his ammonium nitrate-copper-aluminum-plywood standard to his current proposal—each of which can give us optimal results. I am so happy. Since I could hardly hope to present any new insights into Hall's current optimal proposal after he himself has presented it, I think that the best way to show just how substantial is his contribution is by providing some of the old joyless analysis in contrast.

In the old way of thinking, the current level of cyclical output reflects the sum of the effects of autonomous shocks and policy shocks. If policymakers can predict the future autonomous component when their actions have effect with some accuracy, then policy can stabilize the output of the economy by generating policy effects that are negatively correlated with those autonomous shocks. Of course, Friedman taught us in 1951 that optimal policy actions must have not only effects that are negatively correlated but effects that are a fraction of the autonomous effects. If policy actions are too strong, they are destabilizing. The lowest possible variance of output is $(1 - \hat{p}^2)\sigma^2$, where σ^2 is the variance of output due to autonomous shocks and $\hat{p}$ is the largest (in absolute value) attainable correlation of policy effects with autonomous disturbances. If $\hat{p} = -0.2$, then optimal policy would reduce output variance 4 percent and nonoptimal policy would reduce the variance by less or increase the variance of output.

One can see how looking at the problem in this way would lead to a debate over the conduct of stabilization policy. Keynesians traditionally have argued that their models are sufficiently good that a negative correlation could and therefore should be achieved. Monetarists argue that the correlation is at best small and that it is foolish to retain institutions that might, at best, reduce the variance of output trivially but in fact have always responded to political pressures for bold action, which is destabilizing in effect. The new classical school of Lucas, Sargent, and Wallace argues that there are no significant discrepancies between the information available to agents in the private or public sectors, so that $\hat{p} = 0$, and government policies are either nil or destabilizing in effect. That sort of debate can easily get us bogged down in difficult theoretical and empirical issues, which Hall has the vision to avoid.

For example, Hall tells us that policy is optimal only if the percentage deviations of the unemployment rate are always proportional to percentage deviations of the price level from a fixed target. He even presents some calculations to show that postwar results fall short of that touchstone. Had I not seen the numbers, I never would have believed it.

One hypothesis to explain such—by Hall's standard, appalling—performance is that there has not been a fixed target price level. Even a fixed target growth path for the price level combined with an "elastic policy" with respect to deviations from this path and cyclical unemployment would fail miserably by his standard. Since calculations are easier to perform with a zero inflation rate, any policy that does not produce it surely must be a "nonstarter."

Another excuse that people from the Federal Reserve might offer for their miserable performance is that they were trying to follow an "elastic policy" as indicated by standard reaction-function estimates, but they had not figured out how to "simply peg the price level [deviation] at a multiple of the unemployment rate" deviation. They might claim that they were trying to stabilize the economy, given uncertainty about what its state would be when their actions actually took effect.

Hall has foreseen such attempts to shift the debate back to the dismal-science paradigm in which information is not free and people have to make decisions under uncertainty. So he plans to develop an automatic interest-rate policy rule that would overcome these petty cavils. The idea seems to be that rational expectations and perfect foresight are practically the same thing. Therefore the public's expectations can be relied on to force the Federal Reserve into a consistent policy. It is not clear why the induced money demand shifts will be more correctly calibrated than money supply movements, which could alternatively achieve the same effects.

So if policymakers just try hard enough and implement a new interest-rate policy rule to be worked out in the future, the uncertainty problem is solved. Hall considers many important issues, such as whether this policy regime would be optimal in a more general model in which our economy is merely a special—and, I daresay, uninteresting—case. Since some technical issues of impossibility might arise if this proposal were based on actually observed data, Hall rightly suggests the Federal Reserve "target on expectations" because "expectations are instantly responsive to policy"—indeed.

Besides the main issue dealt with by Hall, there is much more in the paper. There is the observation that non-interest-bearing reserves are a "major" source of deadweight loss in an economy such as the United States should be—one in which the government can instead impose nondistorting lump-sum taxes. Certainly the lost interest on some $60 billion of reserves supporting over $380 billion in checkable deposits alone is an indefensible tax burden.

In a similar vein, we can eliminate the deadweight loss due to the government's currency monopoly by permitting private issuance of small bearer securities, whose ownership would be recorded via the Visa system whenever they were transferred so that the owner could receive interest credit on each dollar. Indeed, with the modern technology Hall envisions, we could suppose that the private bearer notes need not actually be printed. And, of course, in the first-best world of lump-sum taxes and perfect honesty, no one would have any reason to prefer anonymous non-interest-bearing currency to debit cards.

Some economists might think that if some tests conclusively reject the null hypothesis that money shocks have no real effects, while other tests fail to reject that same hypothesis, then we should conclude that money shocks do indeed have some real effects even though the latter tests lack the statistical power of the former tests. Hall rises above such simple-minded statistical theory to find the issue in doubt.

I must conclude with a confession that I am not clear about exactly what Hall has in mind about interest-bearing reserves. Since they are to earn a bit under Treasury bills, will banks be required to hold them? Would they actually hold more than the satiety amount? If banks can have as many reserves as they desire in exchange for Treasury bills, and the quantity of reserves is demand-determined, by how much will the tax wedge between the rate paid on reserves and the T-bill rate have to be varied à la Tobin to achieve a determinant price level?

While Hall doubts that his approach has any political appeal whatsoever, he feels that "ventilation of the basic ideas . . . among economists seems like a useful endeavor." I find this instructive too. We Californians have learned that it is bad to bottle up one's gut feelings and are notorious for our methods—thought by some to be bizarre and expensive—of ventilating these feelings to others. Hall has shown that economists, all things considered, are a cheaper sounding board—a discovery from which I am sure we all shall profit in the years to come.

Index

Colin D. Campbell is Loren M. Berry Professor of Economics at Dartmouth College and an adjunct scholar at the American Enterprise Institute. He is the coauthor of *An Introduction to Money and Banking, Fifth Edition* (with R. G. Campbell) and the editor of several other books, most recently *Controlling the Cost of Social Security*. William R. Dougan is Visiting Professor at the Center for the Study of the Economy and the State, Graduate School of Business, University of Chicago. He is the coauthor of *Municipal Management and Budget Methods: An Evaluation of Policy-related Research* (with W. A. Kimmel and J. R. Hall).

THE JOHNS HOPKINS UNIVERSITY PRESS

Alternative Monetary Regimes

This book was composed in Linotron Times Roman by EPS Group from a design
by Susan Bishop. It was printed on 50-lb. Sebago Eggshell Offset Cream paper
and bound by BookCrafters, Inc.